EMEI BURELL

WE SERVED THE PEOPLE™

MY MOTHER'S STORIES

Published by
ARCHAIA™

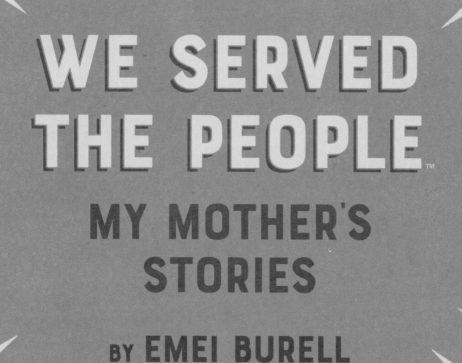

WE SERVED THE PEOPLE™

MY MOTHER'S STORIES

BY EMEI BURELL

ARCHAIA™
Los Angeles, California

COVER BY **EMEI BURELL**

DESIGNER **JILLIAN CRAB**

ASSISTANT EDITOR **GWEN WALLER**

EDITOR **SIERRA HAHN**

ARCHAIA

WE SERVED THE PEOPLE: MY MOTHER'S STORIES, April 2020. Published by Archaia, a division of Boom Entertainment, Inc. We Served the People is ™ & © 2020 Emei Burell. All rights reserved. Archaia™ and the Archaia logo are trademarks of Boom Entertainment, Inc., registered in various countries and categories. BOOM! Studios does not read or accept unsolicited submissions of ideas, stories, or artwork.

BOOM! Studios, 5670 Wilshire Boulevard, Suite 400, Los Angeles, CA 90036-5679. Printed in Hong Kong. First Printing.

ISBN: 978-1-68415-504-0, eISBN: 978-1-64144-662-4

FOR MOM

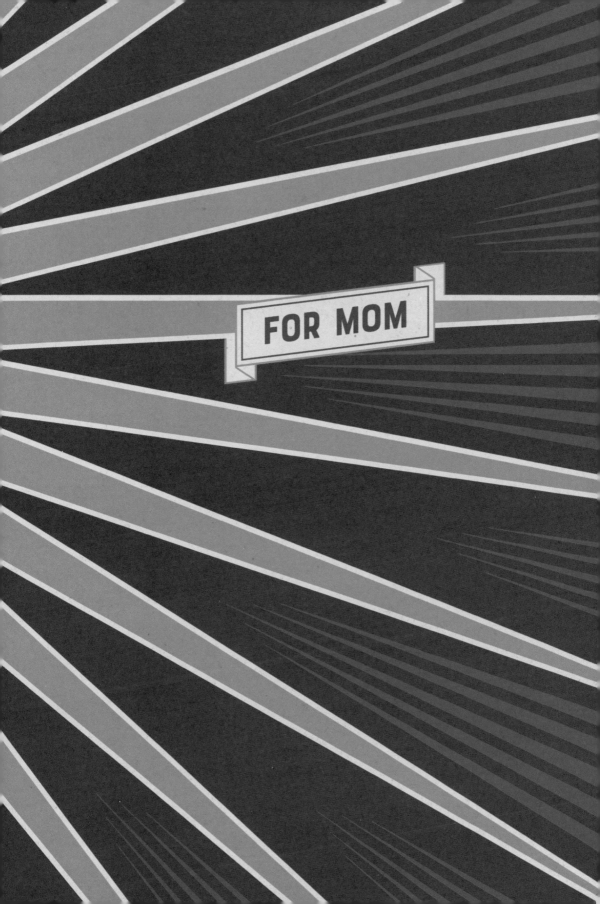

The Cultural Revolution took place in China between 1966 and 1976. According to history books, it was a sociopolitical movement launched by Mao Zedong who was Chairman of the Communist Party of China. The objective was to preserve communism by ridding Chinese society of capitalist ideology and traditional Chinese customs. This period also marked Mao Zedong Thought or Maoism as the dominant ideology of the communist party and was indicative of Mao's return to power after the failures of his Great Leap Forward. Both the Great Leap Forward and the Cultural Revolution lead to millions of lives lost.

For the people that I've talked with about the Cultural Revolution, this period of history is a bit mysterious. Some know it as a communist revolution while others know that ancient artifacts were trashed by the thousands. Most everyone in the world knows that it changed Chinese society forever. But the specifics of that period remain hazy.

Everything I know about the Cultural Revolution is through the stories my mother has told me about her time growing up in China during these tumultuous times. Seen through her adolescent eyes, the Cultural Revolution looks like this:

For those kids living in Beijing the revolution started in June of 1966 when all classes were suddenly cancelled until further notice . I was 14-years-old at the time, just about to graduate from 7th grade. They said they would send notice when classes would resume . . . but they never did.

Our teachers were detained in the school building — they were not allowed to go home and had to live at school. They spent their days under the scrutiny of work groups sent by the municipal government. These groups forced the teachers to write about their pasts and work lives, which would then be compared to the file that the party had on them. If the two documents didn't correspond, the teachers would be openly criticized for their dishonest behaviour and "problematic" pasts.

We still had to attend school, but as we had nothing to do, we'd aimlessly wander the grounds and watch the high schoolers put up so-called "Big-Character Posters" on the walls of the schoolyard . On these posters were all kinds of criticism against the teachers written with big characters.

We spent our days lounging around like this until March of '67 when the military was dispatched to schools to start up classes again. But the "classes" were nothing more than a roll call followed by either reading the newspapers or "Quotations from Chairman Mao" (i.e. Mao's "Little Red Book") so that we could discuss for a bit before going home.

Some days we'd stand around drawing pictures on the blackboard, other days we would go on an excursion to the countryside to help farmers with their crops — we did all kinds of things like this for a year.

In 1968, we were supposed to graduate from junior high — in China this is when you either continue to study or get appointed a job from the government. At this time, we weren't allowed to look for a job, we weren't allowed to choose — we could only wait.
The government couldn't assign us anything —
and by 'us' I'm not only talking about our class or our school —
I'm talking about students all across China.

I'm talking about 16 million students.

There was no way for the government to find enough jobs for us.

So, on December 22nd, 1968, Mao ZeDong launched the Down to the Countryside Movement:

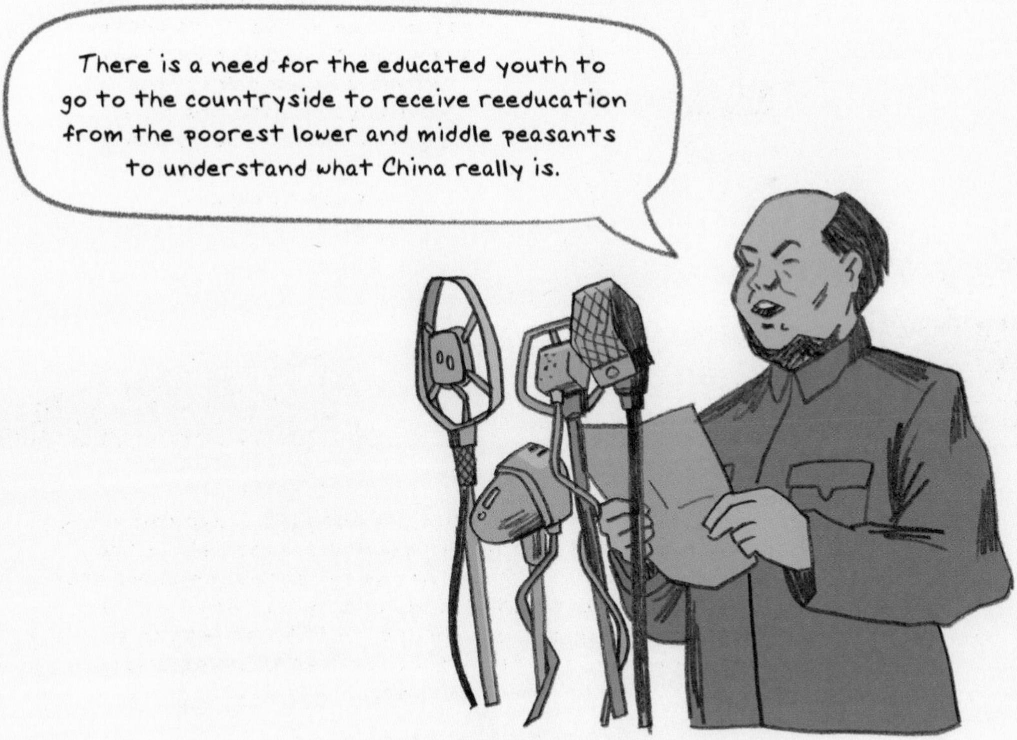
There is a need for the educated youth to go to the countryside to receive reeducation from the poorest lower and middle peasants to understand what China really is.

This was a nationwide movement —
no matter if you wanted to or not, you had to go.

Dozens of teachers would move in big groups from house to house to persuade us all. If any of us would refuse to go, the teachers would turn to our parents and then to their superiors. When the pressure came from all directions, it was hard to stand ground.

Thousands of students from Beijing were sent to the countryside of ShaanXi, ShanXi, and DongBei to start with. There, we were supposed to stay, and work, and be reeducated. We graduates of '68 were supposed to be sent to Jilin, but I had no intention of going. I didn't feel like leaving my family or Beijing at all.

One big problem with leaving the city, was that it was extremely difficult to move back. In China, there is something called the Hukou System — a system of "domestic passports" that was established in 1958 to regulate the rural-to-urban migration. It made moving from the countryside into the city nearly impossible, but moving out of the city was a piece of cake.

I somehow managed to drag out leaving Beijing until '69. I avoided going to the Jilin countryside, but not much time had passed before the teachers came knocking again. This time they were recruiting students to work in state farming corporations in Yunnan, way down in the south of China. My classmates and I agreed that it was better to relocate south than north, and that it was better to go as a paid worker than a farmer.

And so, I ended up in Yunnan. I was stuck there for ten years until the end of the Cultural Revolution.

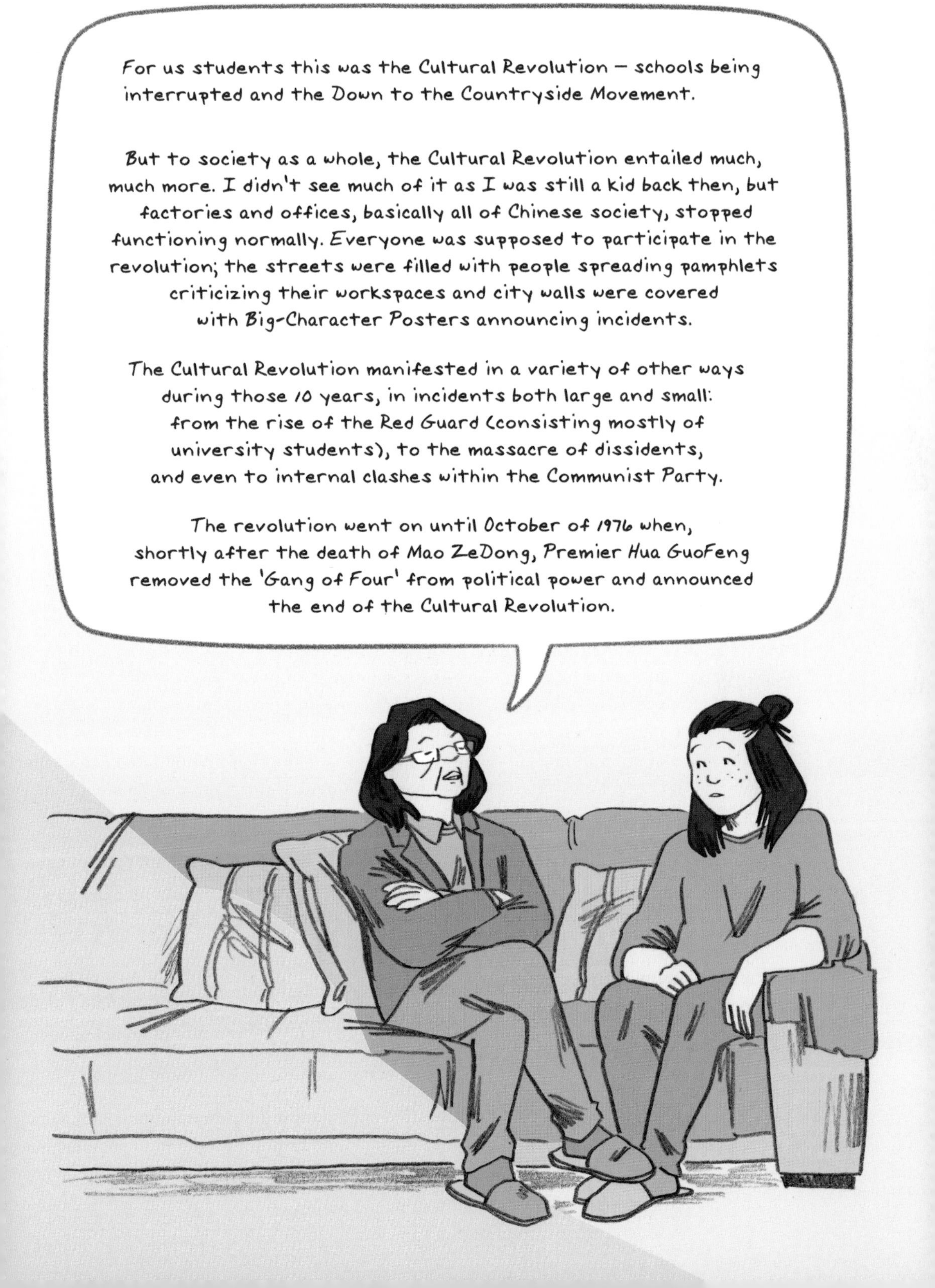
For us students this was the Cultural Revolution — schools being interrupted and the Down to the Countryside Movement.
But to society as a whole, the Cultural Revolution entailed much, much more. I didn't see much of it as I was still a kid back then, but factories and offices, basically all of Chinese society, stopped functioning normally. Everyone was supposed to participate in the revolution; the streets were filled with people spreading pamphlets criticizing their workspaces and city walls were covered with Big-Character Posters announcing incidents.
The Cultural Revolution manifested in a variety of other ways during those 10 years, in incidents both large and small: from the rise of the Red Guard (consisting mostly of university students), to the massacre of dissidents, and even to internal clashes within the Communist Party.
The revolution went on until October of 1976 when, shortly after the death of Mao ZeDong, Premier Hua GuoFeng removed the 'Gang of Four' from political power and announced the end of the Cultural Revolution.

As I said before, I didn't really want to leave Beijing.
But I also didn't have an excuse for not going.

The situation was what it was — we didn't have a choice of whether
to stay or go. All we could do was figure out a way to move somewhere
we thought wasn't too bad.

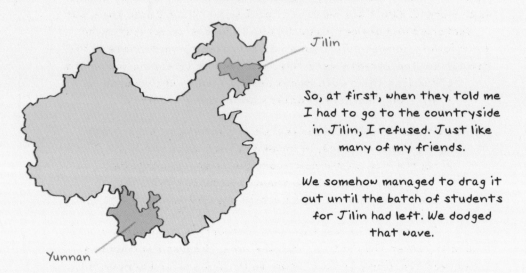

Jilin

So, at first, when they told me
I had to go to the countryside
in Jilin, I refused. Just like
many of my friends.

We somehow managed to drag it
out until the batch of students
for Jilin had left. We dodged
that wave.

Yunnan

But, of course, this couldn't last forever. Our teachers soon came
knocking on our doors again. This time they were sending students
to work at state farming corporations in Yunnan.

My classmates and I agreed that going to
Yunnan wouldn't be too bad — the quality of
life in the south would be higher than in the
north, and because the weather was warm
there, you'd only need to pack a couple
sets of clothes, stuff it into a
wooden crate, and then go
on your way.

My classmates left with the first wave of students going to Yunnan, and I left with the second wave – at least we'd be together.

I left as a regular 17-year-old, who didn't hold too many opinions about the world or what was happening around me. After all, I couldn't do anything about the fact that I was forced to go, and everyone my age was leaving too.

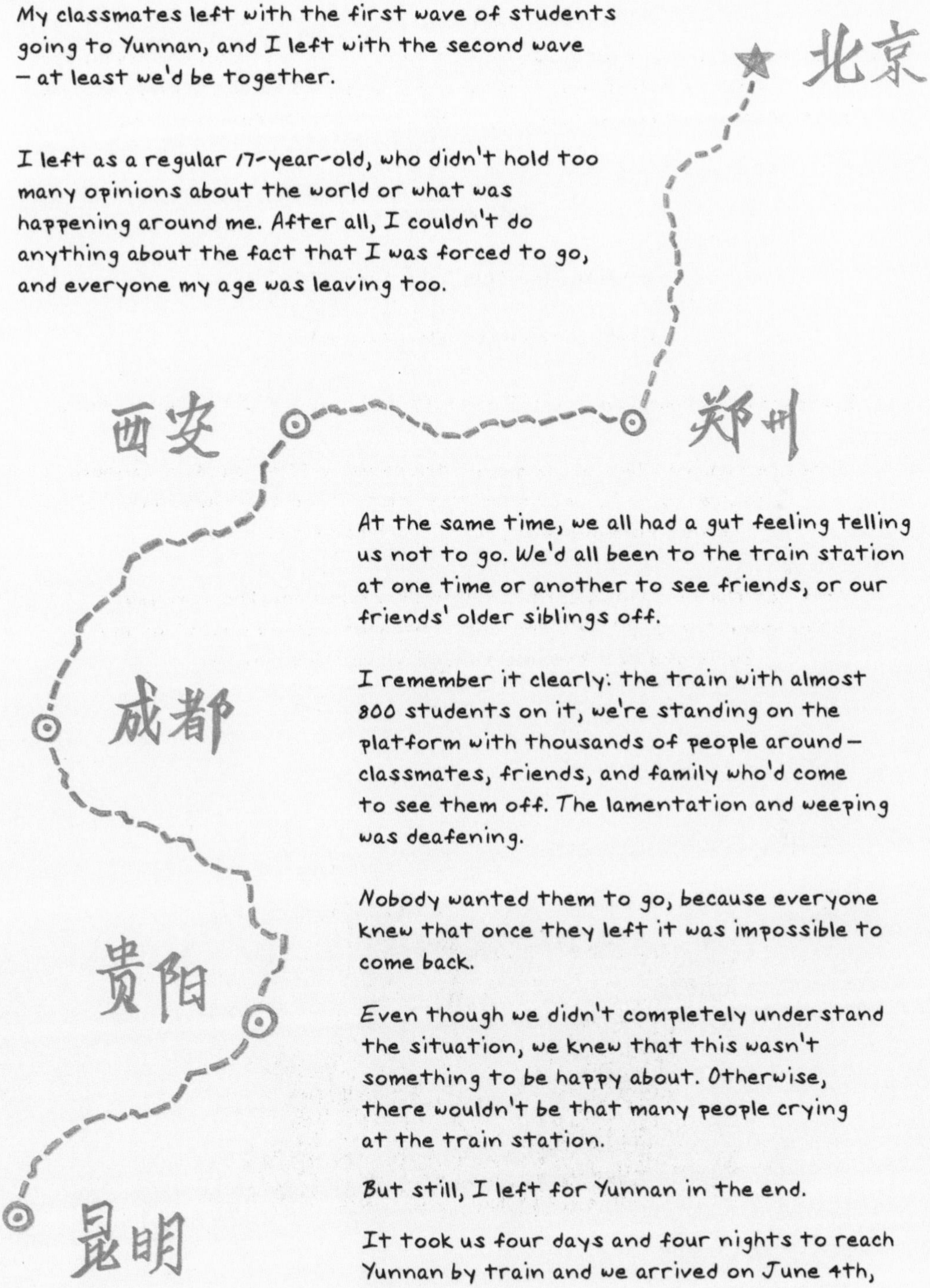
北京
郑州
西安
成都
贵阳
昆明

At the same time, we all had a gut feeling telling us not to go. We'd all been to the train station at one time or another to see friends, or our friends' older siblings off.

I remember it clearly: the train with almost 800 students on it, we're standing on the platform with thousands of people around – classmates, friends, and family who'd come to see them off. The lamentation and weeping was deafening.

Nobody wanted them to go, because everyone knew that once they left it was impossible to come back.

Even though we didn't completely understand the situation, we knew that this wasn't something to be happy about. Otherwise, there wouldn't be that many people crying at the train station.

But still, I left for Yunnan in the end.

It took us four days and four nights to reach Yunnan by train and we arrived on June 4th, 1969 to Kunming train station. On the way, some of us were already thinking "Maybe we were wrong in going".

We rested in Kunming for a day before getting on a bus and going all the
way to the state farms in Xishuangbanna. When we finally arrived at the
state farms and had settled into our quarters, it finally hit me . . .
I regretted leaving Beijing.

I felt so stupid.

Why in the world did I come here?

Maybe I really shouldn't have left?

I understood that now that I had left Beijing, I could never go back.

A desire was instilled in me during those very first days in Yunnan,
a desire to go home, no matter what. I had to figure out
a way to move back, but I just had no clue how.

This was the one thing constantly on my mind for the ten years
I was down there. It was the one thing motivating almost all my
decisions and the one thing I never wavered on.

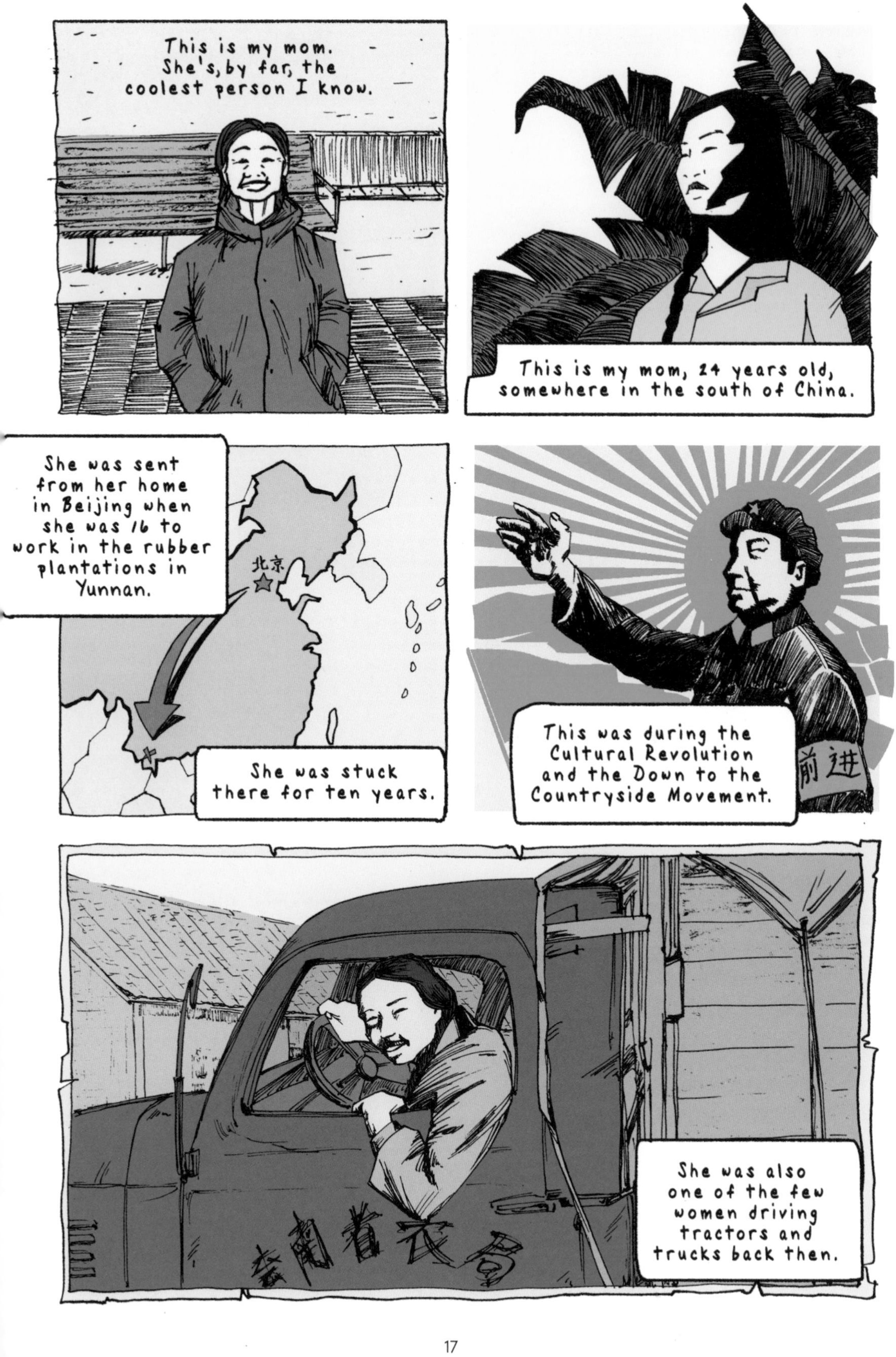
This is my mom.
She's, by far, the
coolest person I know.
This is my mom, 24 years old,
somewhere in the south of China.
She was sent from her home in Beijing when she was 16 to work in the rubber plantations in Yunnan.
北京
She was stuck there for ten years.
This was during the Cultural Revolution and the Down to the Countryside Movement.
前进
She was also one of the few women driving tractors and trucks back then.

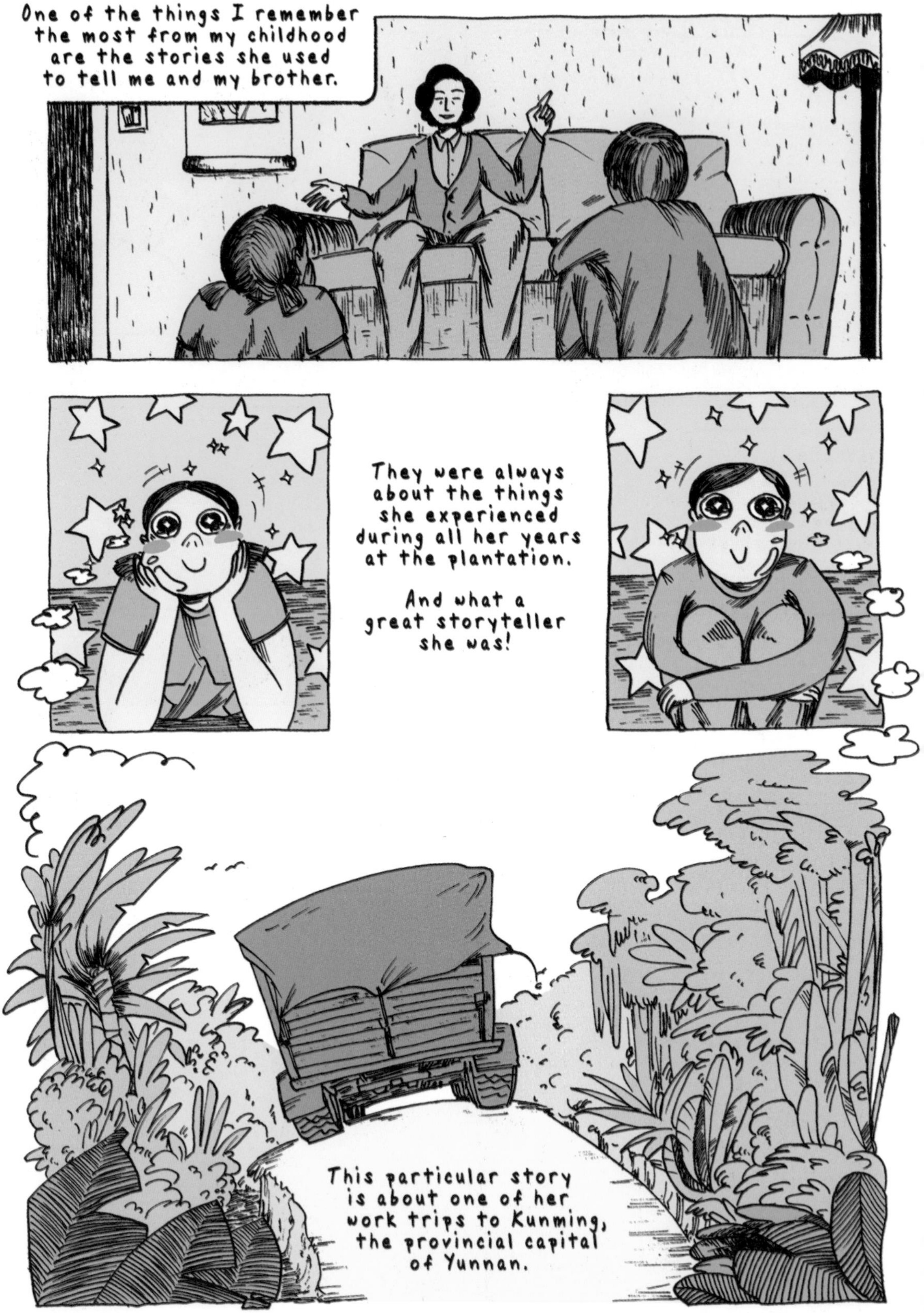
One of the things I remember the most from my childhood are the stories she used to tell me and my brother.
They were always about the things she experienced during all her years at the plantation.
And what a great storyteller she was!
This particular story is about one of her work trips to Kunming, the provincial capital of Yunnan.

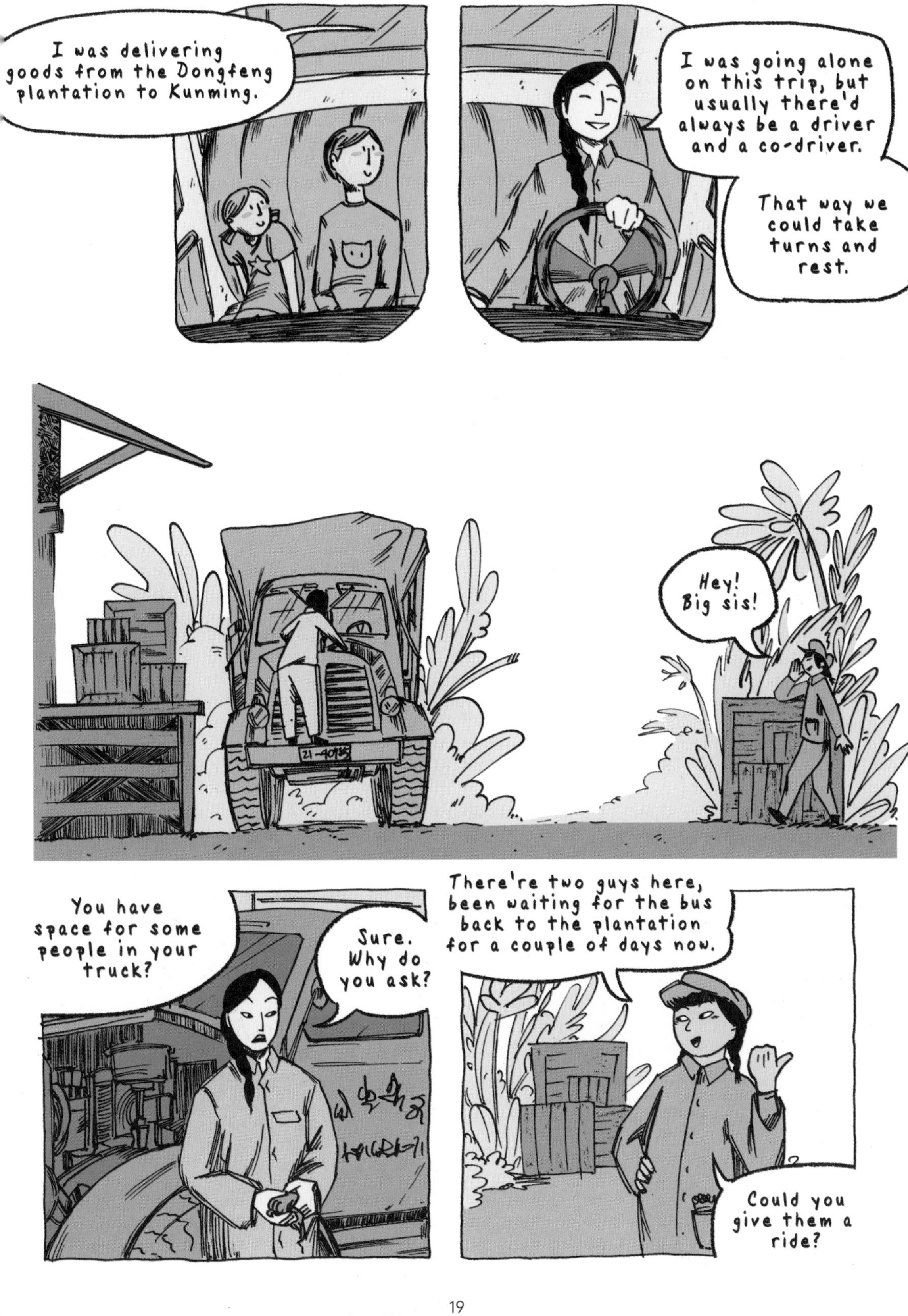
I was delivering goods from the Dongfeng plantation to Kunming.
I was going alone on this trip, but usually there'd always be a driver and a co-driver.
That way we could take turns and rest.
Hey! Big sis!
You have space for some people in your truck?
Sure. Why do you ask?
There're two guys here, been waiting for the bus back to the plantation for a couple of days now.
Could you give them a ride?

KUNMING → DŌNGFENG

MON 20/8			
TUE 21/8			N/A
WEN 22/8			FULL
THU 23/8			N/A
			N/A
SA[T] 25/8			

At that time, the means of communication were pretty bad in the area. There weren't many buses going to and from the plantation.

If you miss one you have to wait at least a couple of days for the next departure.

Yeah, no problem.

Great!

And by the way, one of them is a driver too, so if you get tired on the way — just have him drive for you!

Hm, Ok.

Next morning

I'm Chen Ming.

Hi.

Nice to meet you.

This is my cousin Zhang Jing.

We're the ones Ping mentioned yesterday.

So, this is the famous Chen!

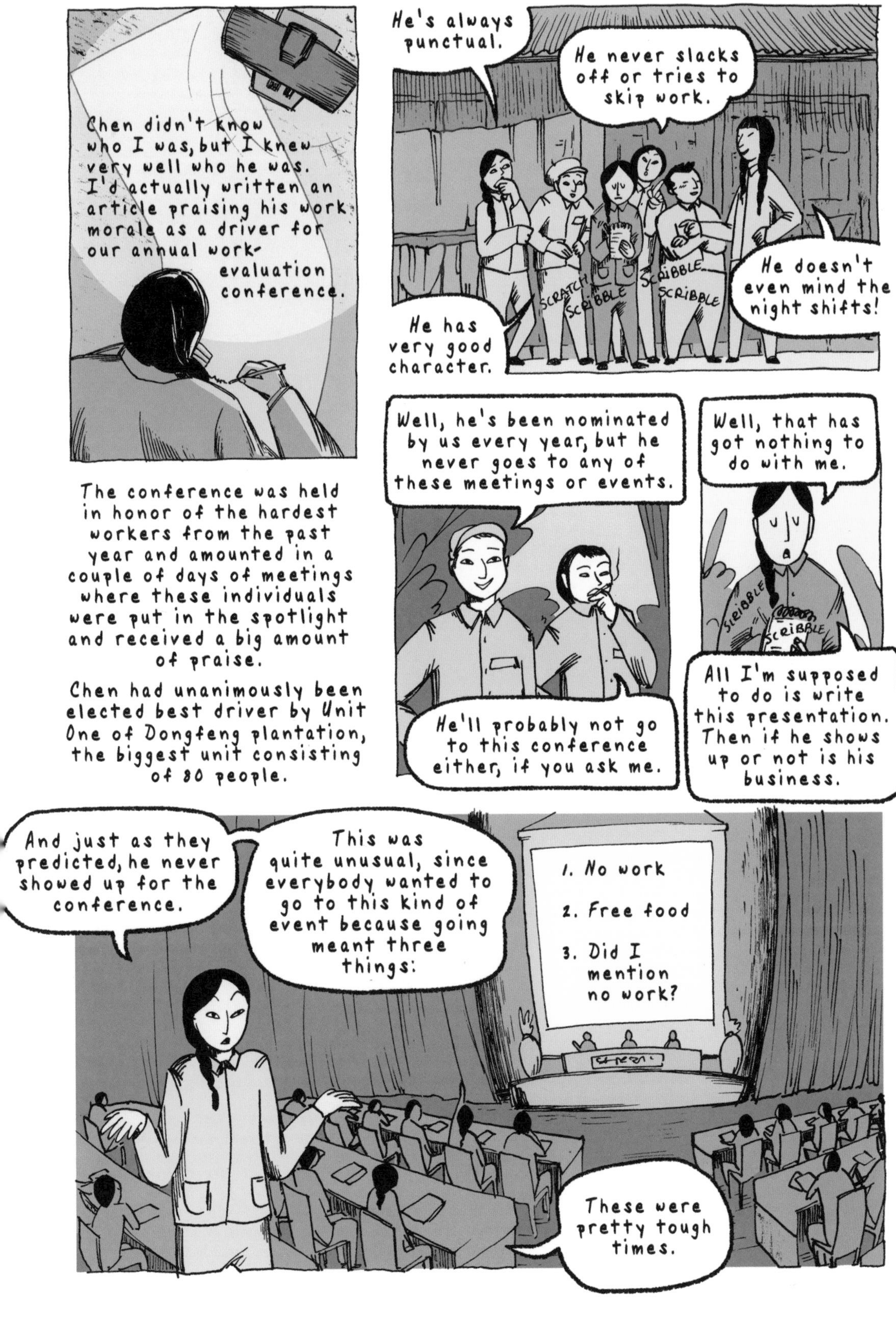
Chen didn't know who I was, but I knew very well who he was. I'd actually written an article praising his work morale as a driver for our annual work-evaluation conference.
He's always punctual.
He never slacks off or tries to skip work.
SCRATCH
SCRIBBLE
SCRIBBLE
SCRIBBLE
He has very good character.
He doesn't even mind the night shifts!
The conference was held in honor of the hardest workers from the past year and amounted in a couple of days of meetings where these individuals were put in the spotlight and received a big amount of praise.
Chen had unanimously been elected best driver by Unit One of Dongfeng plantation, the biggest unit consisting of 80 people.
Well, he's been nominated by us every year, but he never goes to any of these meetings or events.
He'll probably not go to this conference either, if you ask me.
Well, that has got nothing to do with me.
SCRIBBLE
SCRIBBLE
All I'm supposed to do is write this presentation. Then if he shows up or not is his business.
And just as they predicted, he never showed up for the conference.
This was quite unusual, since everybody wanted to go to this kind of event because going meant three things:
1. No work
2. Free food
3. Did I mention no work?
These were pretty tough times.

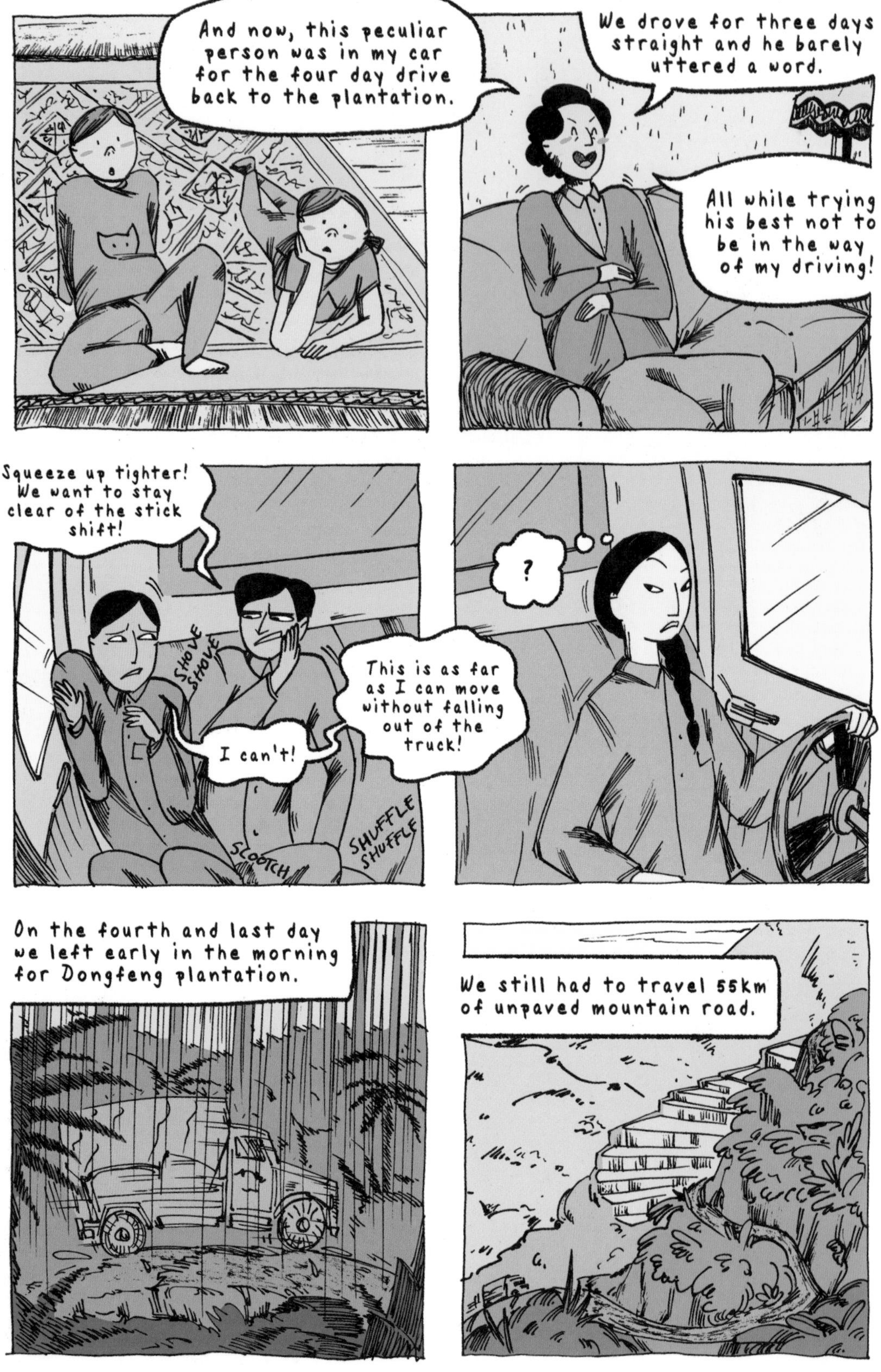
And now, this peculiar person was in my car for the four day drive back to the plantation.
We drove for three days straight and he barely uttered a word.
All while trying his best not to be in the way of my driving!
Squeeze up tighter! We want to stay clear of the stick shift!
SHOVE SHOVE
I can't!
This is as far as I can move without falling out of the truck!
SLOOTCH
SHUFFLE SHUFFLE
?
On the fourth and last day we left early in the morning for Dongfeng plantation.
We still had to travel 55km of unpaved mountain road.

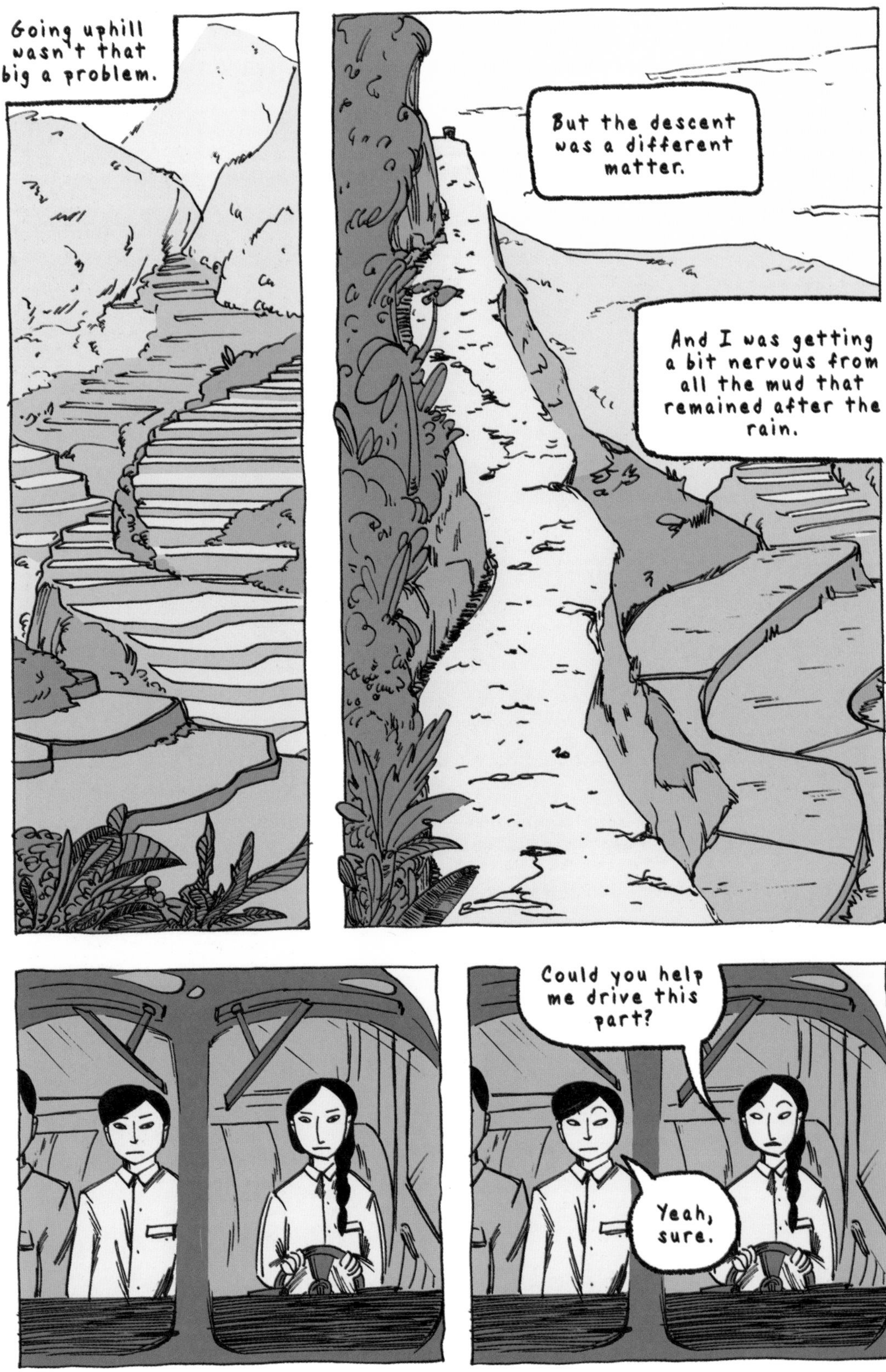
Going uphill wasn't that big a problem.
But the descent was a different matter.
And I was getting a bit nervous from all the mud that remained after the rain.
Could you help me drive this part?
Yeah, sure.

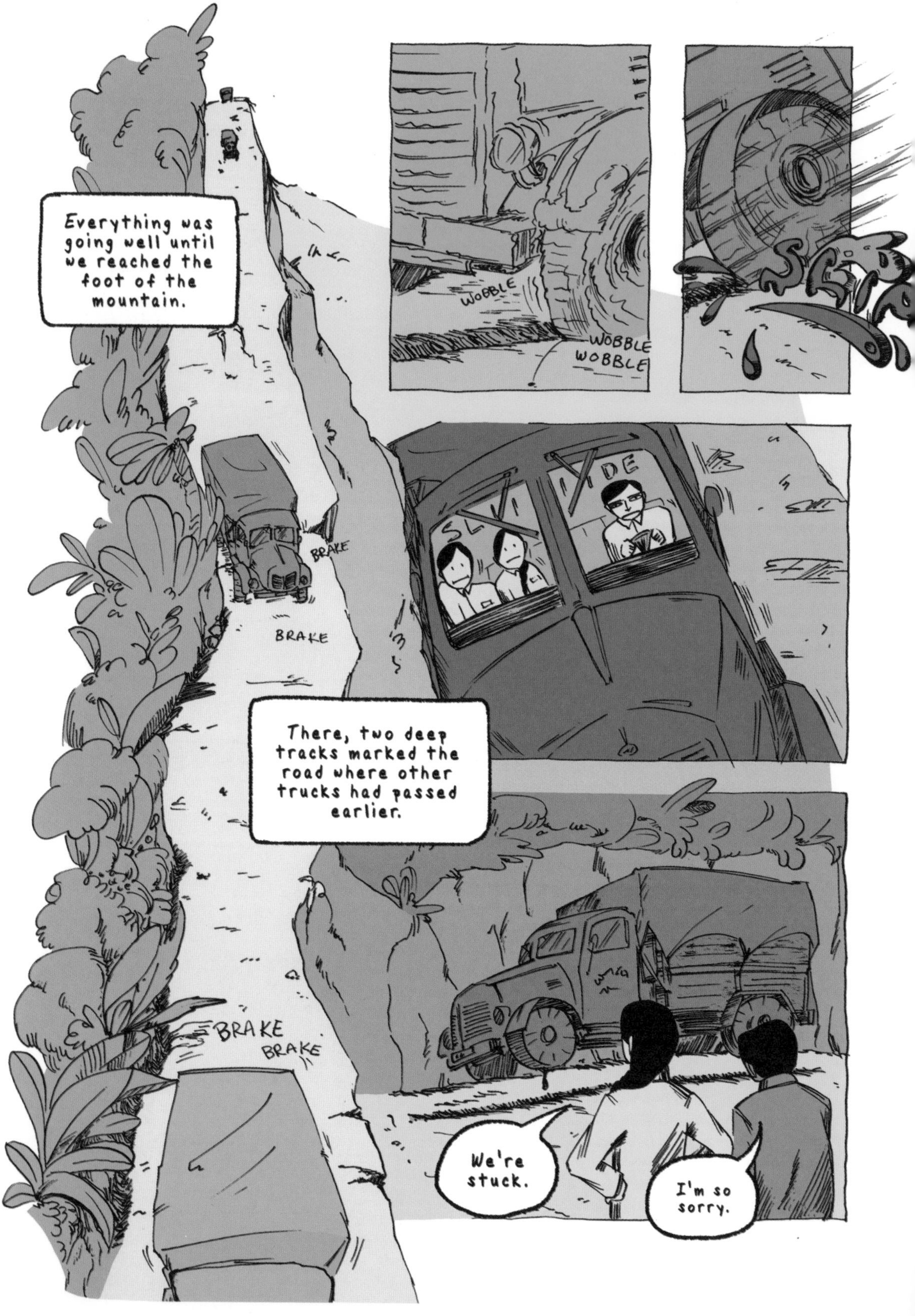
Everything was going well until we reached the foot of the mountain.
WOBBLE
WOBBLE
WOBBLE
BRAKE
BRAKE
BRAKE
BRAKE
There, two deep tracks marked the road where other trucks had passed earlier.
We're stuck.
I'm so sorry.

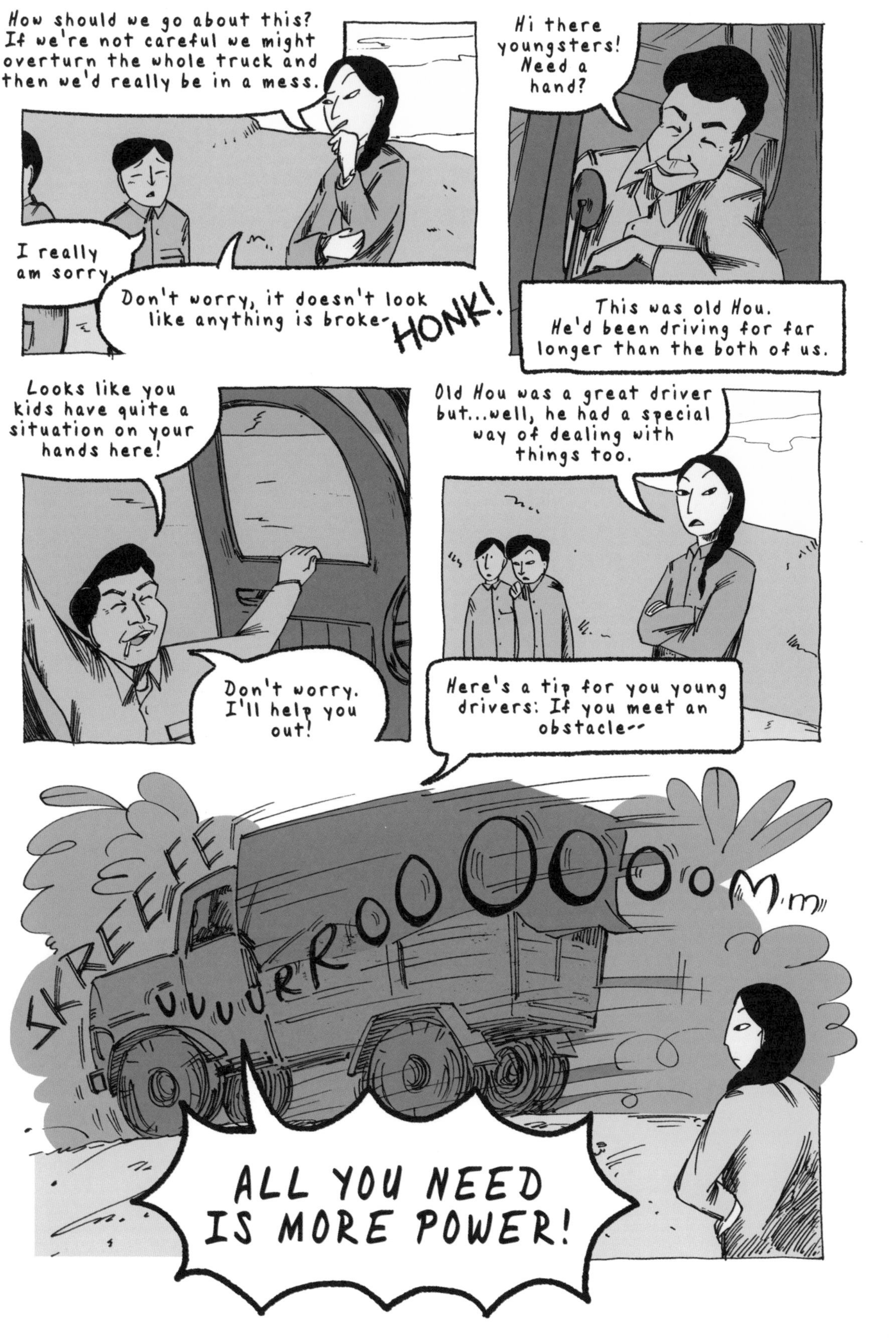
How should we go about this? If we're not careful we might overturn the whole truck and then we'd really be in a mess.
I really am sorry.
Don't worry, it doesn't look like anything is broke-
HONK!
Hi there youngsters! Need a hand?
This was old Hou. He'd been driving for far longer than the both of us.
Looks like you kids have quite a situation on your hands here!
Don't worry. I'll help you out!
Old Hou was a great driver but...well, he had a special way of dealing with things too.
Here's a tip for you young drivers: If you meet an obstacle--
SKREEEE
UUUURROOOOOOoom
ALL YOU NEED IS MORE POWER!

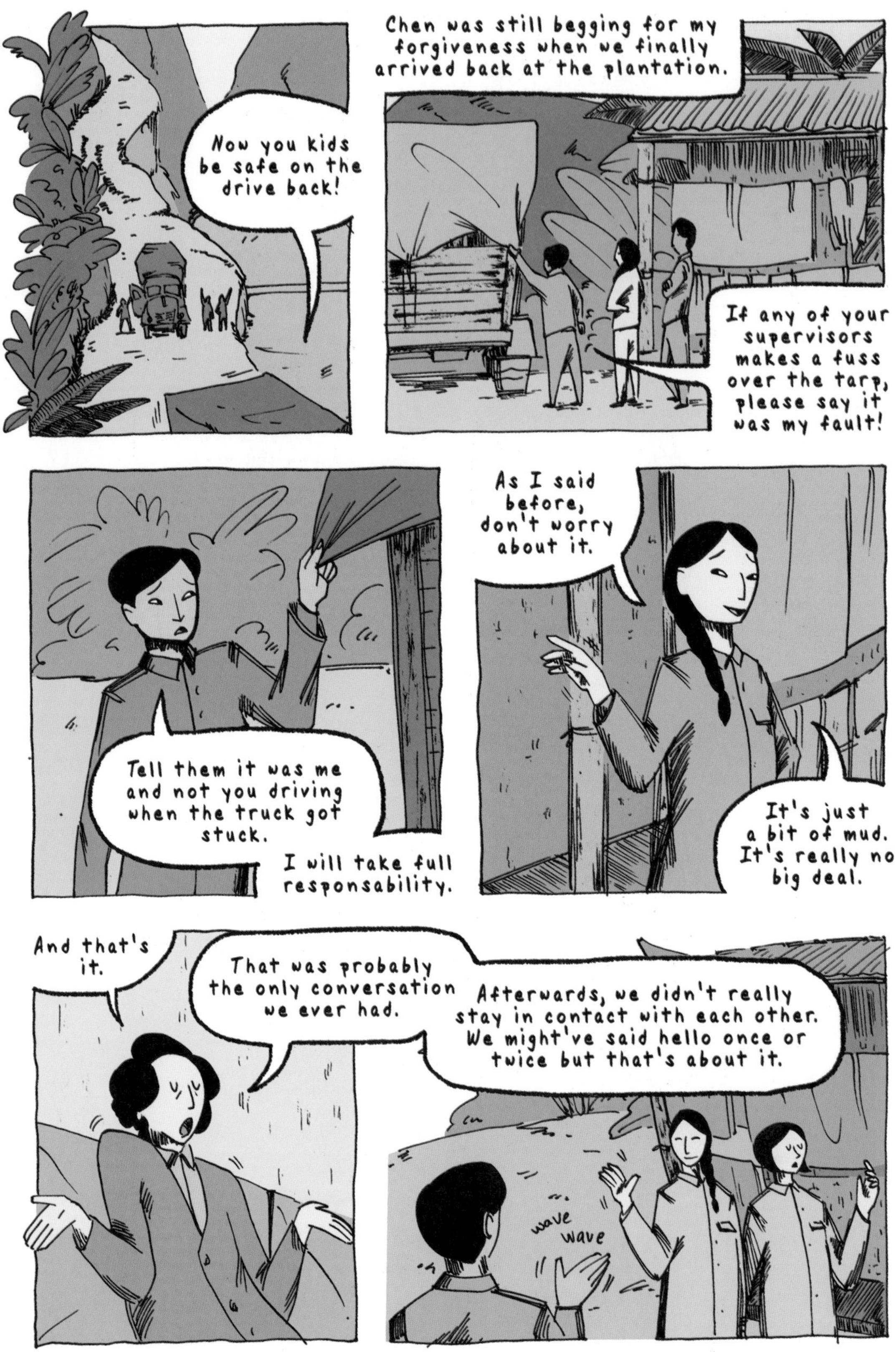
Now you kids be safe on the drive back!
Chen was still begging for my forgiveness when we finally arrived back at the plantation.
If any of your supervisors makes a fuss over the tarp, please say it was my fault!
Tell them it was me and not you driving when the truck got stuck.
I will take full responsability.
As I said before, don't worry about it.
It's just a bit of mud. It's really no big deal.
And that's it.
That was probably the only conversation we ever had.
Afterwards, we didn't really stay in contact with each other. We might've said hello once or twice but that's about it.
wave wave

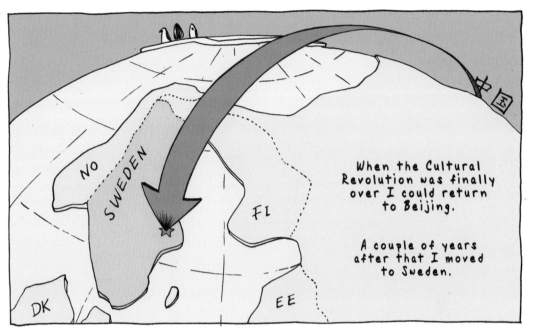

When the Cultural Revolution was finally over I could return to Beijing.

A couple of years after that I moved to Sweden.

I didn't speak to Chen for almost 40 years.

Right, dear?

Yup, that's about right.

This is my mom today, 64-years-old. She's reunited with Chen, the man she met by chance on a road halfway across the world.

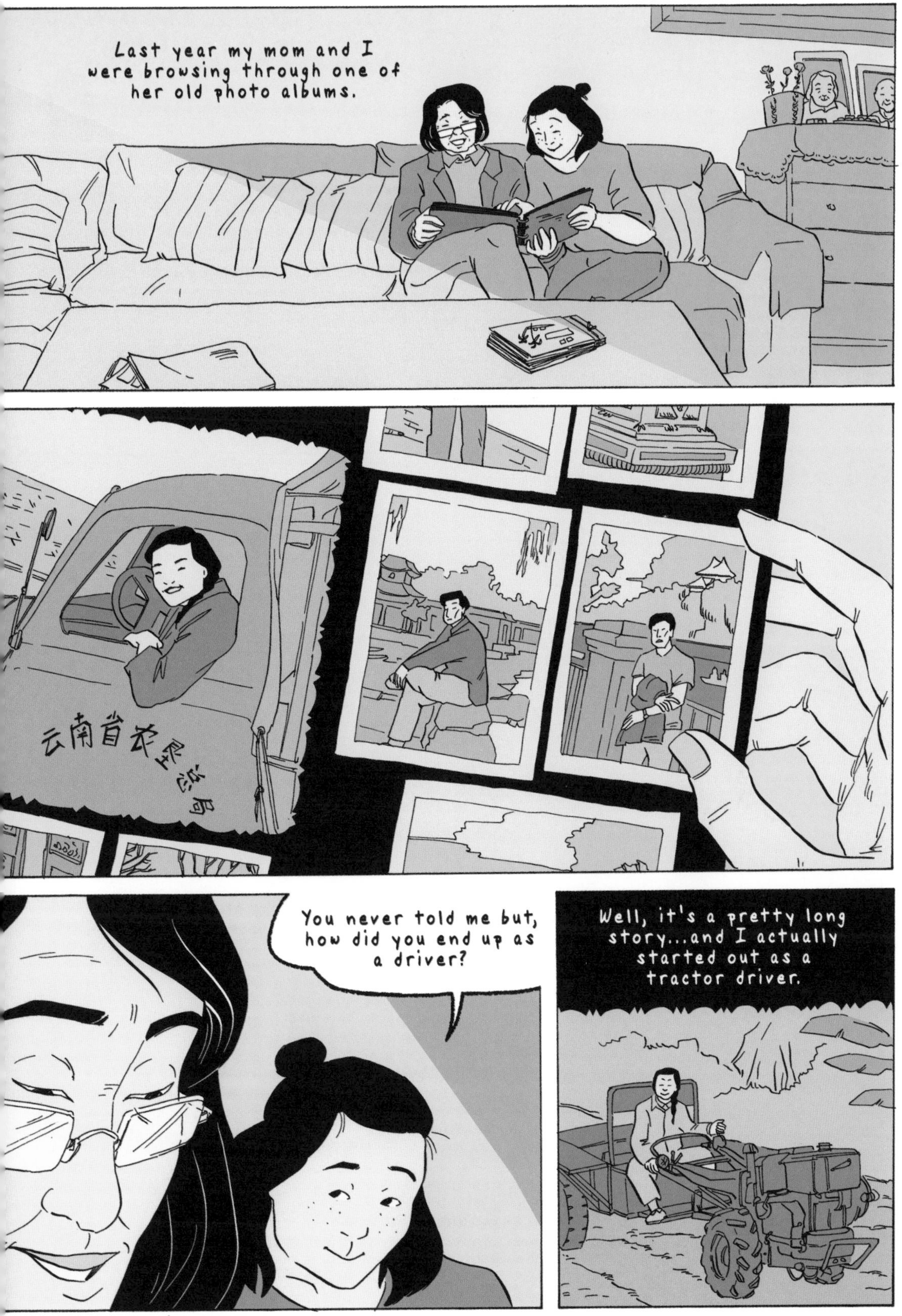

Last year my mom and I were browsing through one of her old photo albums.
云南省农垦总局
You never told me but, how did you end up as a driver?
Well, it's a pretty long story...and I actually started out as a tractor driver.

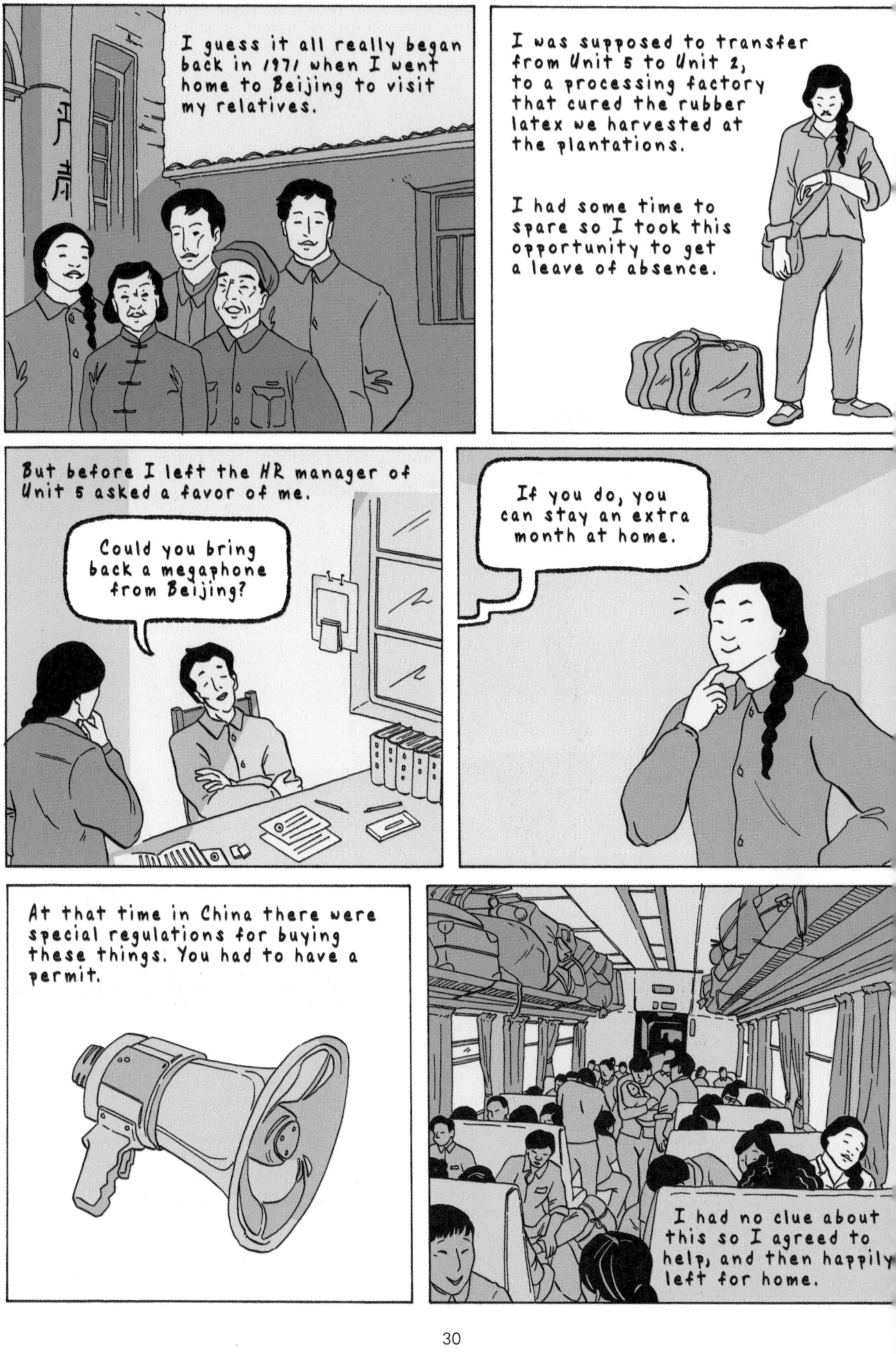
I guess it all really began back in 1971 when I went home to Beijing to visit my relatives.
I was supposed to transfer from Unit 5 to Unit 2, to a processing factory that cured the rubber latex we harvested at the plantations.
I had some time to spare so I took this opportunity to get a leave of absence.
But before I left the HR manager of Unit 5 asked a favor of me.
Could you bring back a megaphone from Beijing?
If you do, you can stay an extra month at home.
At that time in China there were special regulations for buying these things. You had to have a permit.
I had no clue about this so I agreed to help, and then happily left for home.

This was because China was a completely centrally planned economy at the time. An economy like this implied that what was produced, how it was produced, and for whom it was produced was controlled and determined by the central government.

Economic Systems
Planned Economy
Free Market
Communism
Mixed Economies
Capitalism

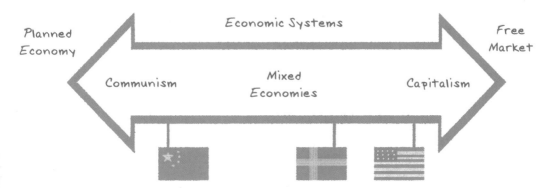

Because of the planned economy there was a lack of many, many things. And this shortage resulted in the requirement of special "buying" permits.

The permit that I needed to buy the megaphone had to be applied for at the corresponding government bureaus well in advance. Only after receiving a permit, could you go to the store and buy the object of your desire.

Other things that required permits included microphones, special camera lenses, foreign educational material, specific tools, cars or trucks, refrigerators or even theater make-up.

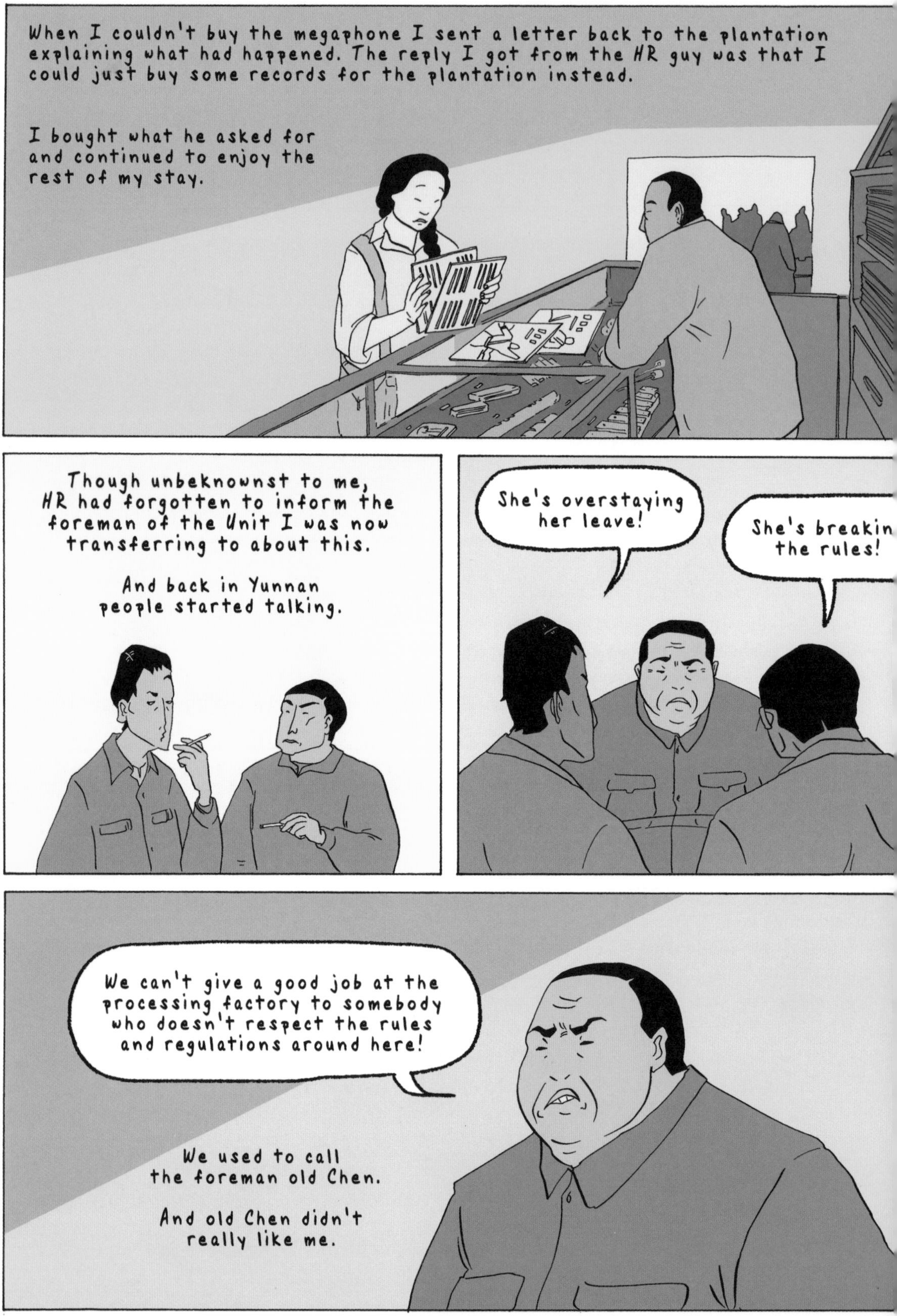

When I couldn't buy the megaphone I sent a letter back to the plantation explaining what had happened. The reply I got from the HR guy was that I could just buy some records for the plantation instead.
I bought what he asked for and continued to enjoy the rest of my stay.
Though unbeknownst to me, HR had forgotten to inform the foreman of the Unit I was now transferring to about this.
And back in Yunnan people started talking.
She's overstaying her leave!
She's breakin the rules!
We can't give a good job at the processing factory to somebody who doesn't respect the rules and regulations around here!
We used to call the foreman old Chen.
And old Chen didn't really like me.

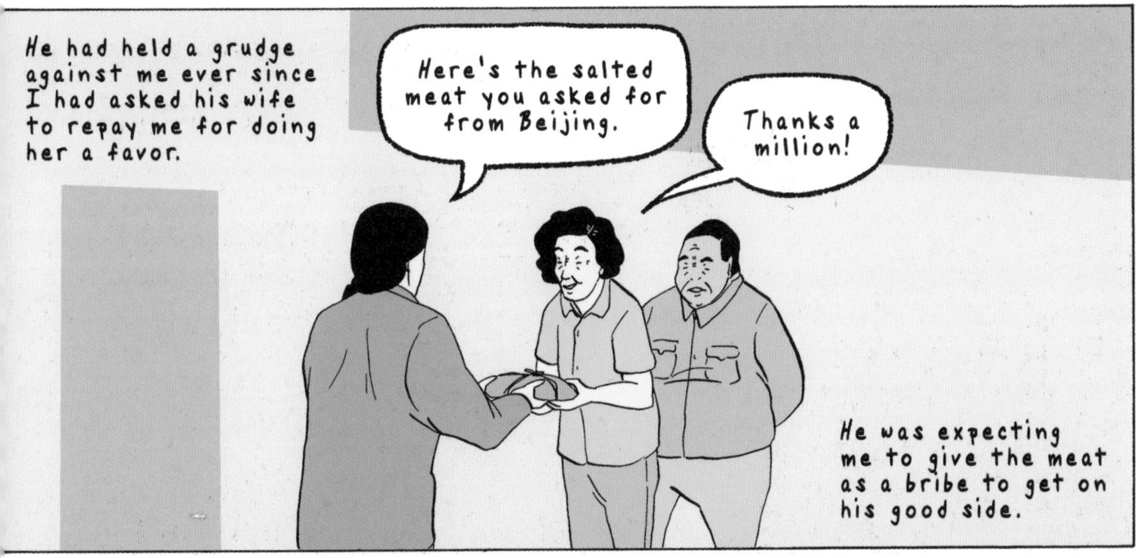
He had held a grudge against me ever since I had asked his wife to repay me for doing her a favor.
Here's the salted meat you asked for from Beijing.
Thanks a million!
He was expecting me to give the meat as a bribe to get on his good side.

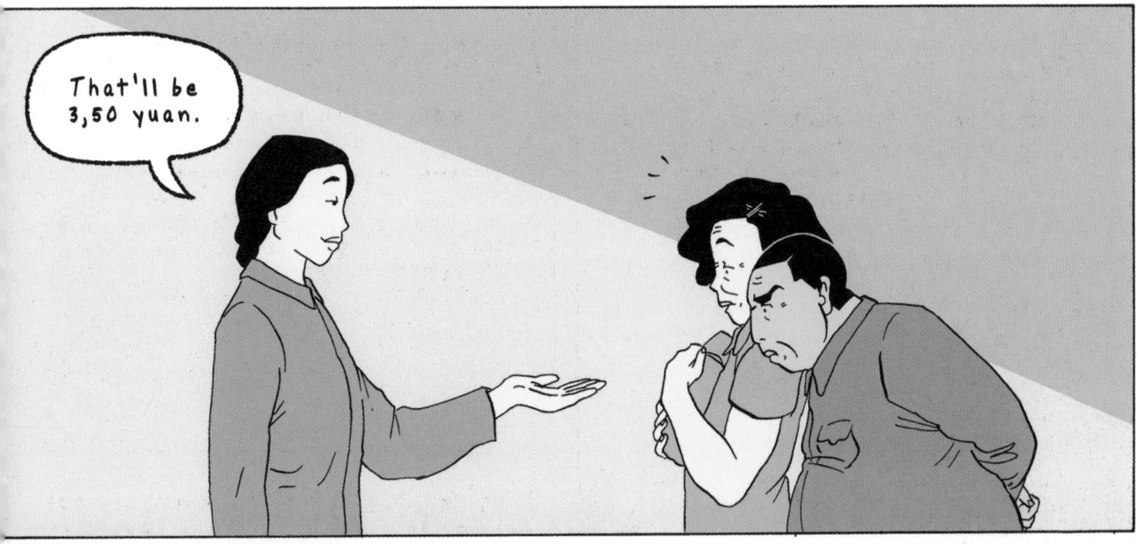
That'll be 3,50 yuan.

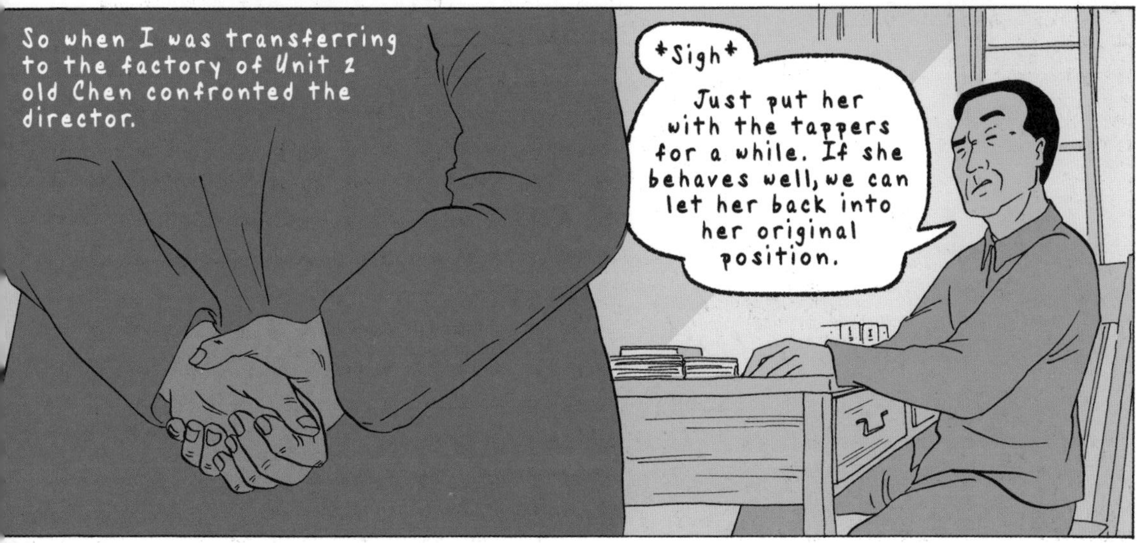
So when I was transferring to the factory of Unit 2 old Chen confronted the director.
Sigh
Just put her with the tappers for a while. If she behaves well, we can let her back into her original position.

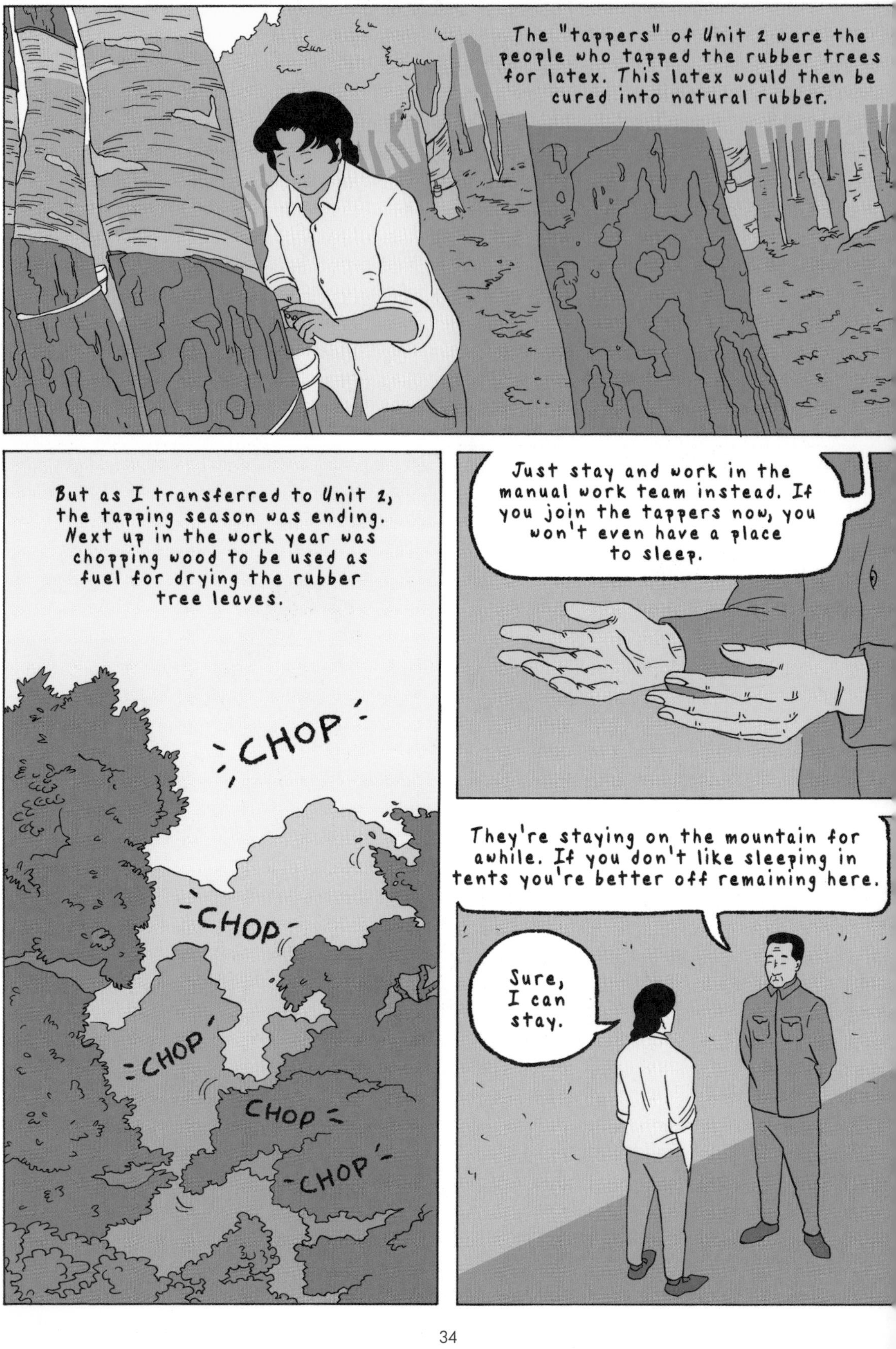
The "tappers" of Unit 2 were the people who tapped the rubber trees for latex. This latex would then be cured into natural rubber.
But as I transferred to Unit 2, the tapping season was ending. Next up in the work year was chopping wood to be used as fuel for drying the rubber tree leaves.
CHOP
CHOP
CHOP
CHOP
CHOP
Just stay and work in the manual work team instead. If you join the tappers now, you won't even have a place to sleep.
They're staying on the mountain for awhile. If you don't like sleeping in tents you're better off remaining here.
Sure, I can stay.

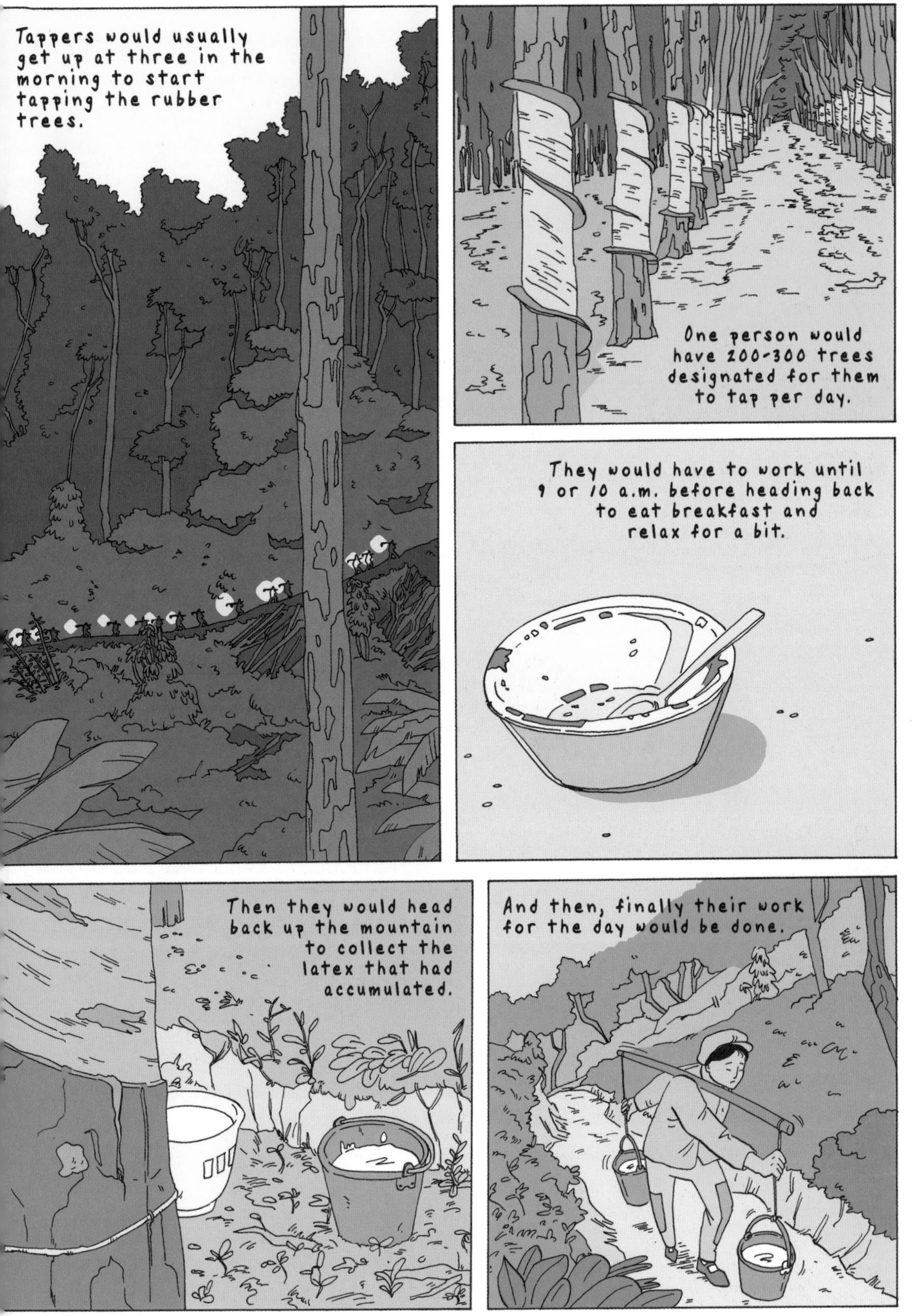
Tappers would usually get up at three in the morning to start tapping the rubber trees.
One person would have 200-300 trees designated for them to tap per day.
They would have to work until 9 or 10 a.m. before heading back to eat breakfast and relax for a bit.
Then they would head back up the mountain to collect the latex that had accumulated.
And then, finally their work for the day would be done.

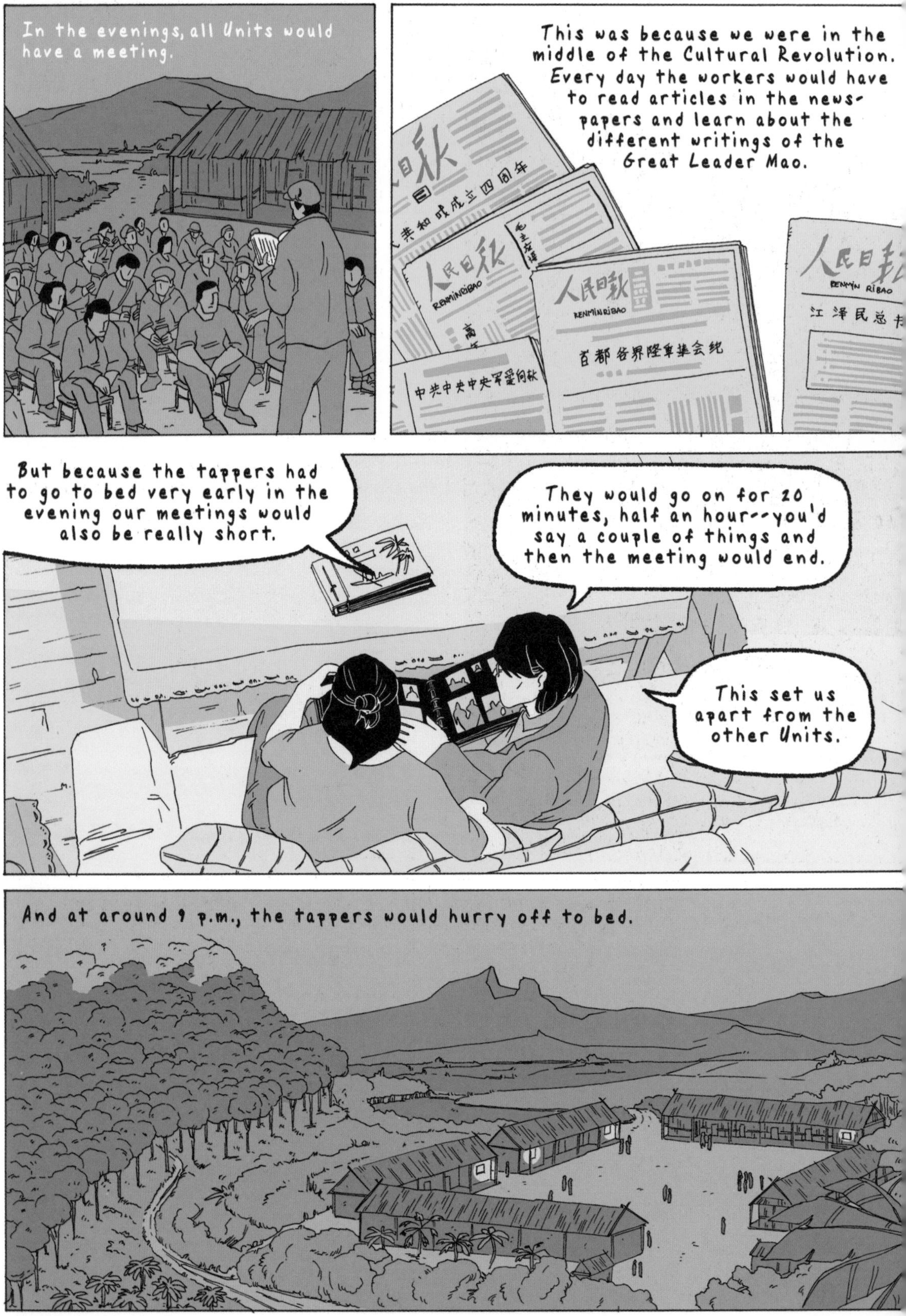
In the evenings, all Units would have a meeting.
This was because we were in the middle of the Cultural Revolution. Every day the workers would have to read articles in the news-papers and learn about the different writings of the Great Leader Mao.
But because the tappers had to go to bed very early in the evening our meetings would also be really short.
They would go on for 20 minutes, half an hour--you'd say a couple of things and then the meeting would end.
This set us apart from the other Units.
And at around 9 p.m., the tappers would hurry off to bed.

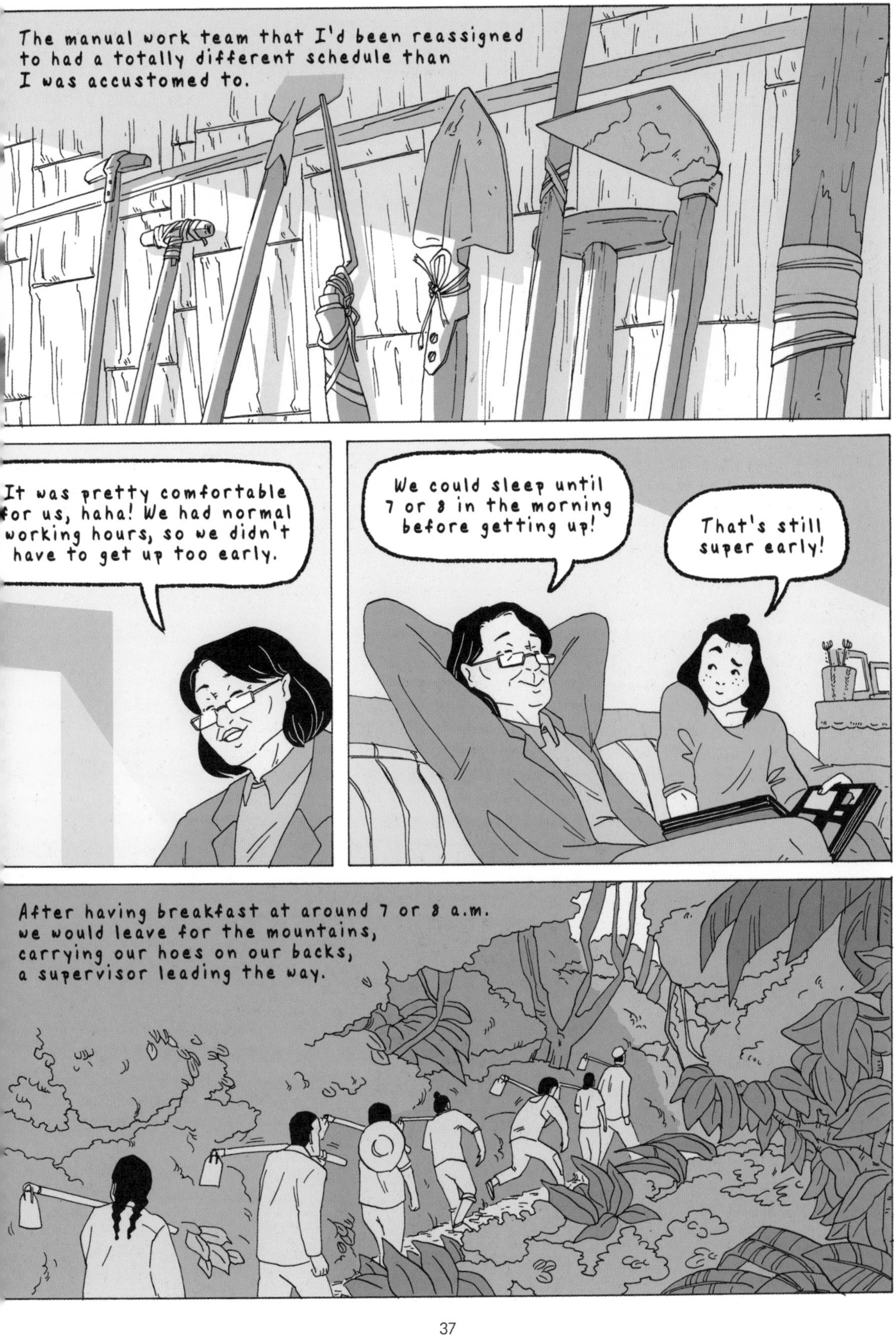
The manual work team that I'd been reassigned to had a totally different schedule than I was accustomed to.
It was pretty comfortable for us, haha! We had normal working hours, so we didn't have to get up too early.
We could sleep until 7 or 8 in the morning before getting up!
That's still super early!
After having breakfast at around 7 or 8 a.m. we would leave for the mountains, carrying our hoes on our backs, a supervisor leading the way.

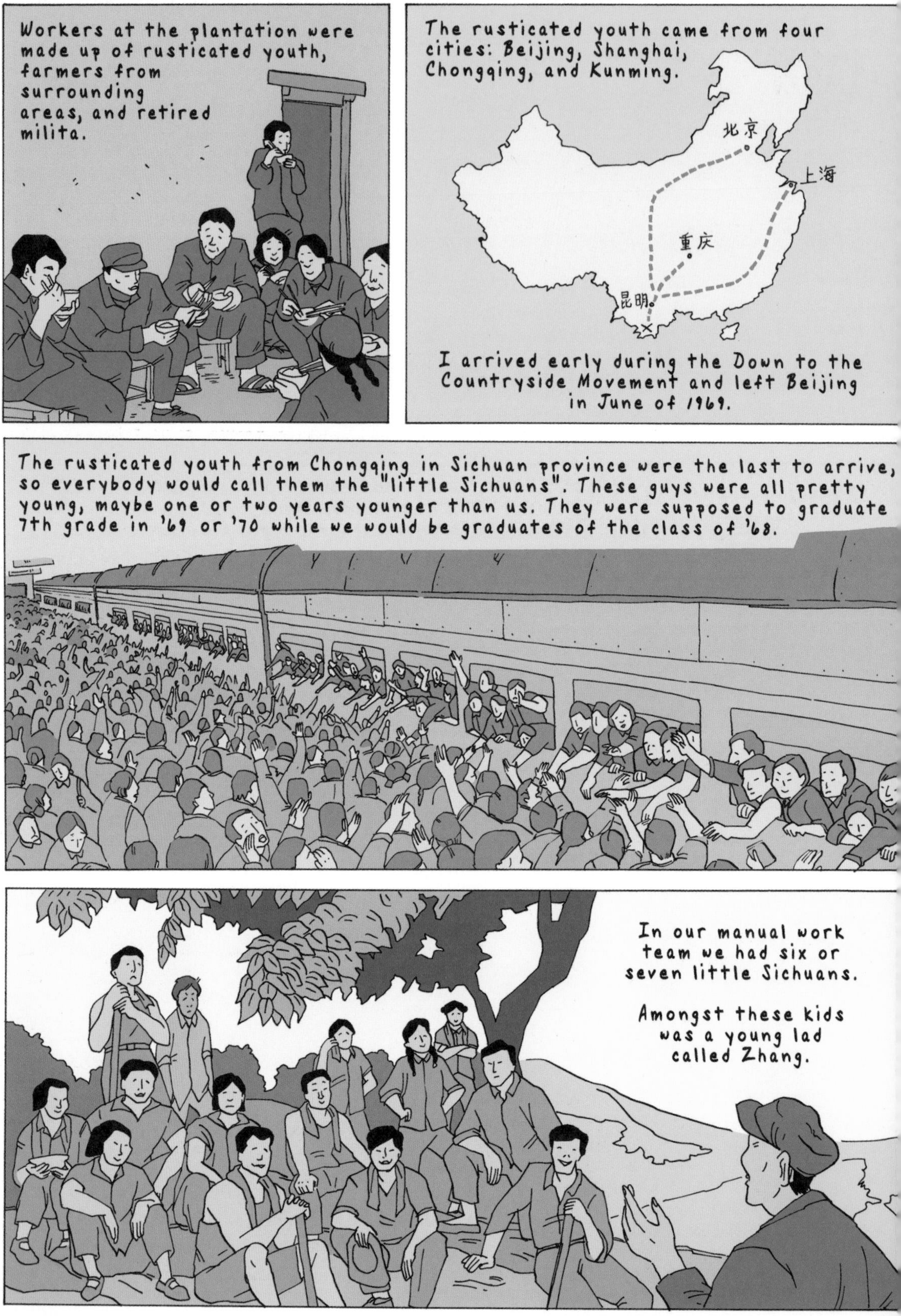

Workers at the plantation were made up of rusticated youth, farmers from surrounding areas, and retired milita.
The rusticated youth came from four cities: Beijing, Shanghai, Chongqing, and Kunming.
北京
上海
重庆
昆明
I arrived early during the Down to the Countryside Movement and left Beijing in June of 1969.
The rusticated youth from Chongqing in Sichuan province were the last to arrive, so everybody would call them the "little Sichuans". These guys were all pretty young, maybe one or two years younger than us. They were supposed to graduate 7th grade in '69 or '70 while we would be graduates of the class of '68.
In our manual work team we had six or seven little Sichuans.
Amongst these kids was a young lad called Zhang.

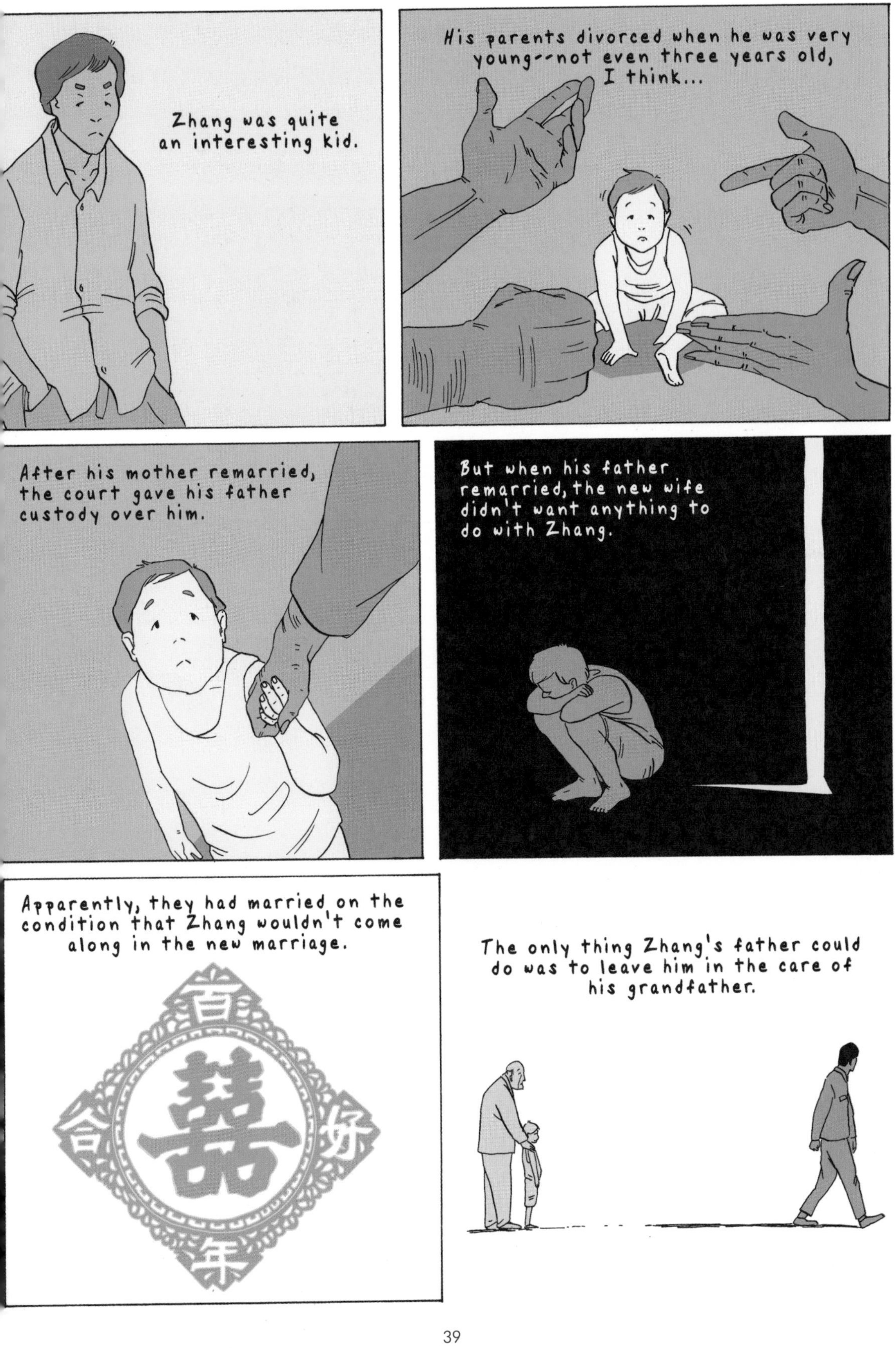
Zhang was quite an interesting kid.
His parents divorced when he was very young--not even three years old, I think...
After his mother remarried, the court gave his father custody over him.
But when his father remarried, the new wife didn't want anything to do with Zhang.
Apparently, they had married on the condition that Zhang wouldn't come along in the new marriage.
百
合
囍
好
年
The only thing Zhang's father could do was to leave him in the care of his grandfather.

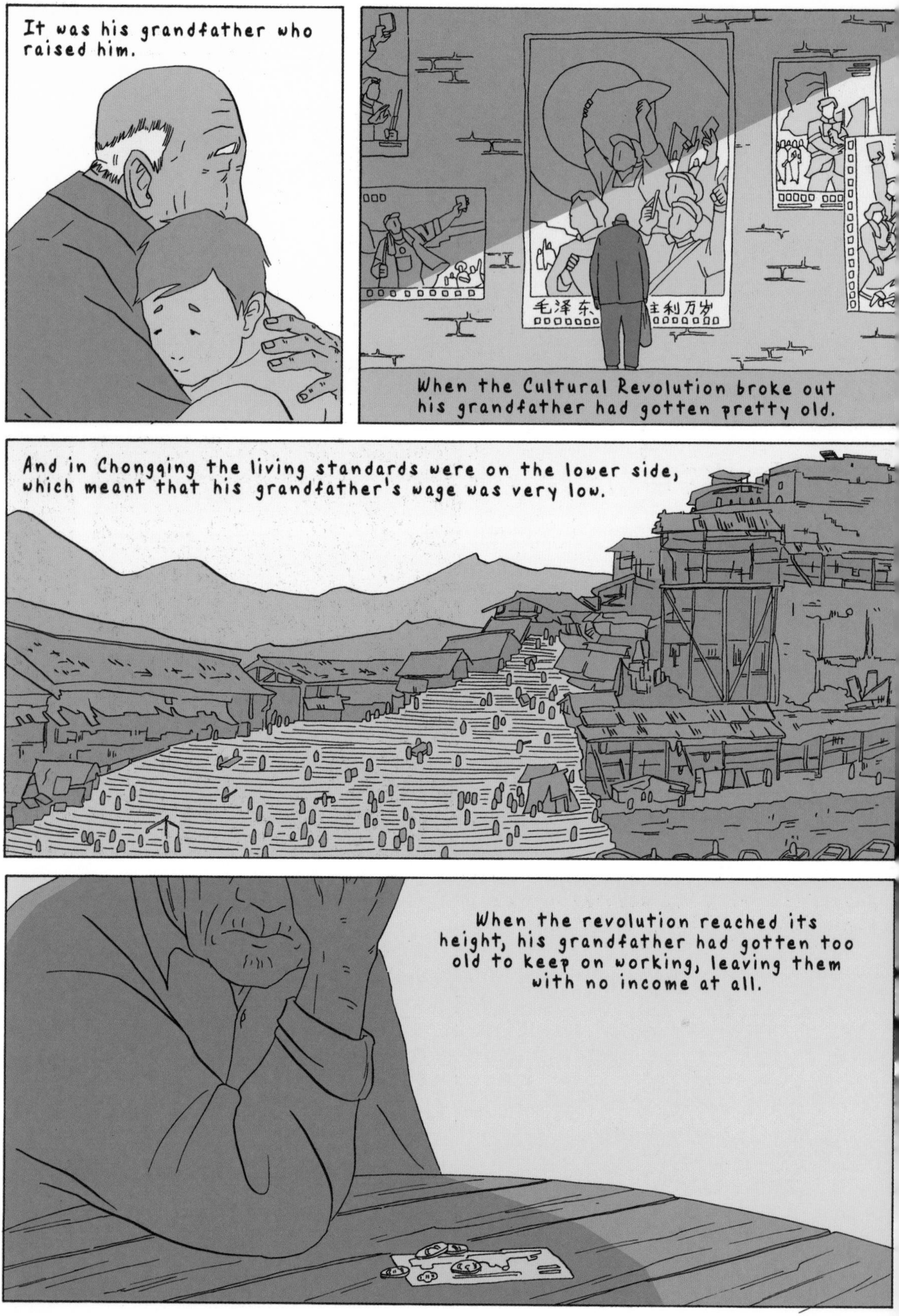

It was his grandfather who raised him.
When the Cultural Revolution broke out his grandfather had gotten pretty old.
And in Chongqing the living standards were on the lower side, which meant that his grandfather's wage was very low.
When the revolution reached its height, his grandfather had gotten too old to keep on working, leaving them with no income at all.

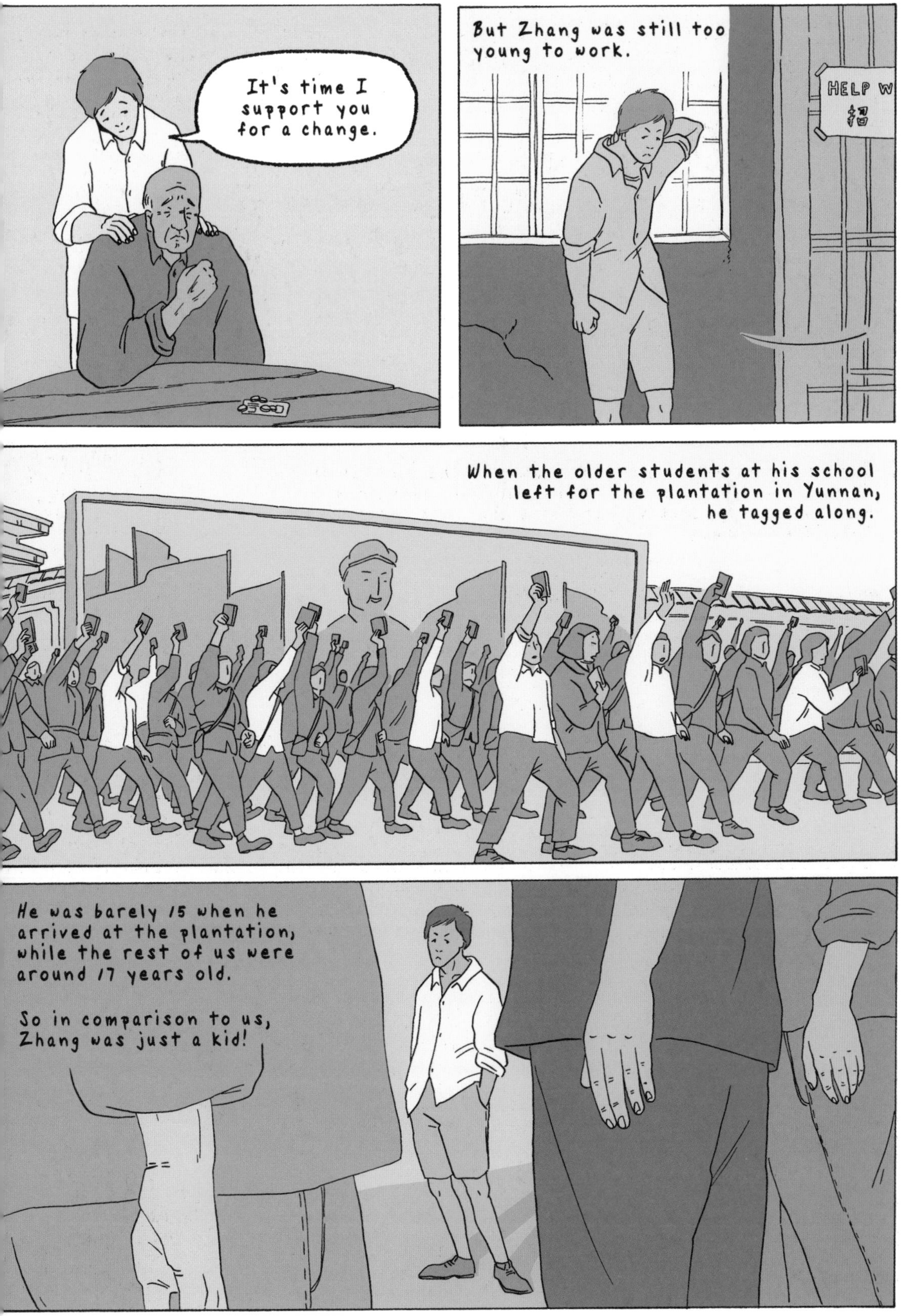
It's time I support you for a change.
But Zhang was still too young to work.
HELP W
招
When the older students at his school left for the plantation in Yunnan, he tagged along.
He was barely 15 when he arrived at the plantation, while the rest of us were around 17 years old.
So in comparison to us, Zhang was just a kid!

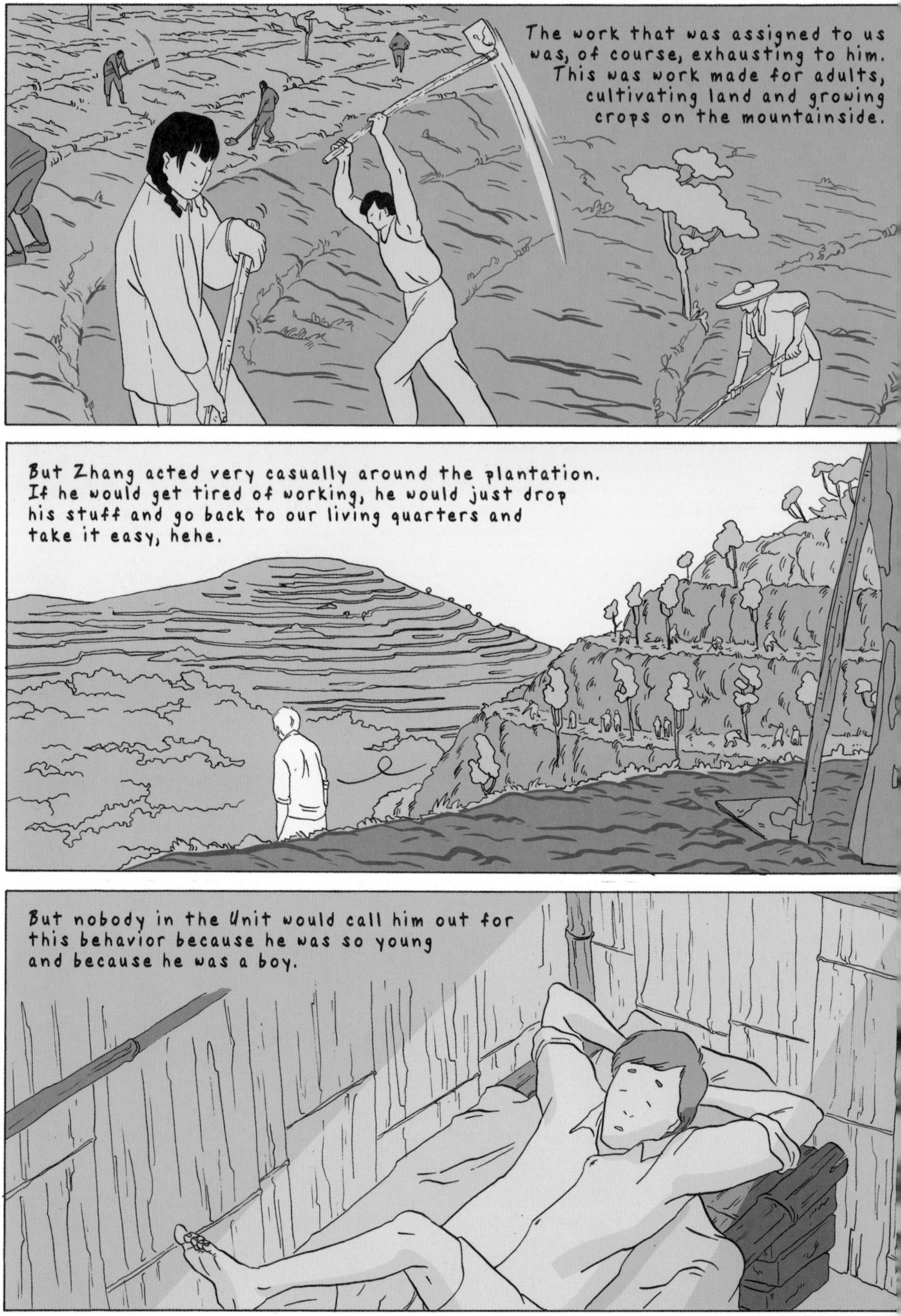
The work that was assigned to us was, of course, exhausting to him. This was work made for adults, cultivating land and growing crops on the mountainside.
But Zhang acted very casually around the plantation. If he would get tired of working, he would just drop his stuff and go back to our living quarters and take it easy, hehe.
But nobody in the Unit would call him out for this behavior because he was so young and because he was a boy.

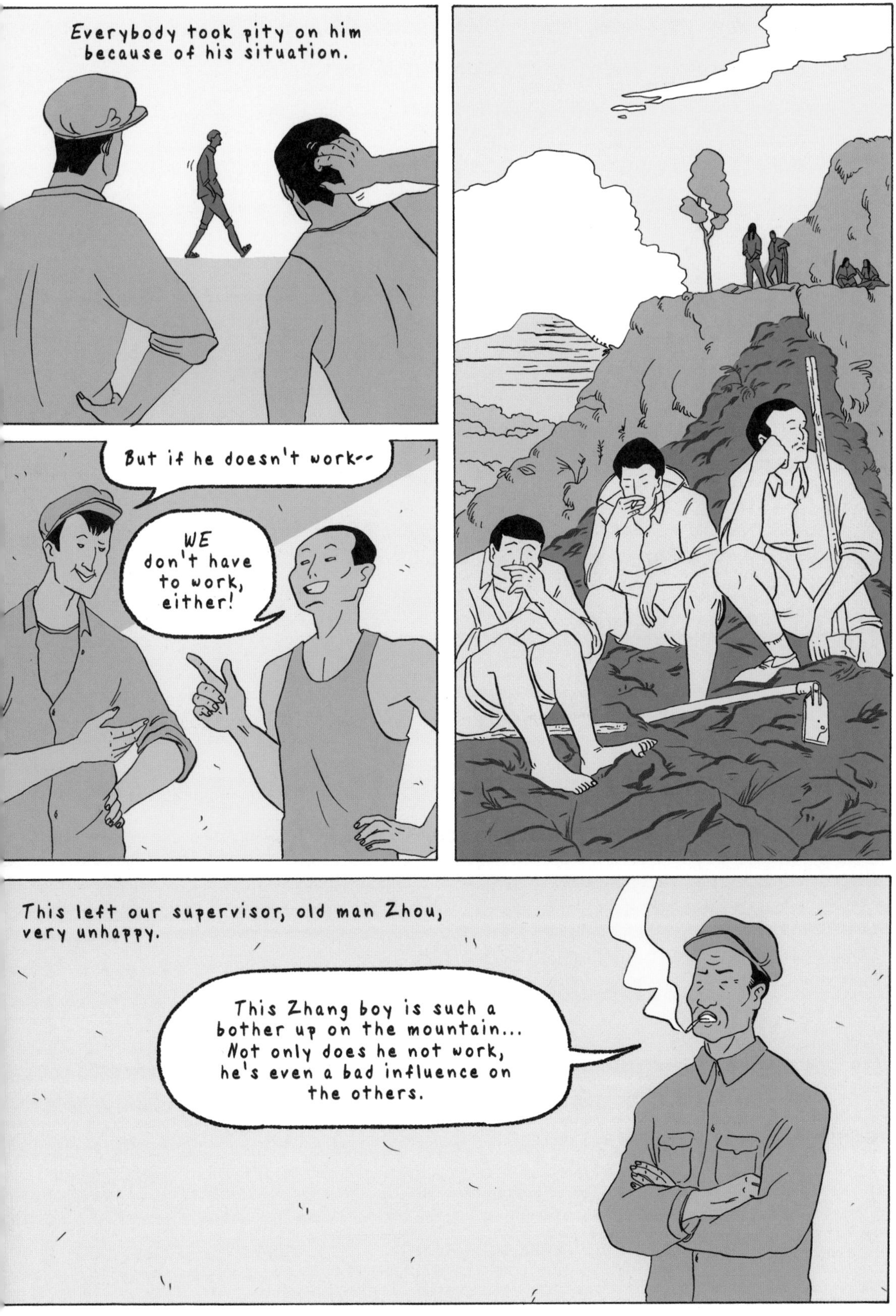
Everybody took pity on him because of his situation.
But if he doesn't work--
WE don't have to work, either!
This left our supervisor, old man Zhou, very unhappy.
This Zhang boy is such a bother up on the mountain... Not only does he not work, he's even a bad influence on the others.

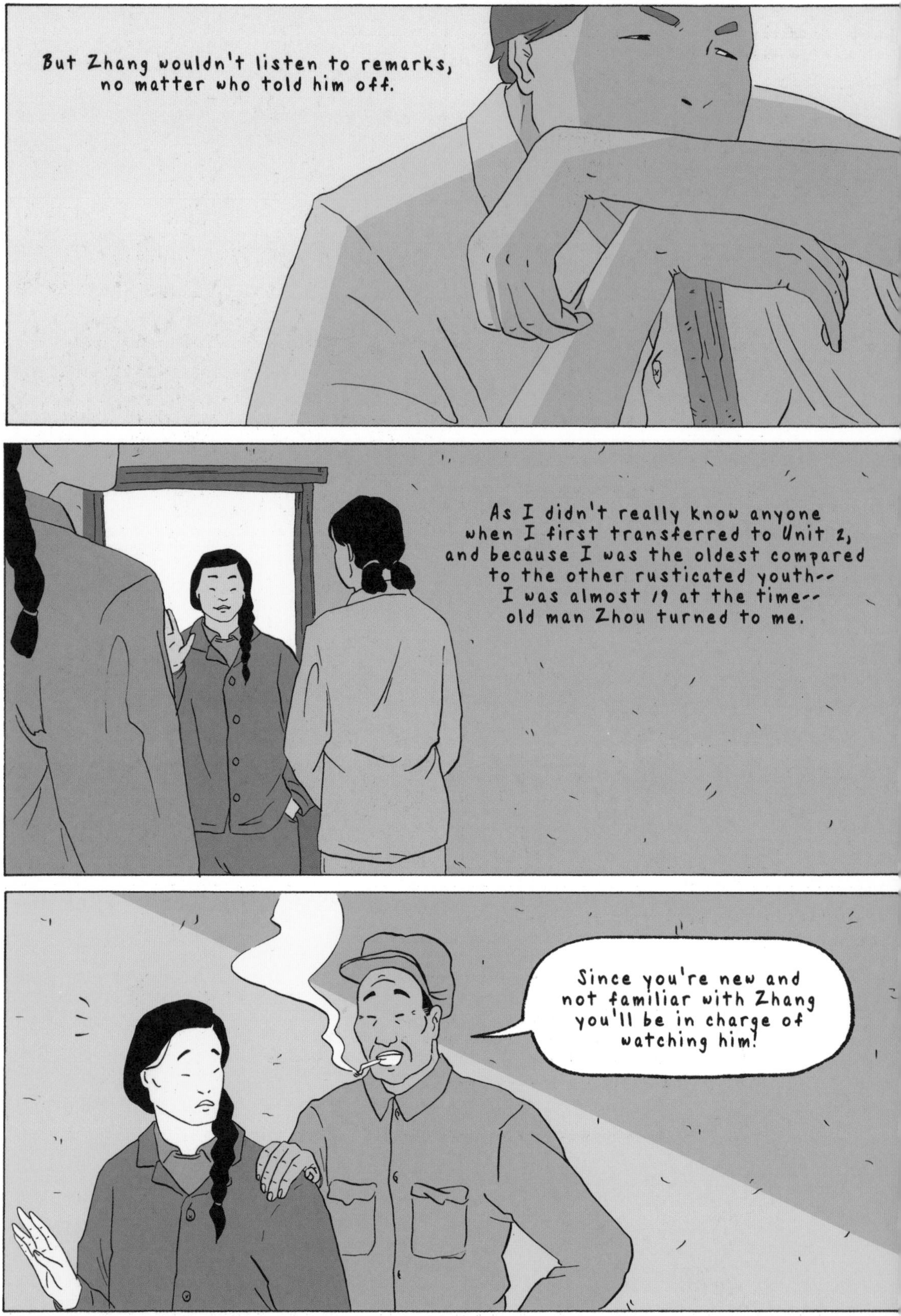
But Zhang wouldn't listen to remarks, no matter who told him off.
As I didn't really know anyone when I first transferred to Unit 2, and because I was the oldest compared to the other rusticated youth-- I was almost 19 at the time-- old man Zhou turned to me.
Since you're new and not familiar with Zhang you'll be in charge of watching him!

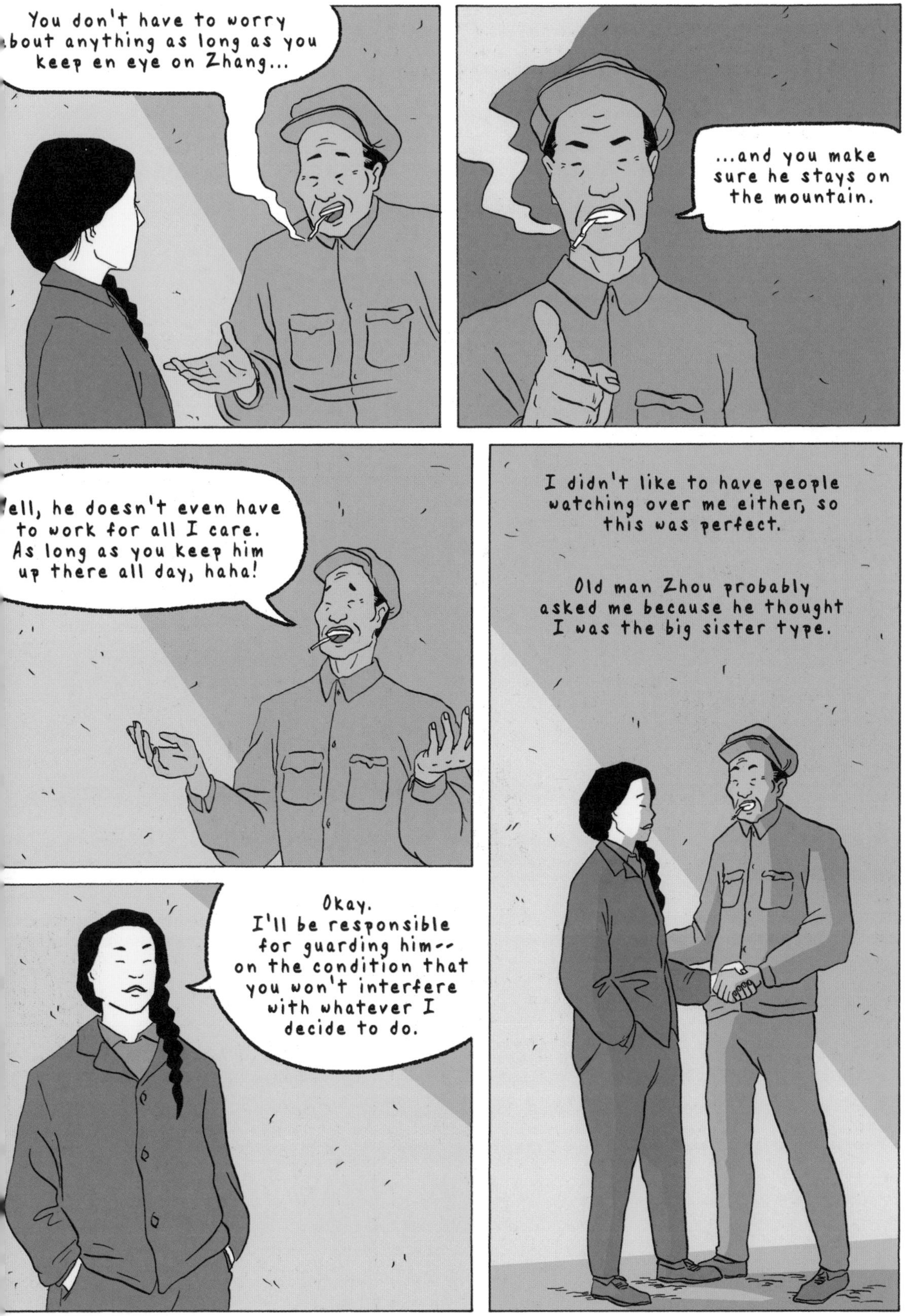
You don't have to worry bout anything as long as you keep en eye on Zhang...
...and you make sure he stays on the mountain.
ell, he doesn't even have to work for all I care. As long as you keep him up there all day, haha!
Okay. I'll be responsible for guarding him--on the condition that you won't interfere with whatever I decide to do.
I didn't like to have people watching over me either, so this was perfect.
Old man Zhou probably asked me because he thought I was the big sister type.

We were in the midst of spring and the task at hand for the manual work team was to turn the soil over so that we could plant new seeds. But because it was the mountainside we couldn't use cows or machines, only manpower.

We'll divide the land between us and you'll be working in groups of two.

Zhang, You dig with her--

What?

If w   t   there I'll go I'm   e   y part. So e befo   th   day is over. rest o th   ! I won't done,   . I'll just sit on the mountain and relax a   won't lift   her finger to d or   lp   e m   for the day an ju h   ure   handle the res he

Ok, Ok, whatever. You two are still a group.

nod

Let's make this a contest.

If we dig together there's no way to tell who worked more and who worked less. And I don't want to carry your load!

She's a woman, so of course she'll be weaker than me.

There's no way I'll lose to her!

Whoever finishes his part first gets to take the rest of the afternoon off.

So, we gave our lot of land a good look and drew a line with sticks approximately in the middle.

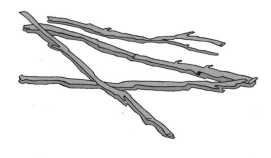

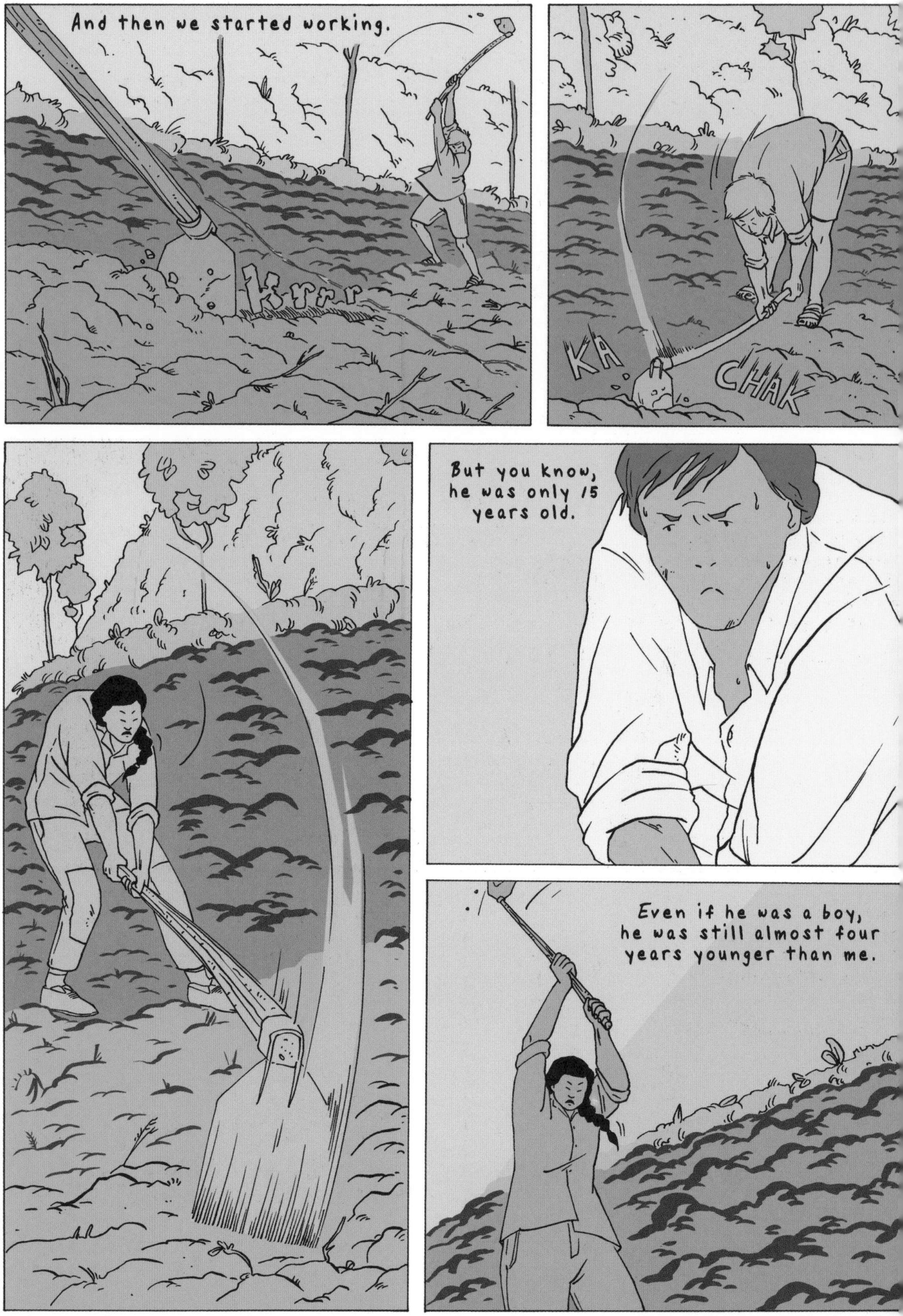
And then we started working.
Krrr
KA
CHAK
But you know, he was only 15 years old.
Even if he was a boy, he was still almost four years younger than me.

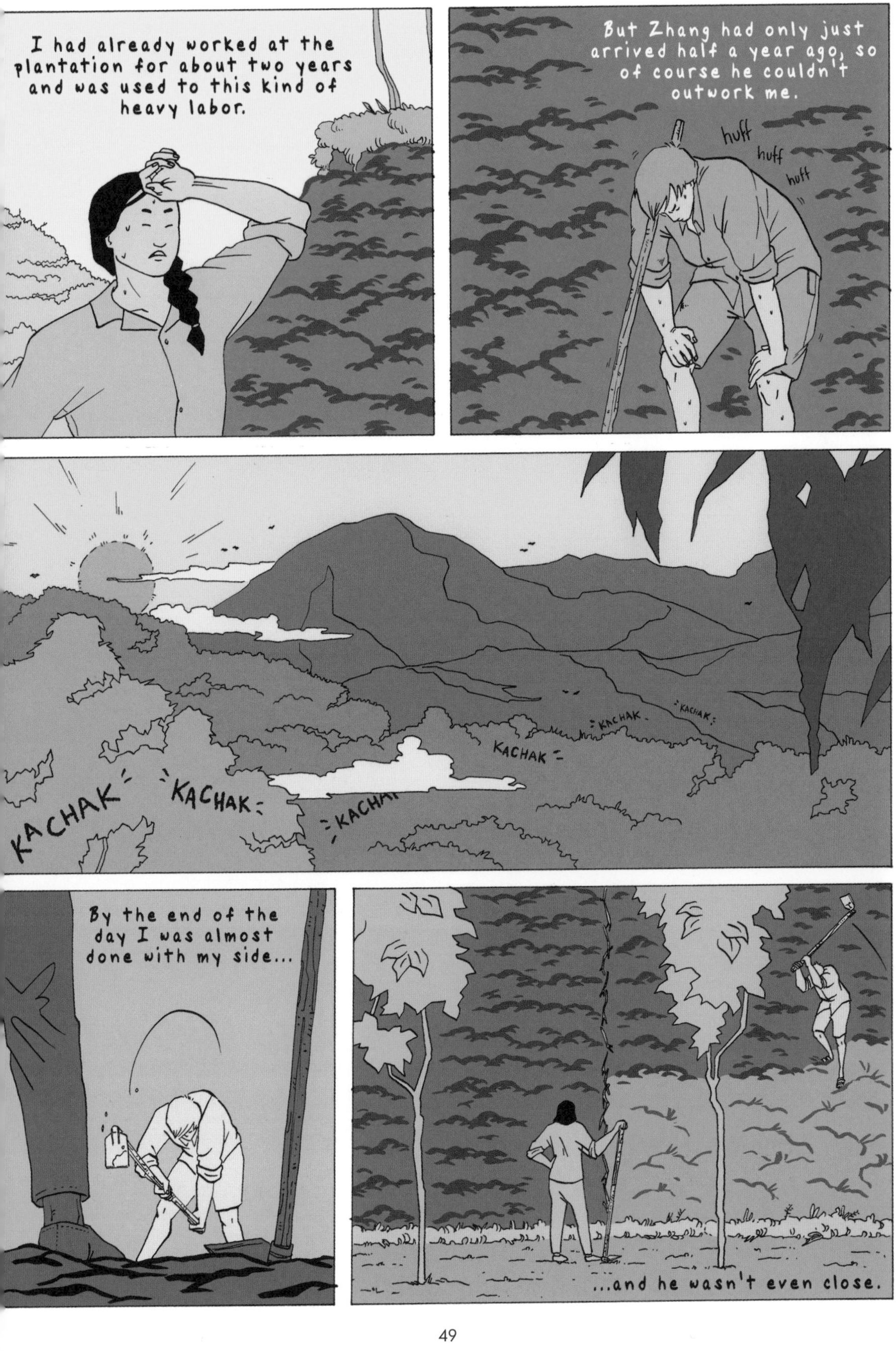
I had already worked at the plantation for about two years and was used to this kind of heavy labor.
But Zhang had only just arrived half a year ago, so of course he couldn't outwork me.
huff
huff
huff
KACHAK
KACHAK
KACHAK
KACHAK
KACHAK
KACHAK
By the end of the day I was almost done with my side...
...and he wasn't even close.

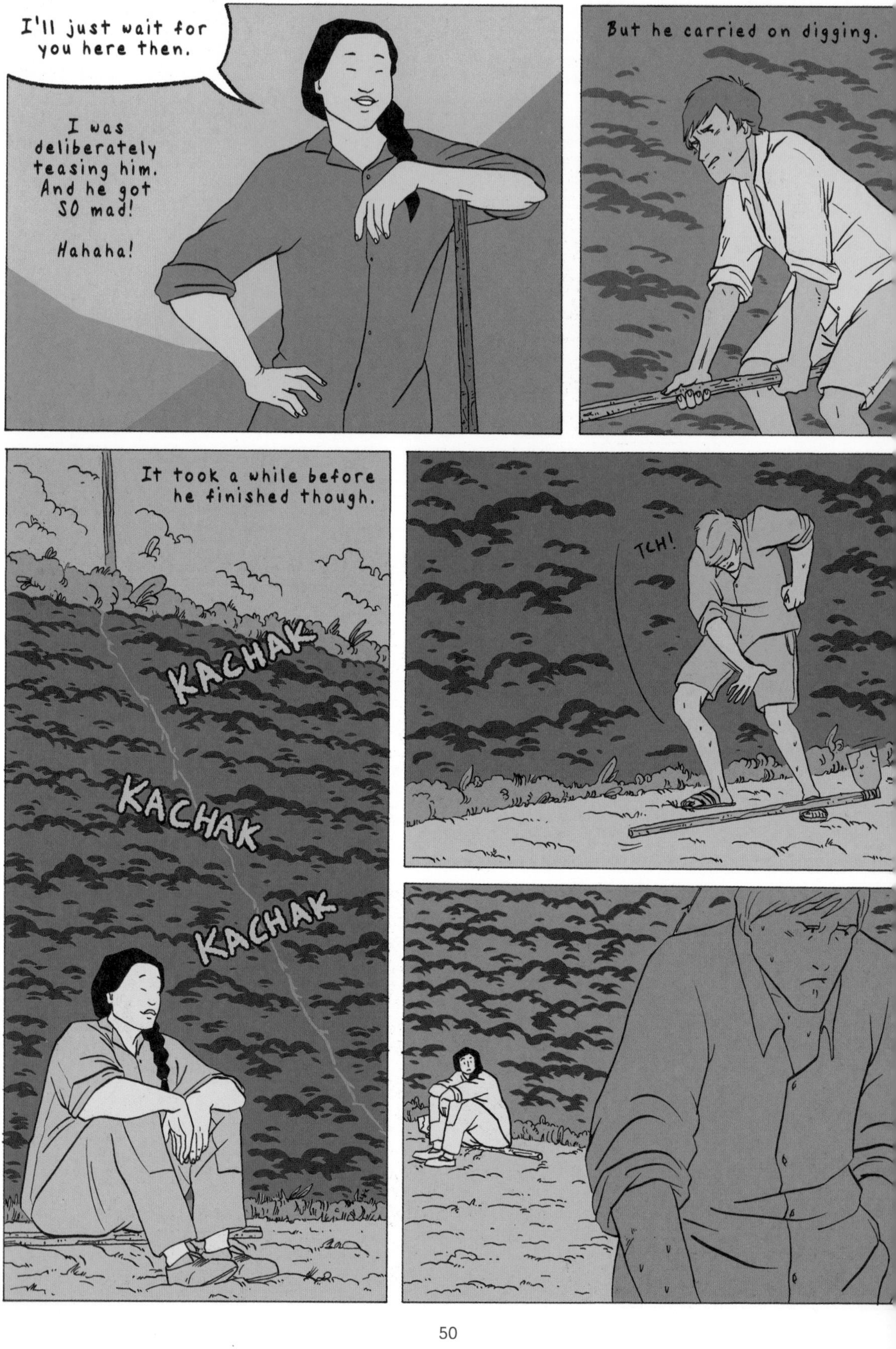
I'll just wait for you here then.
I was deliberately teasing him. And he got SO mad!
Hahaha!
But he carried on digging.
It took a while before he finished though.
KACHAK
KACHAK
KACHAK
TCH!

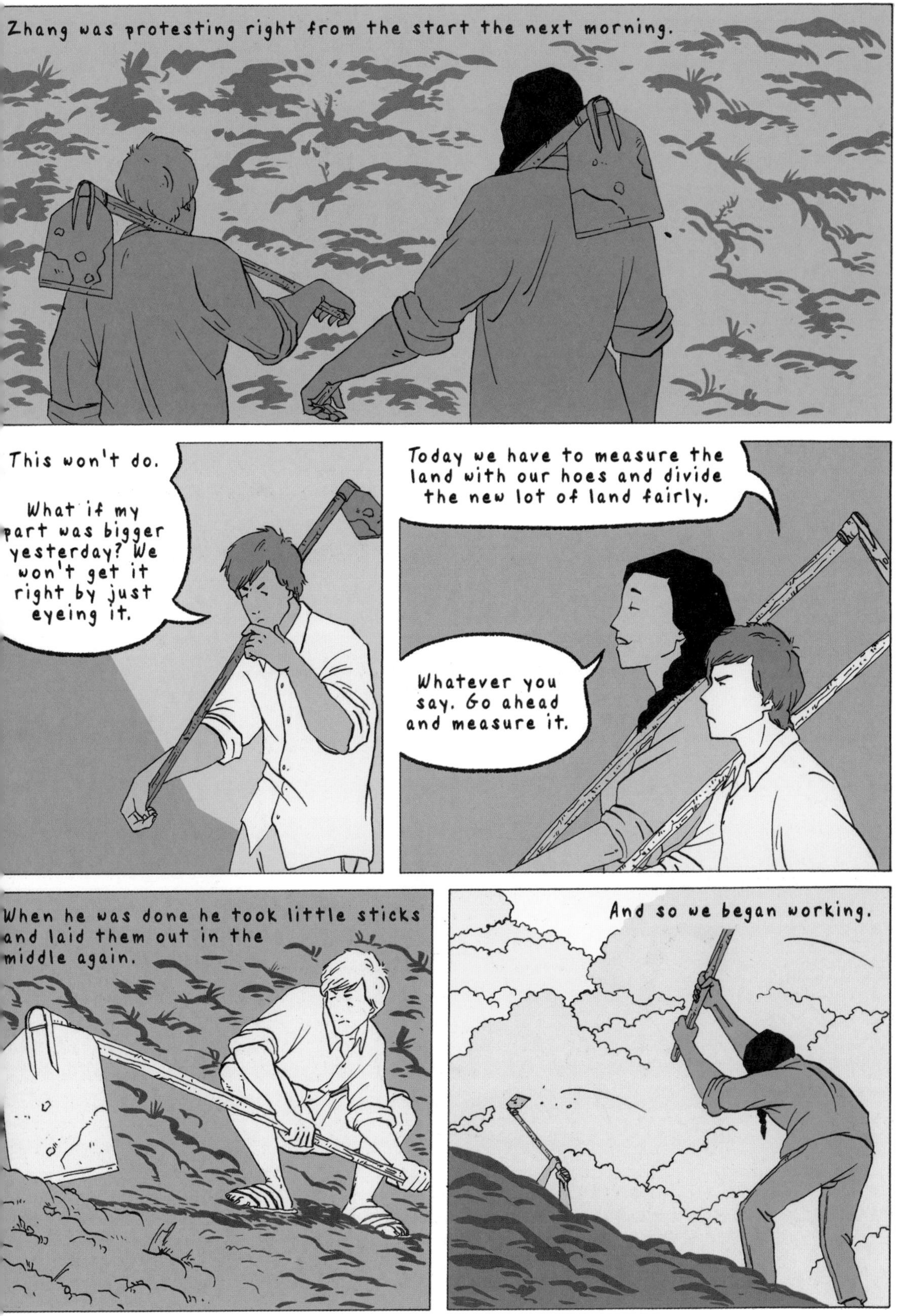

Zhang was protesting right from the start the next morning.
This won't do.
What if my part was bigger yesterday? We won't get it right by just eyeing it.
Today we have to measure the land with our hoes and divide the new lot of land fairly.
Whatever you say. Go ahead and measure it.
When he was done he took little sticks and laid them out in the middle again.
And so we began working.

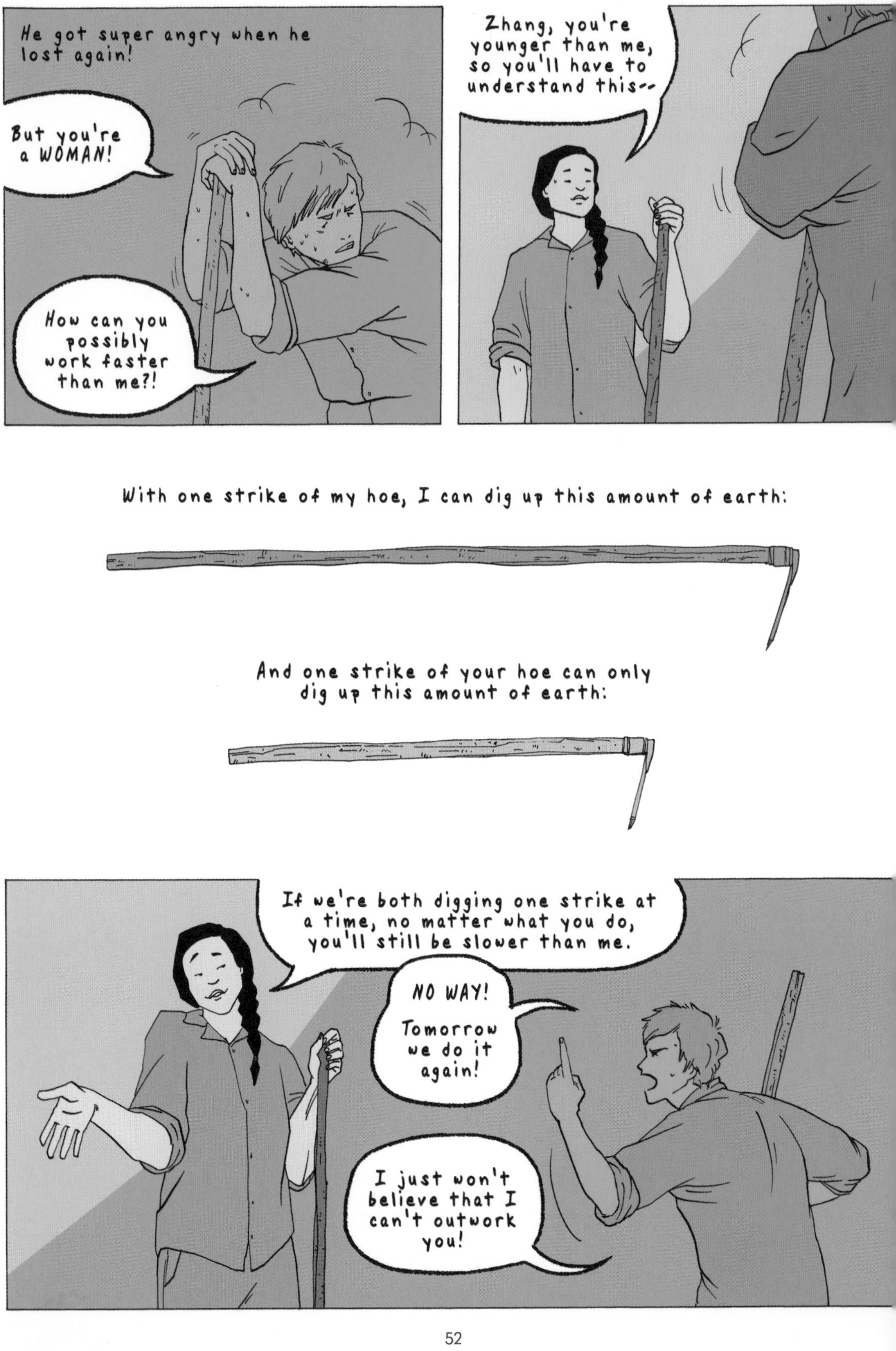
He got super angry when he lost again!
But you're a WOMAN!
How can you possibly work faster than me?!
Zhang, you're younger than me, so you'll have to understand this--
With one strike of my hoe, I can dig up this amount of earth:
And one strike of your hoe can only dig up this amount of earth:
If we're both digging one strike at a time, no matter what you do, you'll still be slower than me.
NO WAY!
Tomorrow we do it again!
I just won't believe that I can't outwork you!

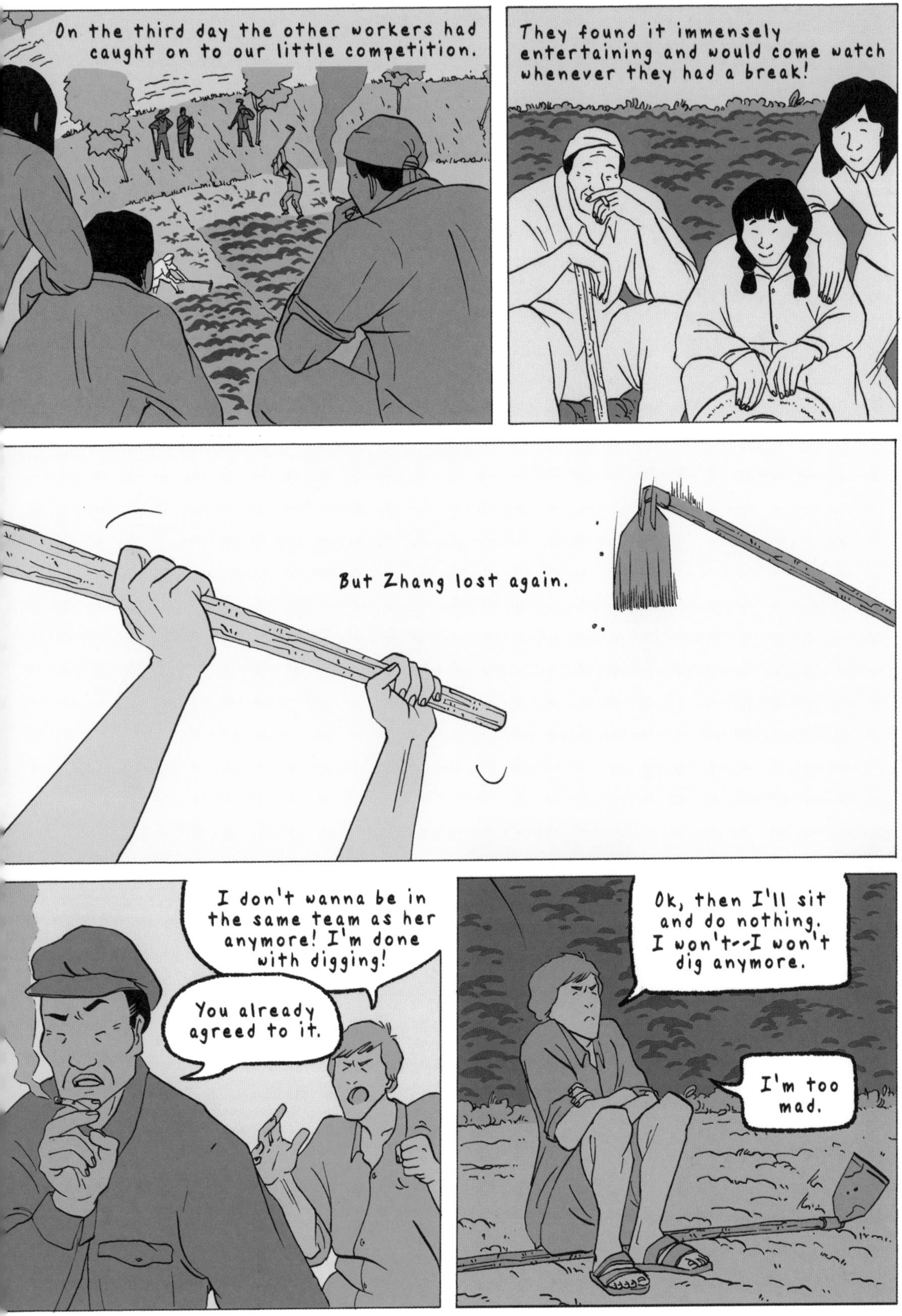
On the third day the other workers had caught on to our little competition.
They found it immensely entertaining and would come watch whenever they had a break!
But Zhang lost again.
I don't wanna be in the same team as her anymore! I'm done with digging!
You already agreed to it.
Ok, then I'll sit and do nothing. I won't--I won't dig anymore.
I'm too mad.

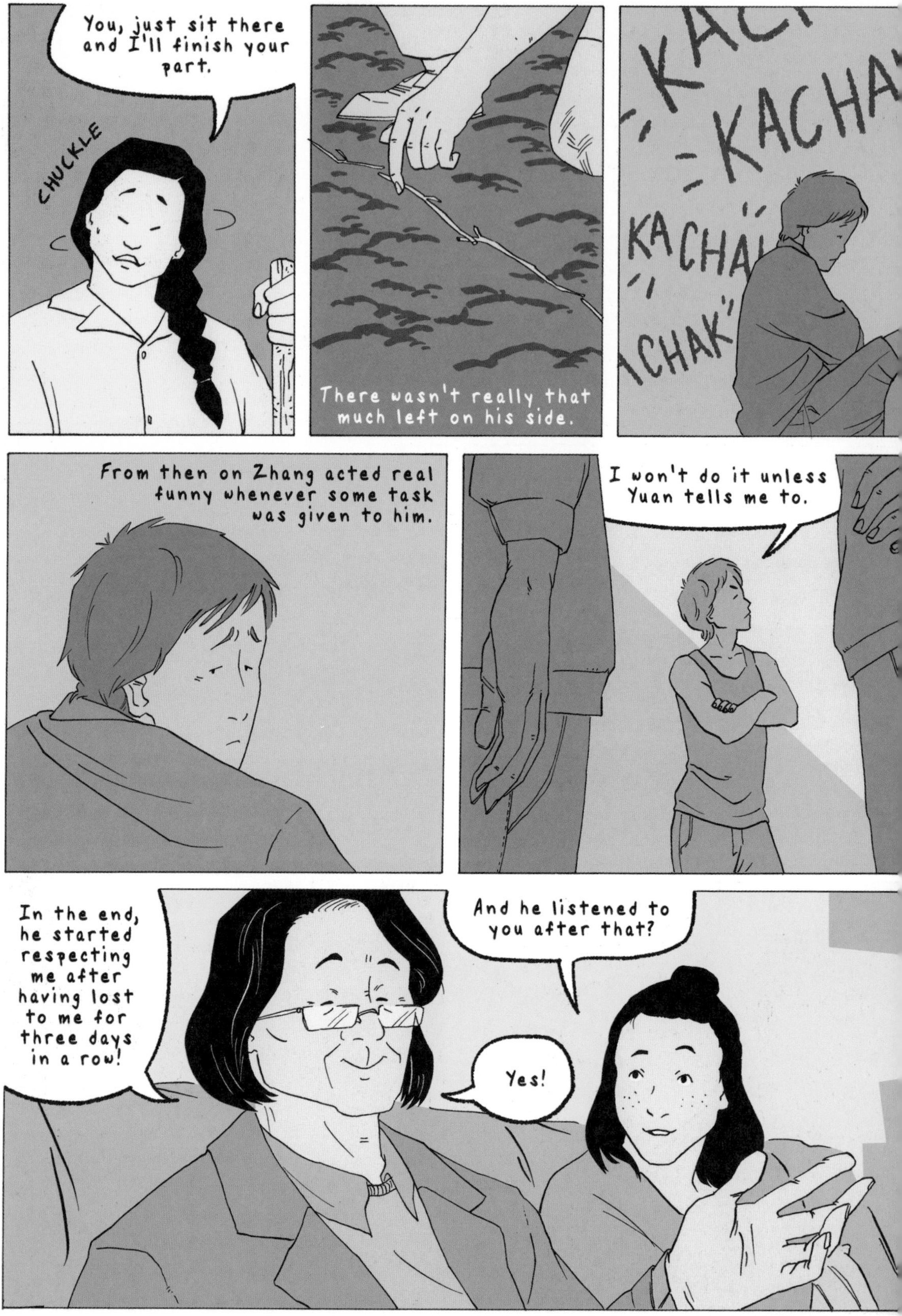
You, just sit there and I'll finish your part.
CHUCKLE
There wasn't really that much left on his side.
KACHAK
KACHAK
KACHAK
KACHAK
From then on Zhang acted real funny whenever some task was given to him.
I won't do it unless Yuan tells me to.
In the end, he started respecting me after having lost to me for three days in a row!
And he listened to you after that?
Yes!

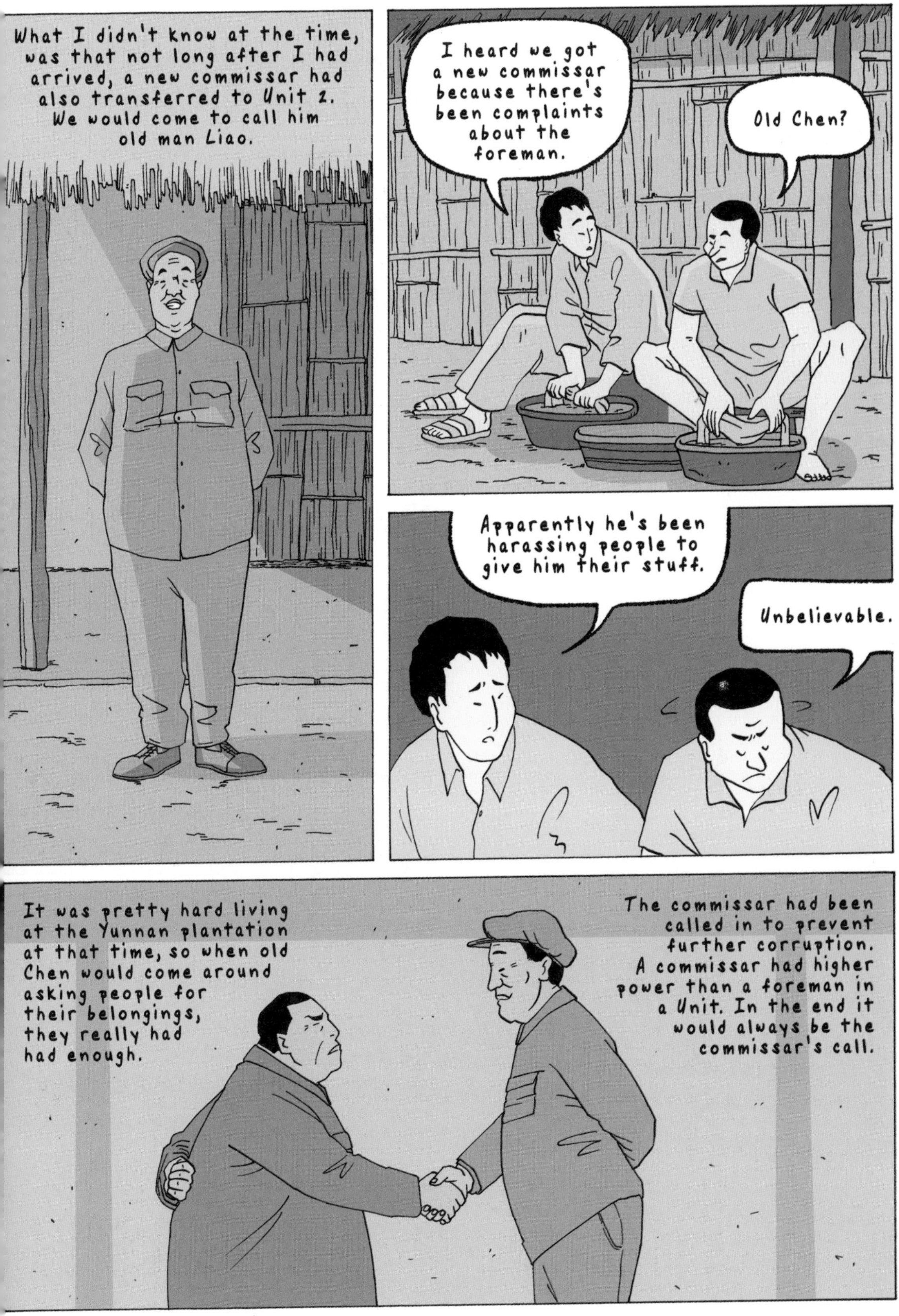
What I didn't know at the time, was that not long after I had arrived, a new commissar had also transferred to Unit 2. We would come to call him old man Liao.
I heard we got a new commissar because there's been complaints about the foreman.
Old Chen?
Apparently he's been harassing people to give him their stuff.
Unbelievable.
It was pretty hard living at the Yunnan plantation at that time, so when old Chen would come around asking people for their belongings, they really had had enough.
The commissar had been called in to prevent further corruption. A commissar had higher power than a foreman in a Unit. In the end it would always be the commissar's call.

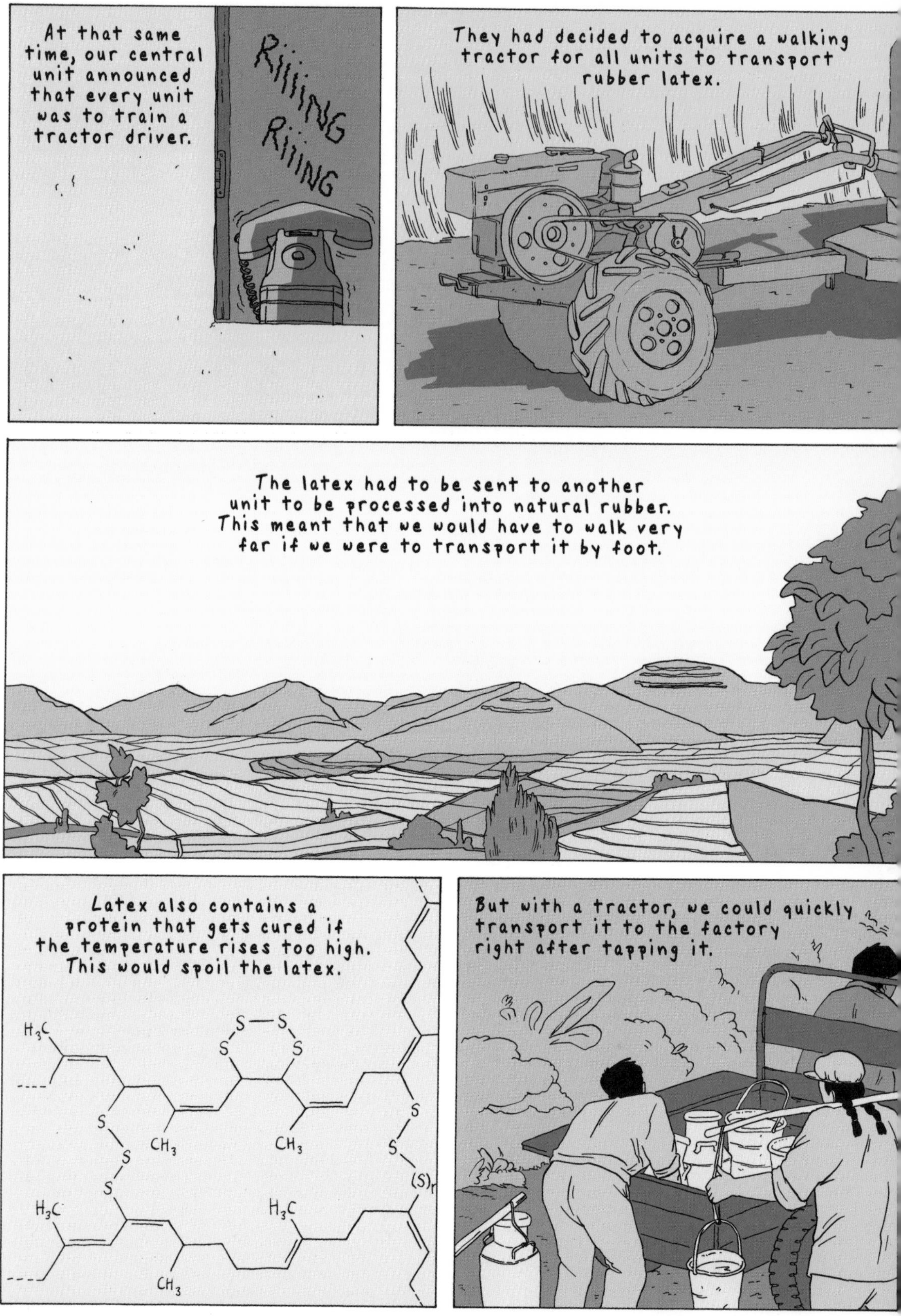
At that same time, our central unit announced that every unit was to train a tractor driver.
RIIIING RIIIING
They had decided to acquire a walking tractor for all units to transport rubber latex.
The latex had to be sent to another unit to be processed into natural rubber. This meant that we would have to walk very far if we were to transport it by foot.
Latex also contains a protein that gets cured if the temperature rises too high. This would spoil the latex.
H_3C
S—S
S S
S
S
S
CH_3
CH_3
S
S
(S)
H_3C
H_3C
CH_3
But with a tractor, we could quickly transport it to the factory right after tapping it.

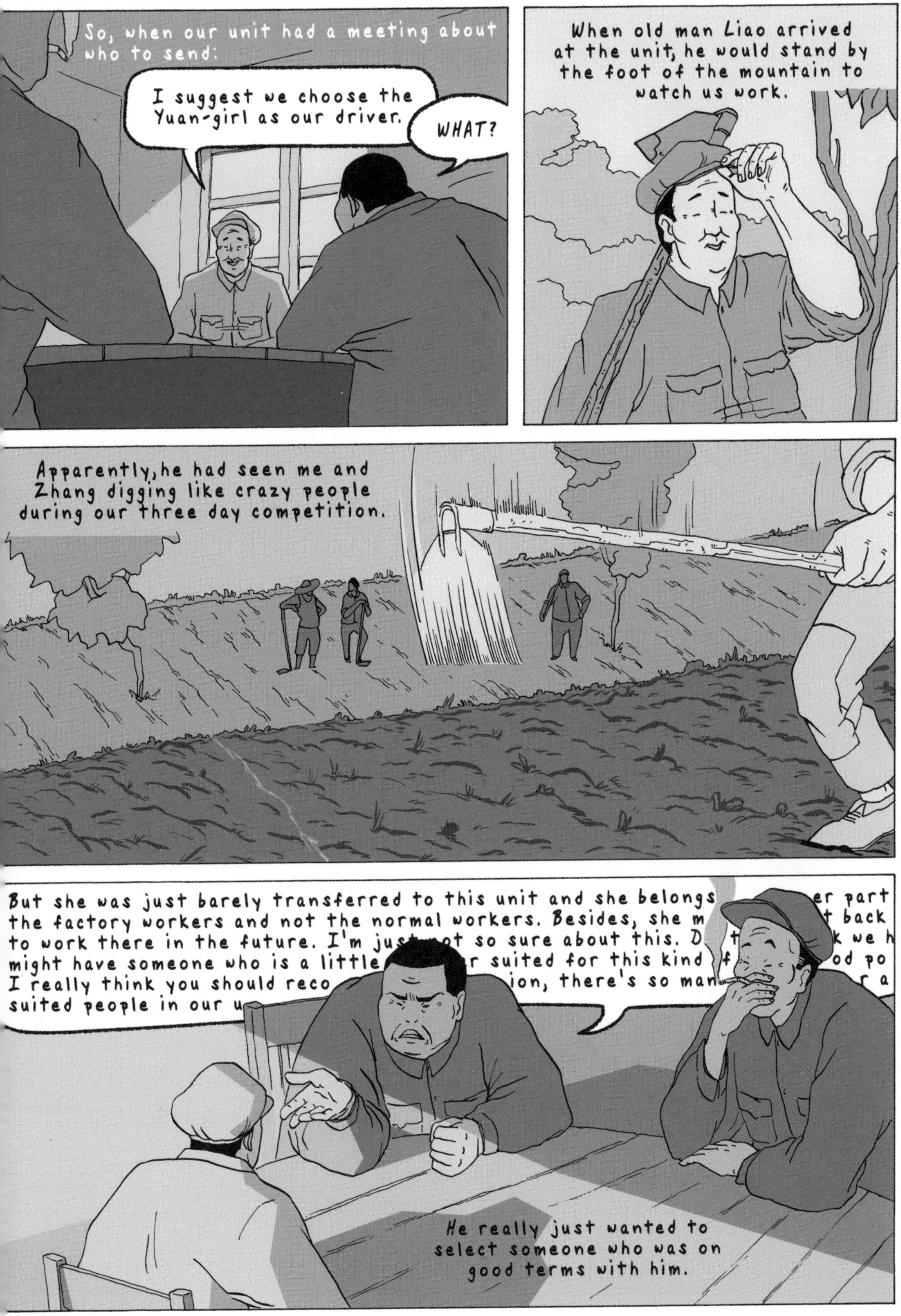
So, when our unit had a meeting about who to send:
I suggest we choose the Yuan-girl as our driver.
WHAT?
When old man Liao arrived at the unit, he would stand by the foot of the mountain to watch us work.
Apparently, he had seen me and Zhang digging like crazy people during our three day competition.
But she was just barely transferred to this unit and she belongs er part
the factory workers and not the normal workers. Besides, she m t back
to work there in the future. I'm ju t so sure about this. D t k we h
might have someone who is a little r suited for this kind f od po
I really think you should reco ion, there's so man r a
suited people in our u
He really just wanted to select someone who was on good terms with him.

But as old man Liao had the last say, he declared:

I choose her to go.

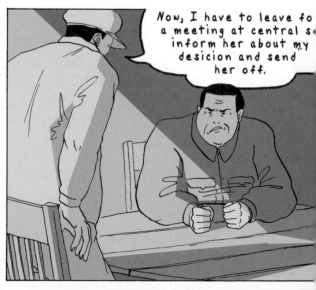

Now, I have to leave for a meeting at central so inform her about my desicion and send her off.

...well?

Yes, sir.

But Yuan is on sick leave, so I best not disturb her rest.

I was bedridden with a high fever because I had caught malaria.

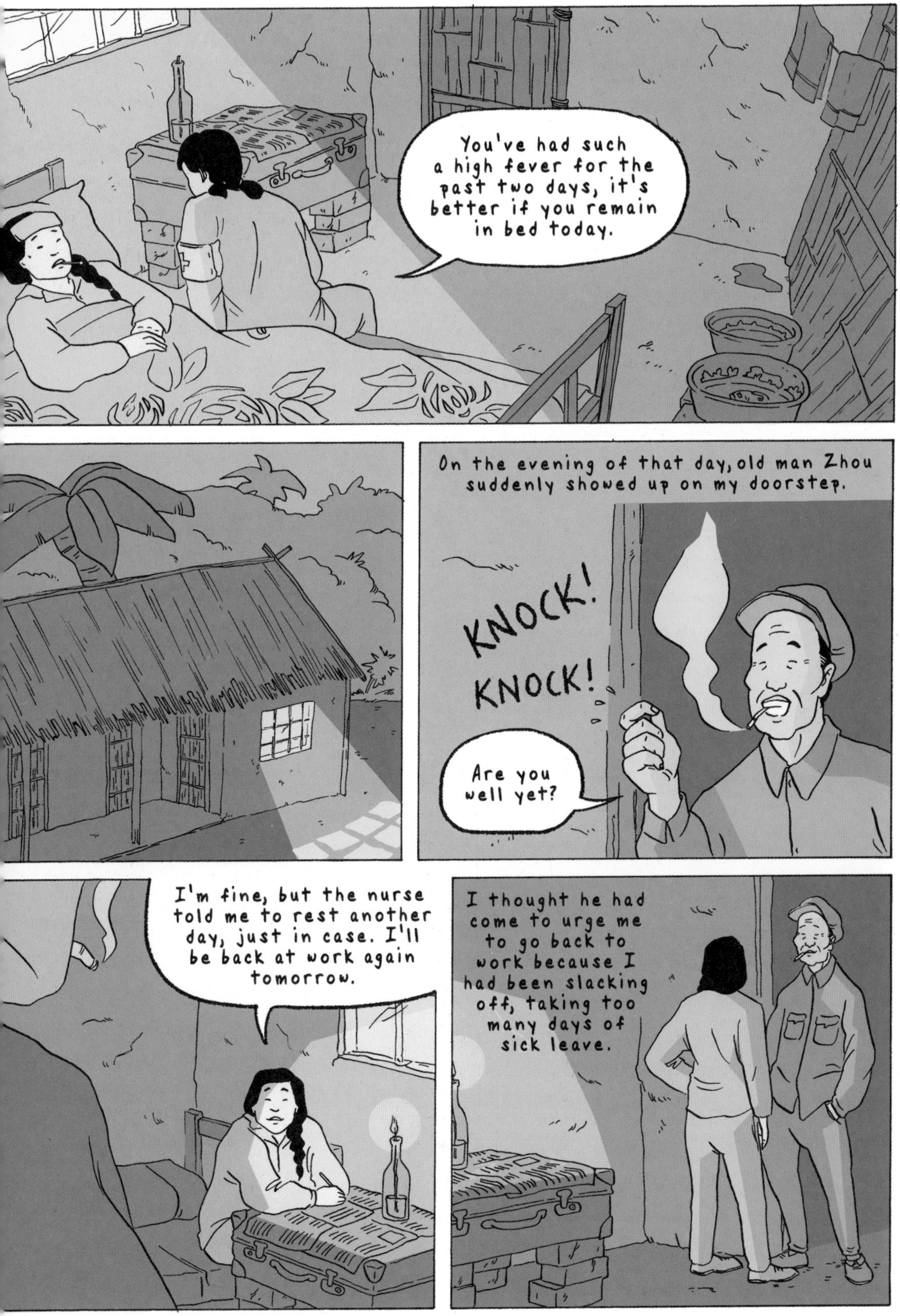
You've had such a high fever for the past two days, it's better if you remain in bed today.
On the evening of that day, old man Zhou suddenly showed up on my doorstep.
KNOCK! KNOCK!
Are you well yet?
I'm fine, but the nurse told me to rest another day, just in case. I'll be back at work again tomorrow.
I thought he had come to urge me to go back to work because I had been slacking off, taking too many days of sick leave.

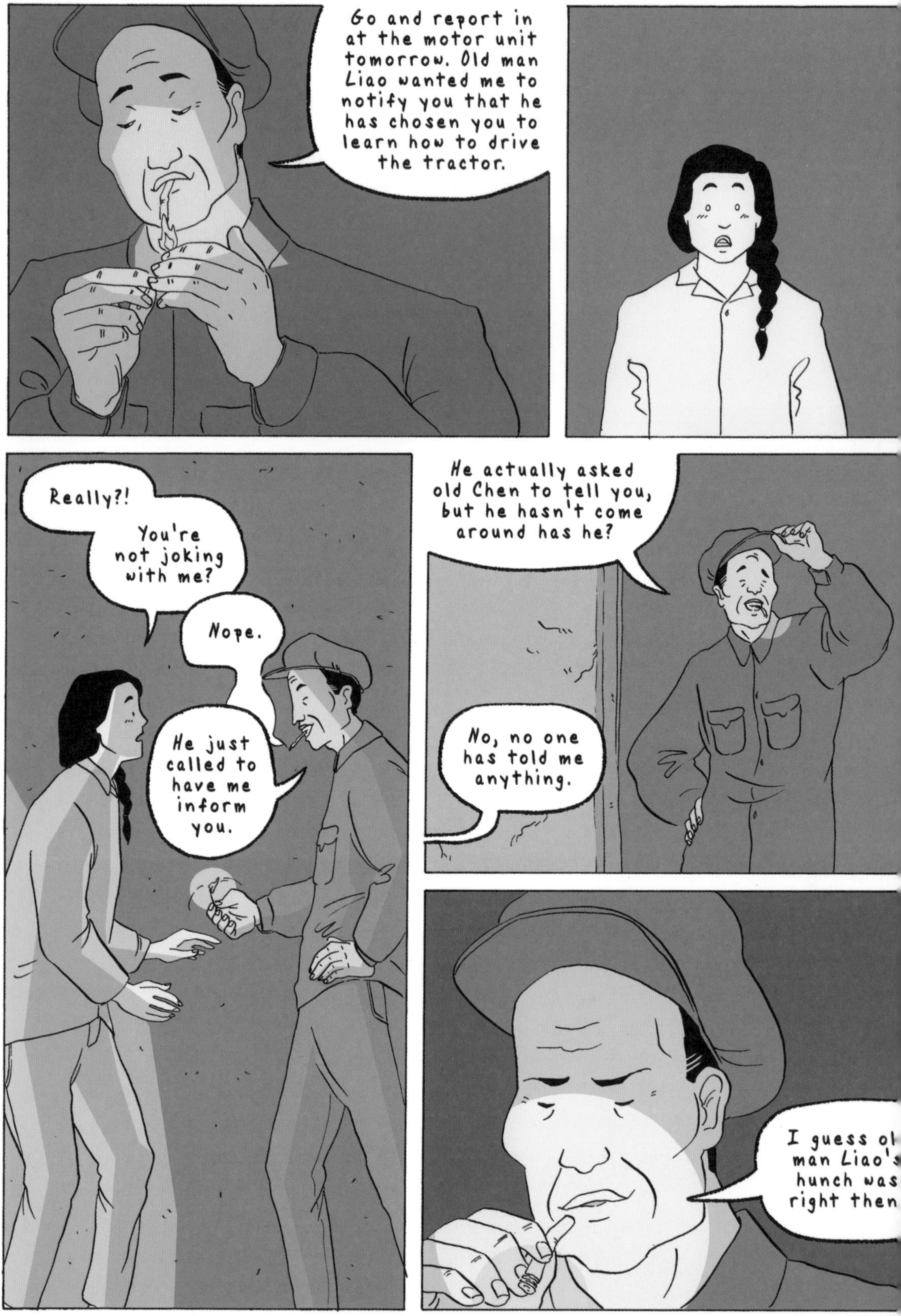
Go and report in at the motor unit tomorrow. Old man Liao wanted me to notify you that he has chosen you to learn how to drive the tractor.
Really?!
You're not joking with me?
Nope.
He just called to have me inform you.
He actually asked old Chen to tell you, but he hasn't come around has he?
No, no one has told me anything.
I guess ol
man Liao's
hunch was
right then

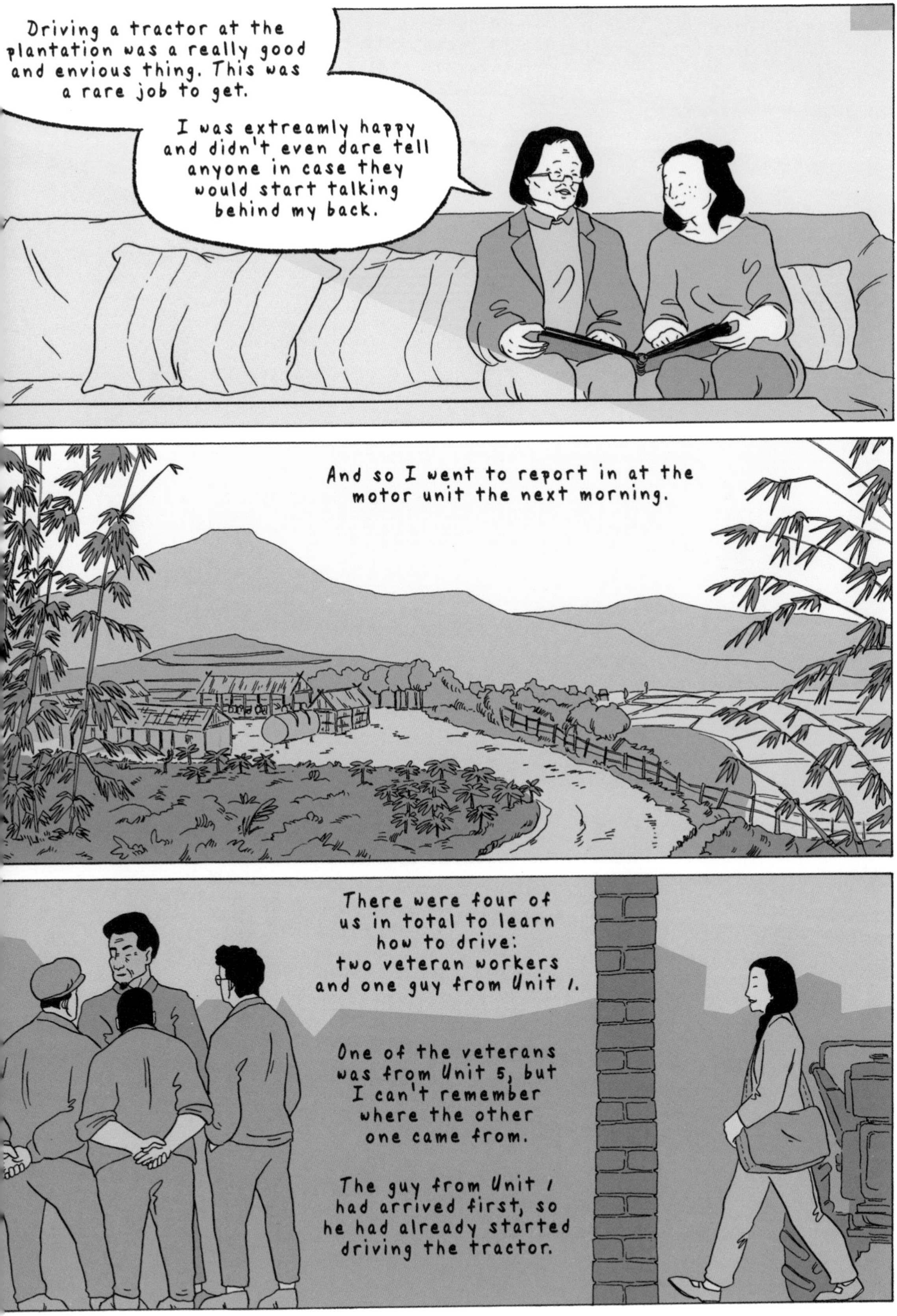
Driving a tractor at the plantation was a really good and envious thing. This was a rare job to get.
I was extreamly happy and didn't even dare tell anyone in case they would start talking behind my back.
And so I went to report in at the motor unit the next morning.
There were four of us in total to learn how to drive: two veteran workers and one guy from Unit 1.
One of the veterans was from Unit 5, but I can't remember where the other one came from.
The guy from Unit 1 had arrived first, so he had already started driving the tractor.

I'll teach you how to drive, but I refuse to teach those two geezers.

When those two finally leave, I'll start teaching you.

Old Hou was the foreman at the motor unit and he looked down on the veterans.

He believed that they had a low education because most of them came from the countryside. Generally, this meant that they wouldn't have attended school for long.

Old Hou was of the view that driving a walking tractor required a certain level of technical skill.

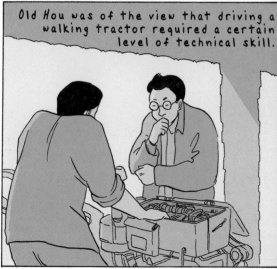

He also thought that it would be for the best if the person was younger as they would be dealing with basic motor theory.

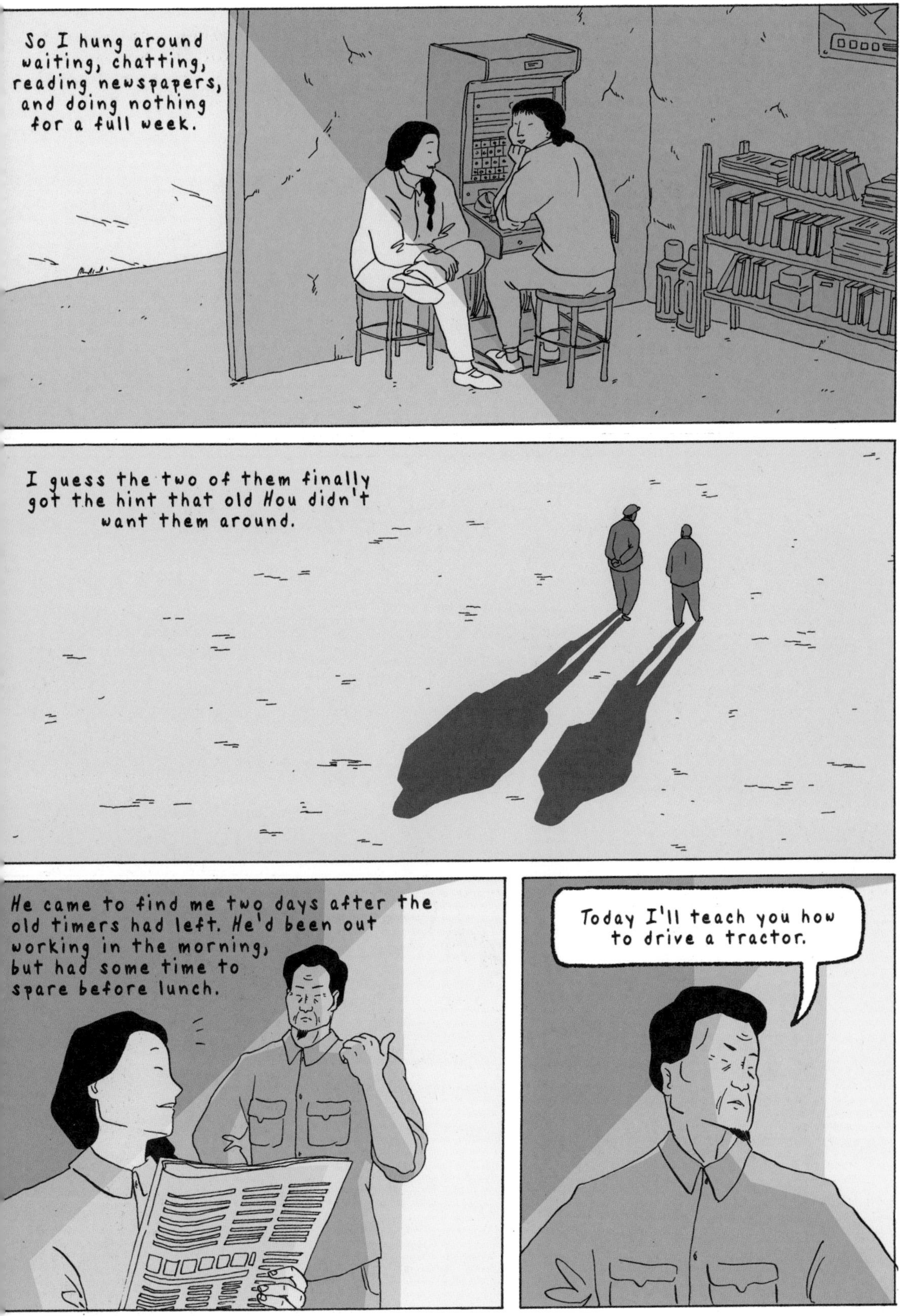
So I hung around waiting, chatting, reading newspapers, and doing nothing for a full week.
I guess the two of them finally got the hint that old Hou didn't want them around.
He came to find me two days after the old timers had left. He'd been out working in the morning, but had some time to spare before lunch.
Today I'll teach you how to drive a tractor.

The walking tractor is a single engine machine, so it's pretty simple compared to other tractors. It has the same driving mechanism as a bicycle.

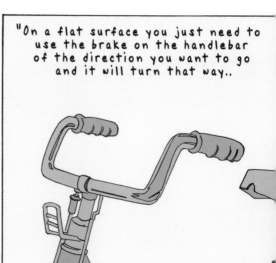

"On a flat surface you just need to use the brake on the handlebar of the direction you want to go and it will turn that way.."

"But when going downhill this mechanism will be inverted, so you'll need to brake on the left side if you want to go right and vice versa."

And now you drive.

Just like that?

Yes.

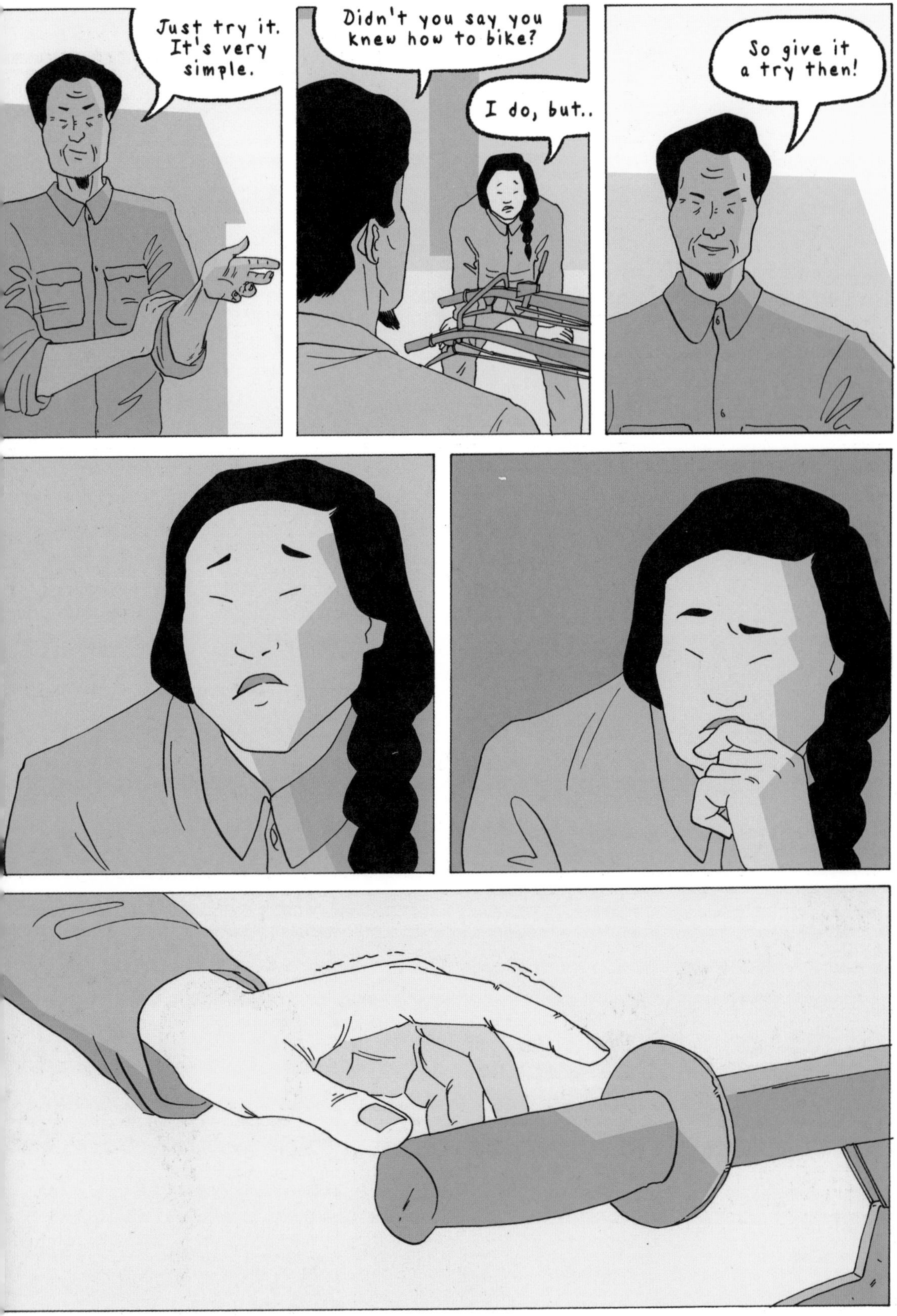
Just try it. It's very simple.
Didn't you say you knew how to bike?
I do, but..
So give it a try then!

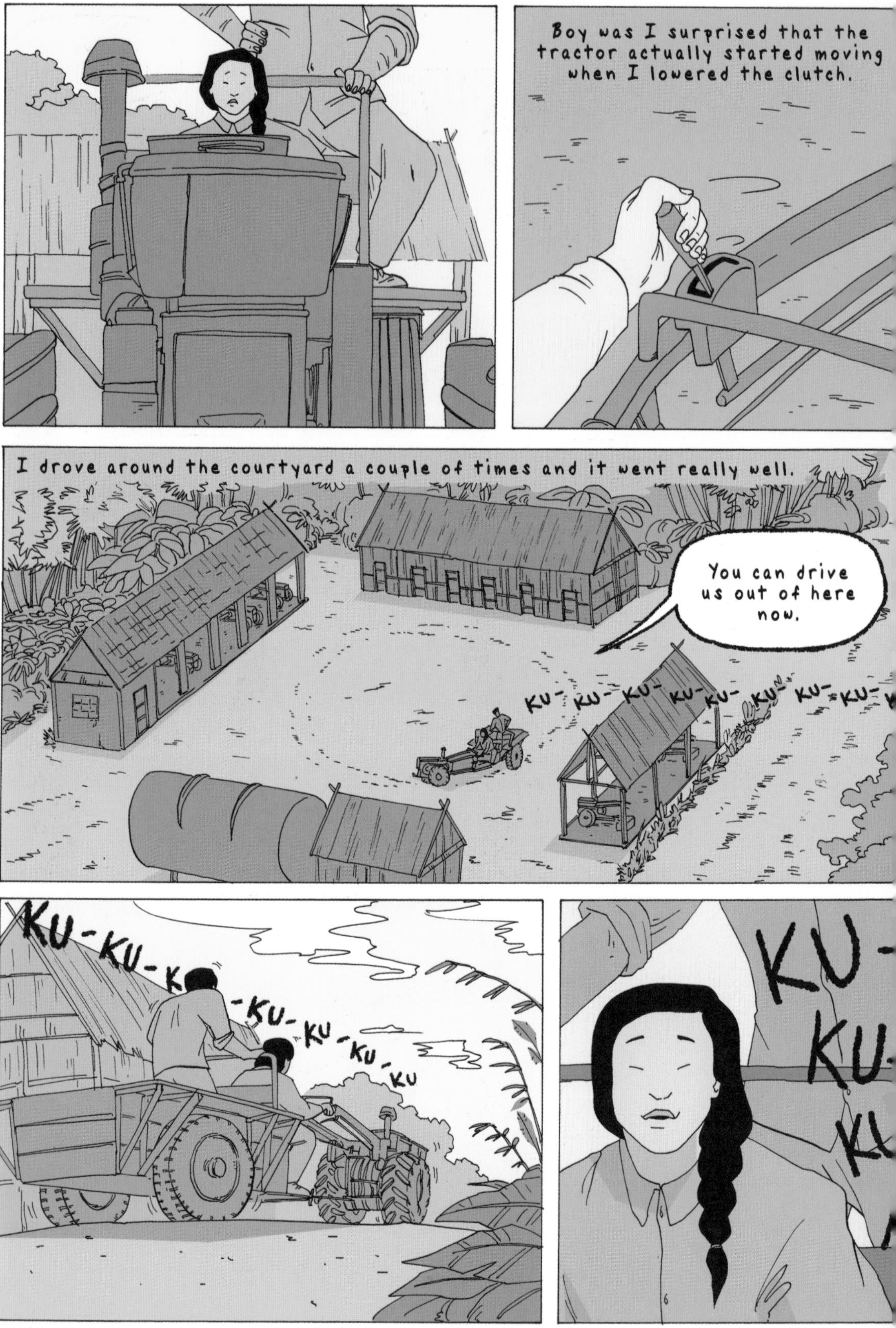
Boy was I surprised that the tractor actually started moving when I lowered the clutch.
I drove around the courtyard a couple of times and it went really well.
You can drive us out of here now.
KU- KU- KU- KU- KU- KU- KU- KU-
KU-KU-KU-K
-KU-KU-KU-KU
KU-
KU

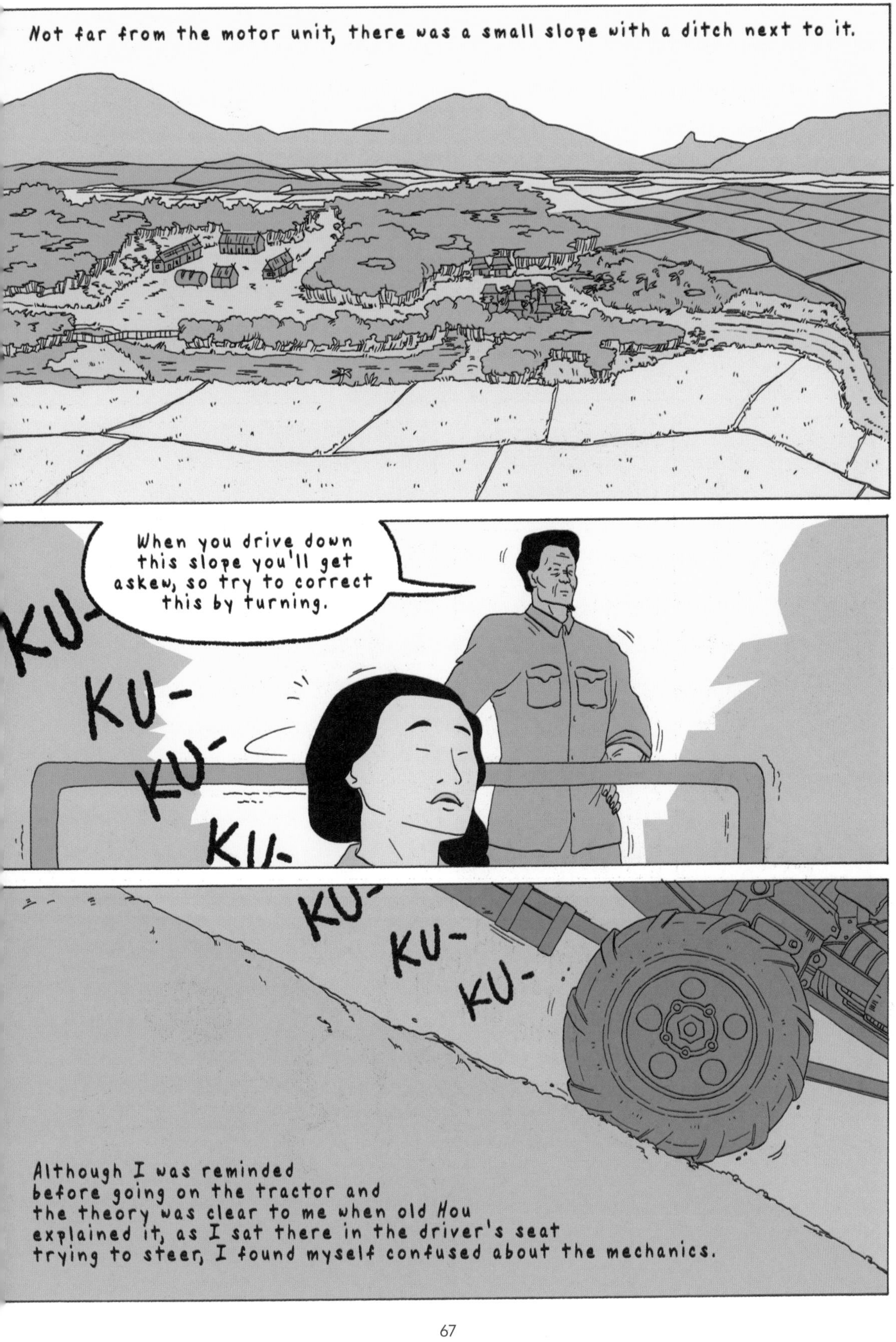
Not far from the motor unit, there was a small slope with a ditch next to it.
When you drive down this slope you'll get askew, so try to correct this by turning.
KU-
KU-
KU-
KU-
KU-
KU-
KU-
Although I was reminded before going on the tractor and the theory was clear to me when old Hou explained it, as I sat there in the driver's seat trying to steer, I found myself confused about the mechanics.

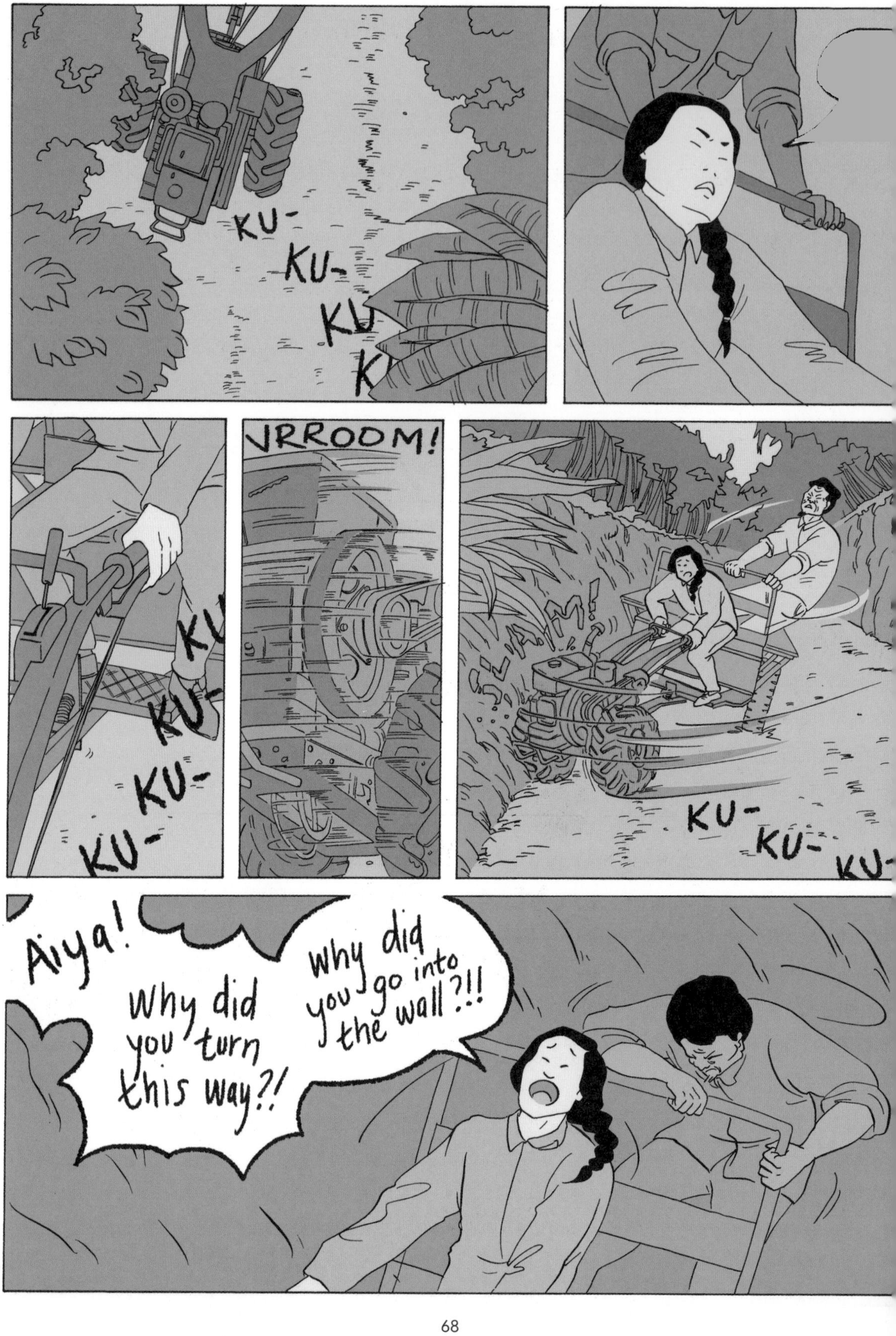
KU-
KU-
KU
KU
KU-
KU-
KU-
KU-
VRROOM!
KU-
KU-
KU-
Aiya!
Why did you turn this way?!
Why did you go into the wall?!!

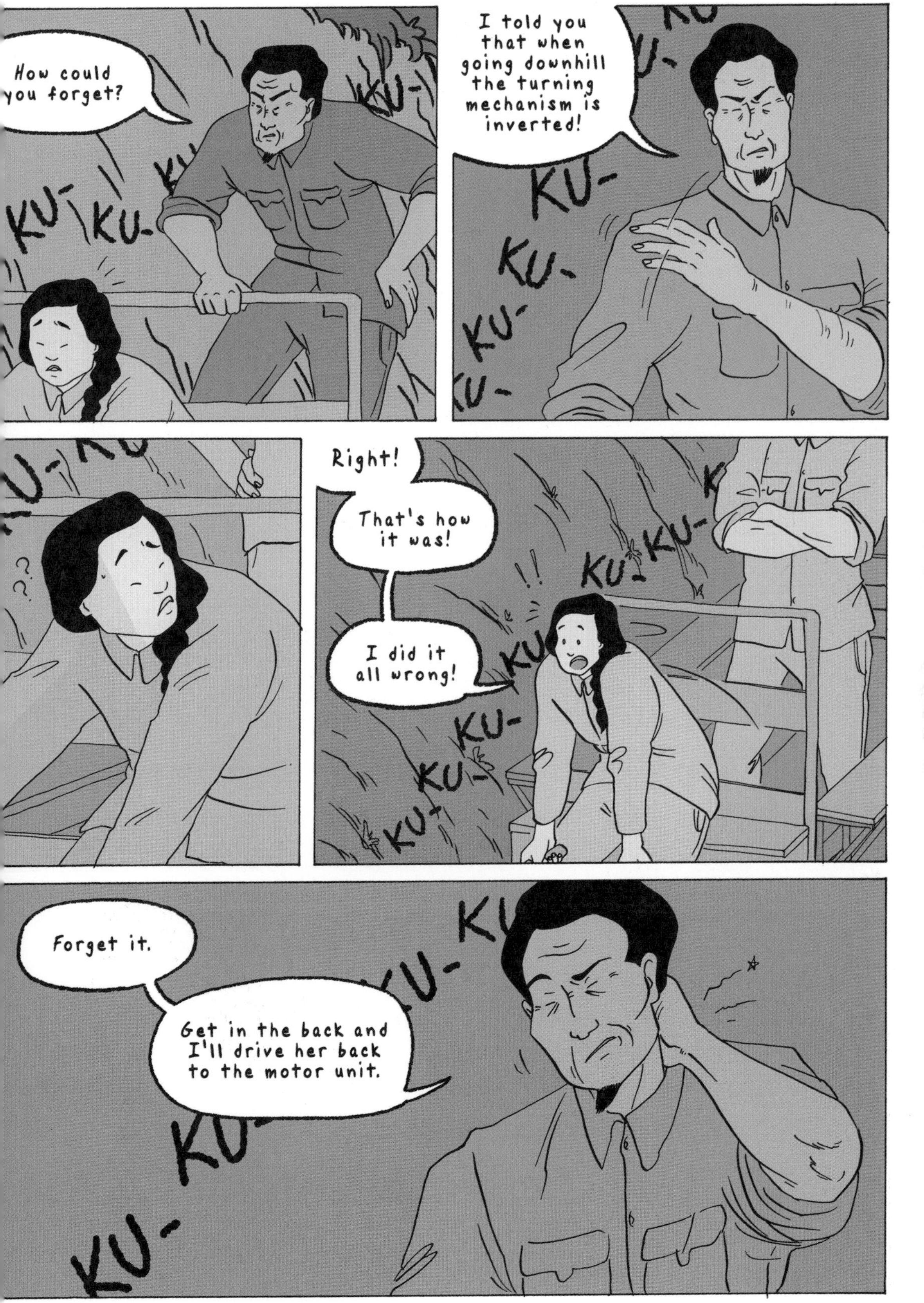
How could you forget?
KU-
KU-
I told you that when going downhill the turning mechanism is inverted!
KU-
KU-
KU-
Right!
That's how it was!
I did it all wrong!
!!
KU-
KU-
KU-
KU-
Forget it.
Get in the back and I'll drive her back to the motor unit.
KU-
KU-

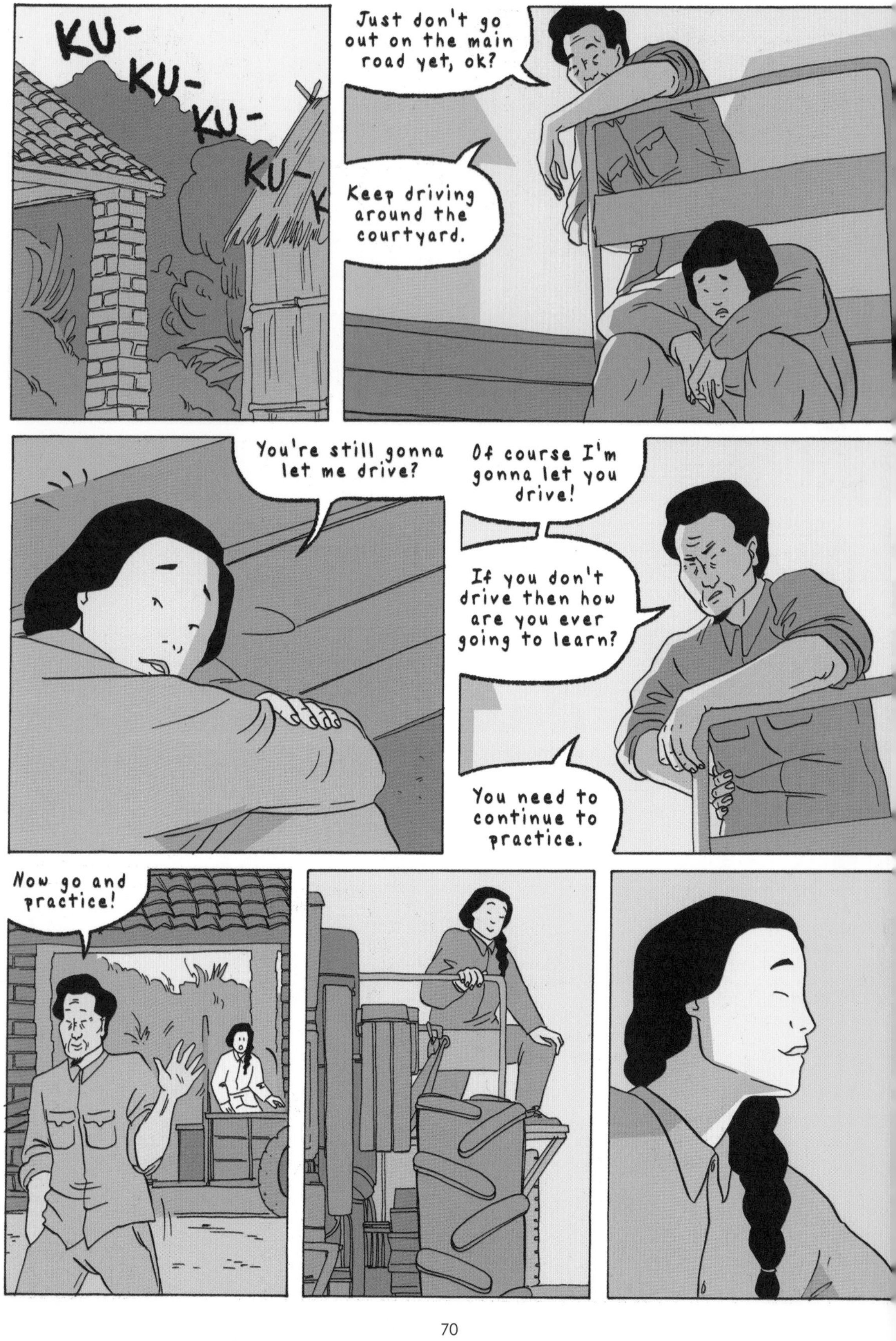
KU-
KU-
KU-
KU-
K
Just don't go out on the main road yet, ok?
Keep driving around the courtyard.
You're still gonna let me drive?
Of course I'm gonna let you drive!
If you don't drive then how are you ever going to learn?
You need to continue to practice.
Now go and practice!

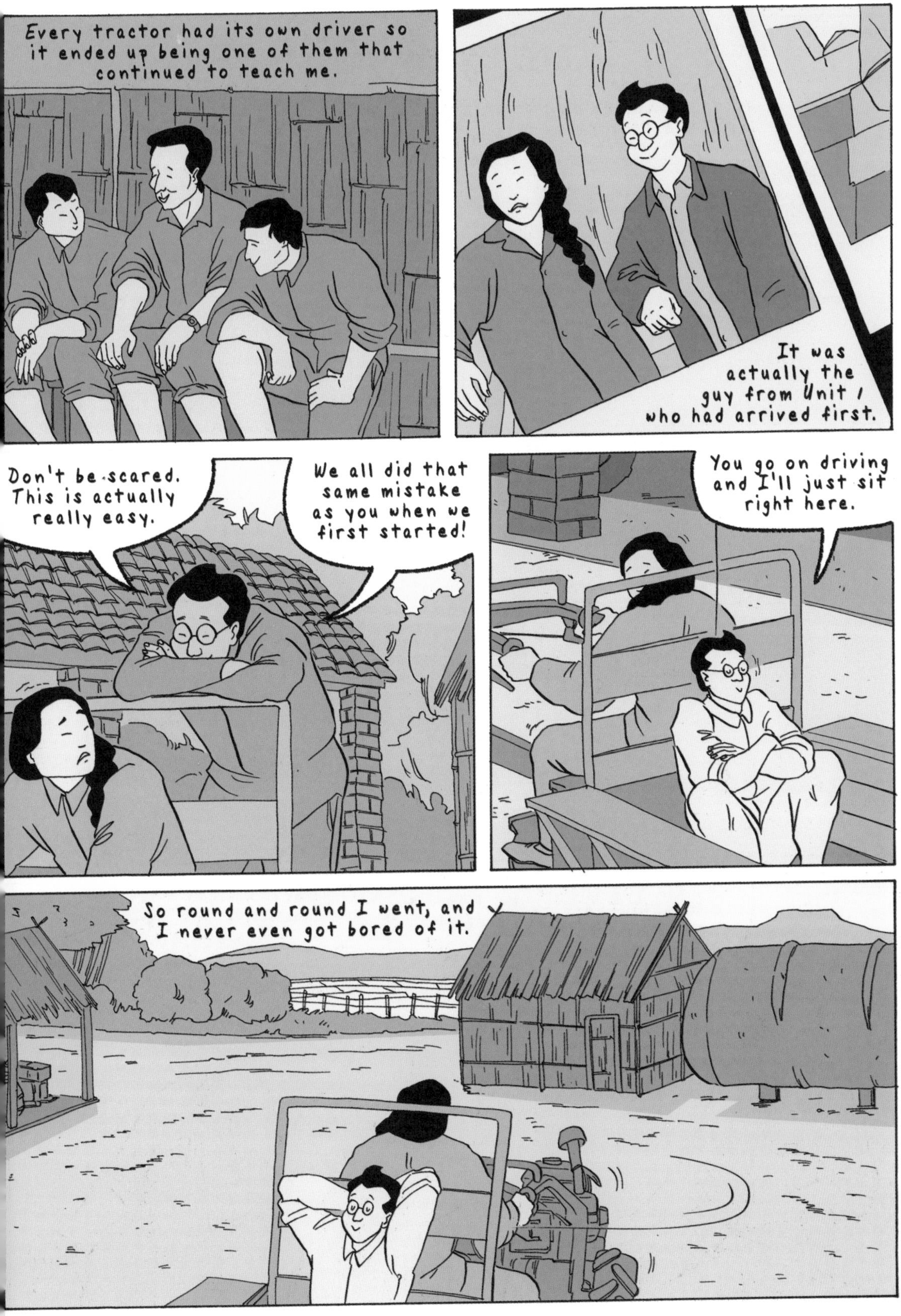
Every tractor had its own driver so it ended up being one of them that continued to teach me.
It was actually the guy from Unit 1 who had arrived first.
Don't be scared. This is actually really easy.
We all did that same mistake as you when we first started!
You go on driving and I'll just sit right here.
So round and round I went, and I never even got bored of it.

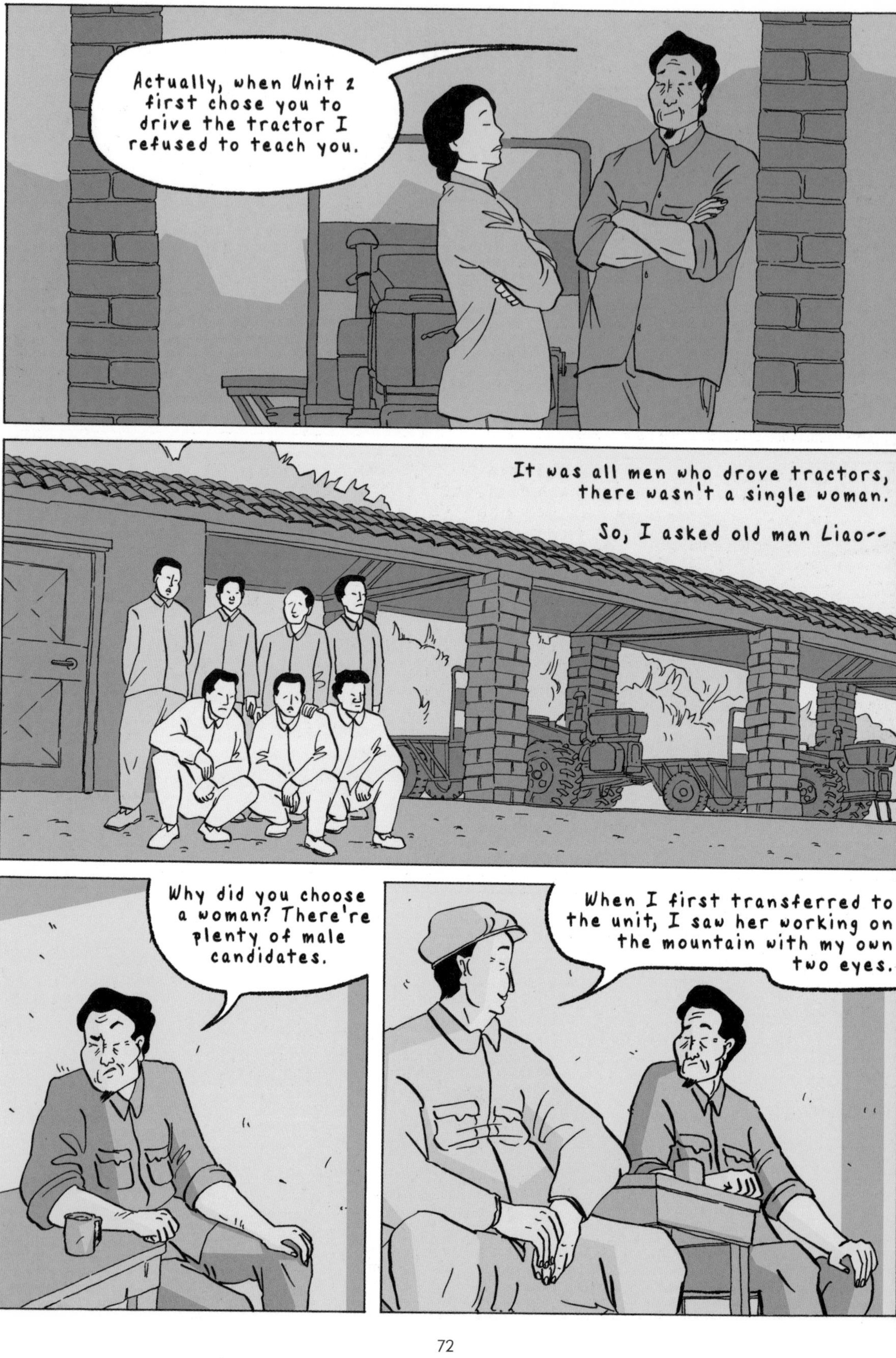
Actually, when Unit 2 first chose you to drive the tractor I refused to teach you.
It was all men who drove tractors, there wasn't a single woman.
So, I asked old man Liao--
Why did you choose a woman? There're plenty of male candidates.
When I first transferred to the unit, I saw her working on the mountain with my own two eyes.

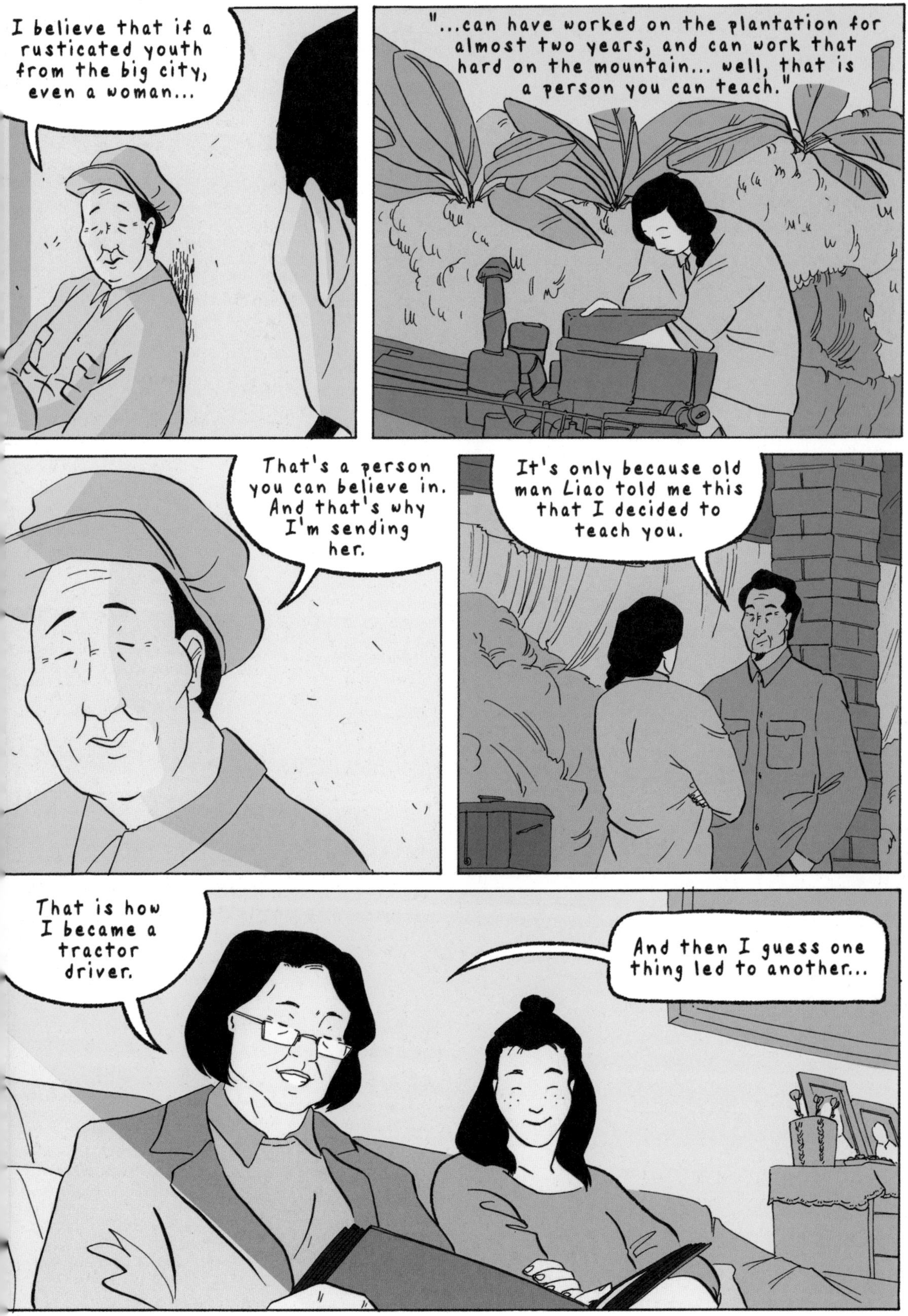
I believe that if a rusticated youth from the big city, even a woman...
"...can have worked on the plantation for almost two years, and can work that hard on the mountain... well, that is a person you can teach."
That's a person you can believe in. And that's why I'm sending her.
It's only because old man Liao told me this that I decided to teach you.
That is how I became a tractor driver.
And then I guess one thing led to another...

Mao Zedong died on September 9, 1976.

Soon after, it was officially announced that the Cultural Revolution had ended.

Rumor had it at our plantation that Premier Hua GuoFeng wanted the Down to the Countryside movement to go on while Vice-Premier Deng Xiaoping supported bringing home all of the rusticated youth.

If the movement was to continue, students would no longer be sent to state farming corporations like the one we were at.

This meant the government wouldn't recognize students who were paid workers at these state farms as rusticated youth. They would only acknowledge the students who worked without pay.

As this rumor spread, the rusticated youth working at state farms became agitated:

"We've been out here for almost ten years..."

"Why in the world don't we count as rusticated youth?!"

All they wanted was to go home.

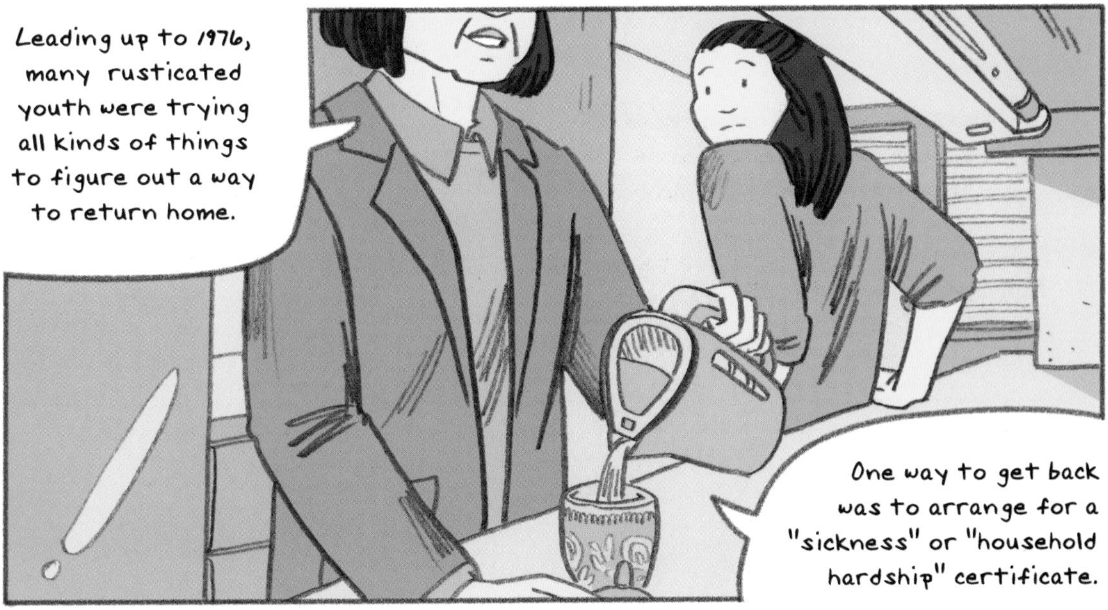
Leading up to 1976, many rusticated youth were trying all kinds of things to figure out a way to return home.
One way to get back was to arrange for a "sickness" or "household hardship" certificate.

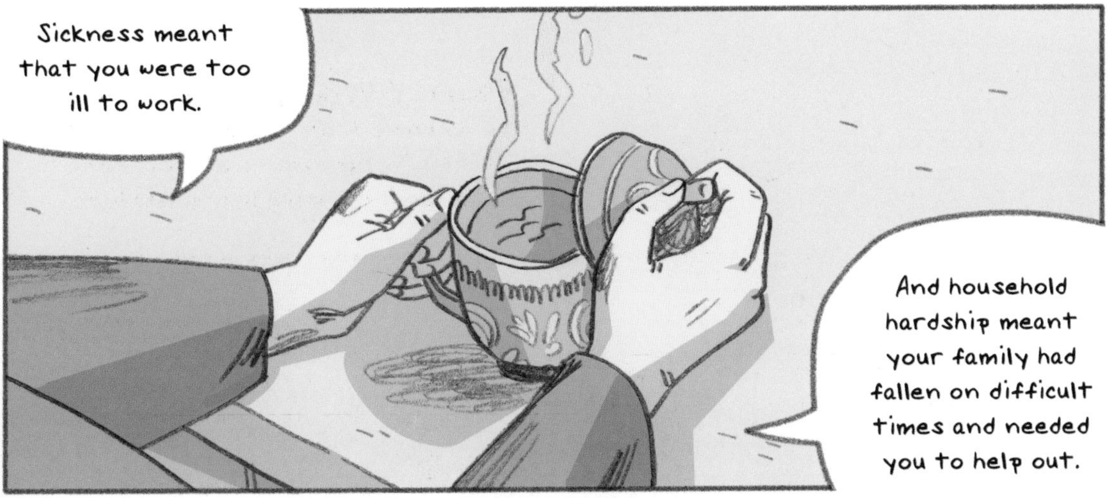
Sickness meant that you were too ill to work.
And household hardship meant your family had fallen on difficult times and needed you to help out.

As regulations were slowly relaxed, these certificates, which were previously very hard to produce, were suddenly accessible. And in '77 and '78, when the Cultural Revolution was finally over, everyone was scrambling to obtain them.

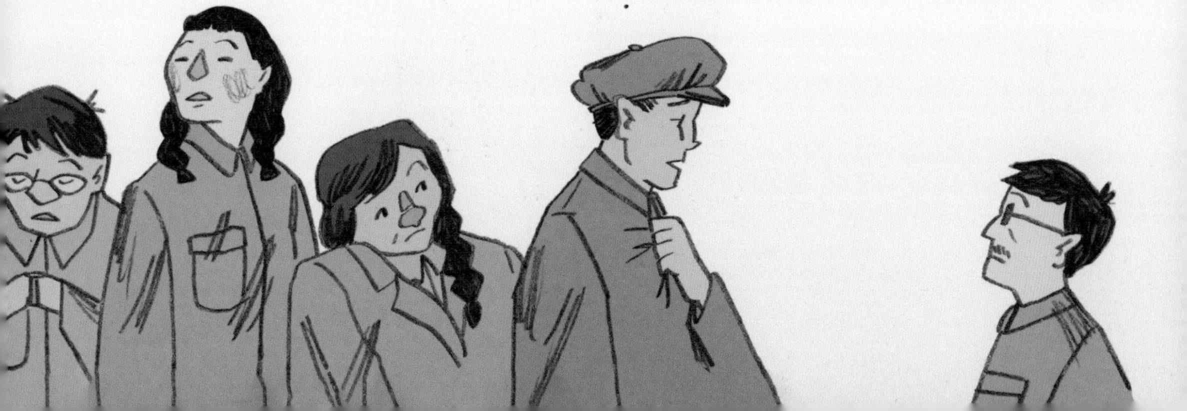

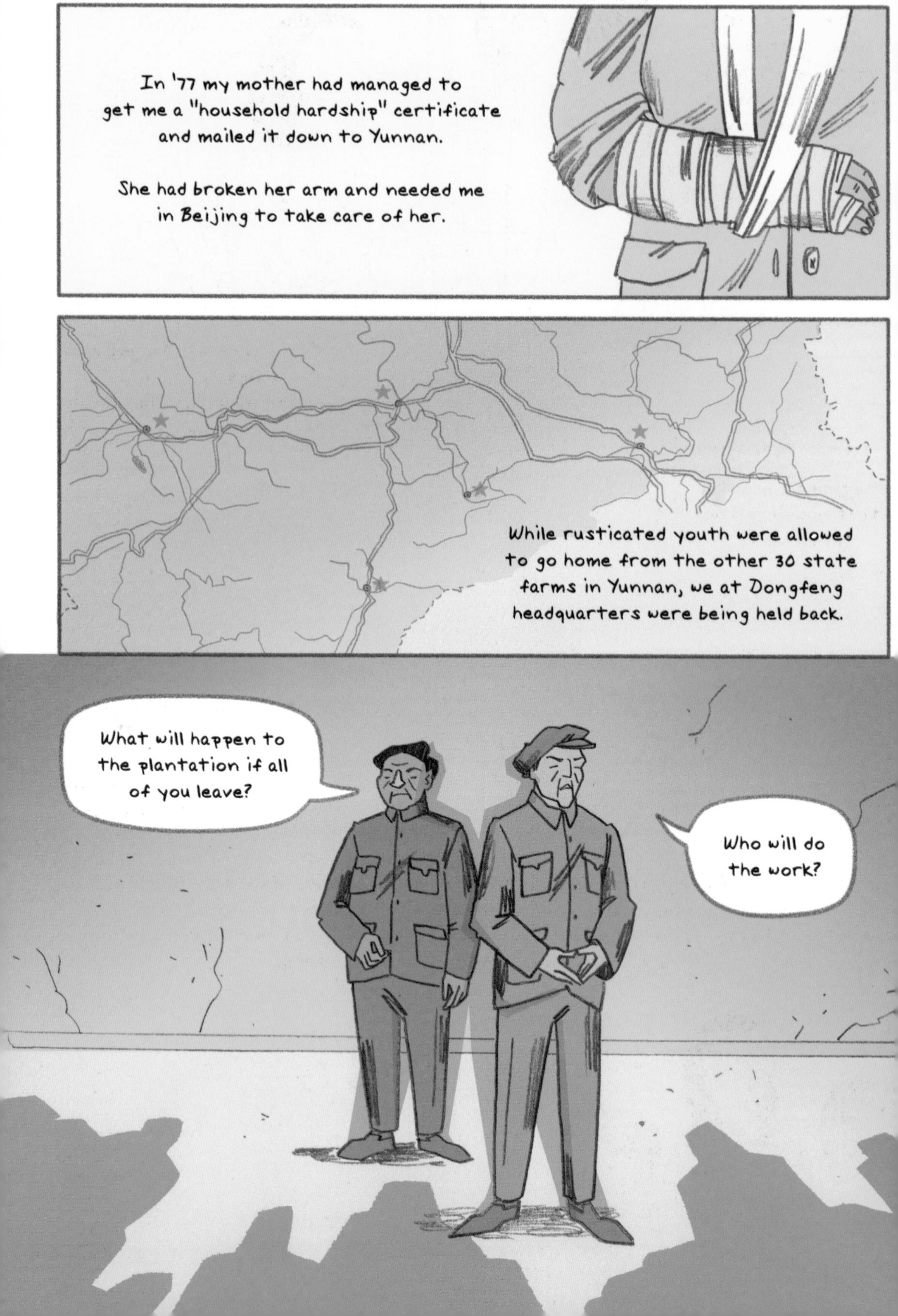
In '77 my mother had managed to get me a "household hardship" certificate and mailed it down to Yunnan.
She had broken her arm and needed me in Beijing to take care of her.
While rusticated youth were allowed to go home from the other 30 state farms in Yunnan, we at Dongfeng headquarters were being held back.
What will happen to the plantation if all of you leave?
Who will do the work?

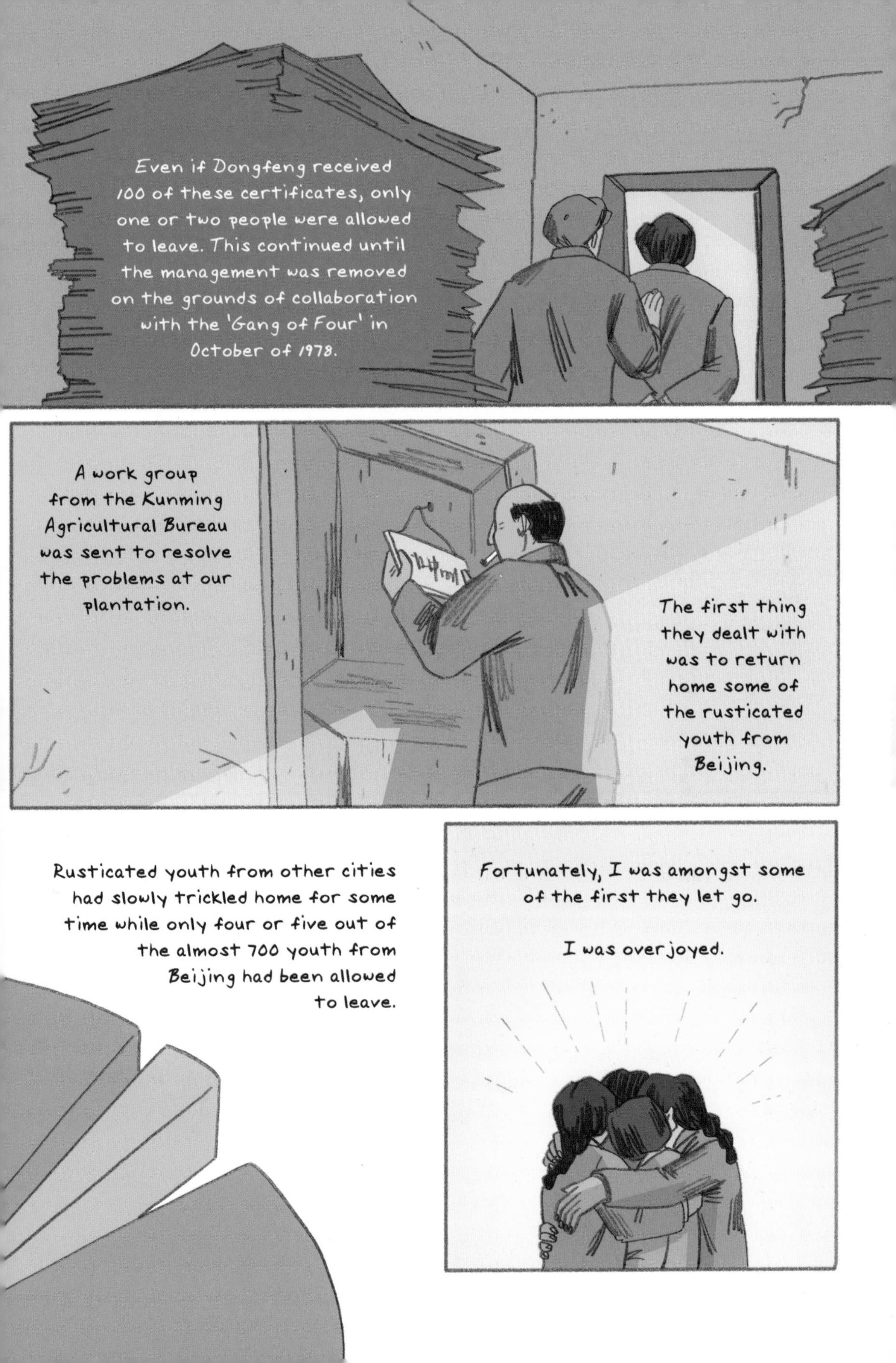
Even if Dongfeng received 100 of these certificates, only one or two people were allowed to leave. This continued until the management was removed on the grounds of collaboration with the 'Gang of Four' in October of 1978.
A work group from the Kunming Agricultural Bureau was sent to resolve the problems at our plantation.
The first thing they dealt with was to return home some of the rusticated youth from Beijing.
Rusticated youth from other cities had slowly trickled home for some time while only four or five out of the almost 700 youth from Beijing had been allowed to leave.
Fortunately, I was amongst some of the first they let go.
I was overjoyed.

公安 POLICE

I rushed to get my documents in order and get my Hukou changed at the local police station.

I waited just long enough to get my wages for that month before hitting the road.

After I left, I heard about an incident where the Vice Minister of the Central Agricultural Bureau came from Beijing to visit the state farms in Yunnan.

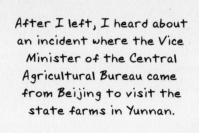

He was met by 1,500 rusticated youth bowing in front of him.

They were crying and begging-- they wanted to go home.

They moved him to tears.

He knew how hard their life had been these past ten years.

His own children had also been sent away.

After quite a few stops on the way home, I finally
arrived in Beijing in December of 1978.

At this time in China, you weren't allowed to find a job by yourself;
you'd have to wait for the government to arrange a job placement
for you. They would notify you when they knew which office or
factory you had been assigned to.

Since so many rusticated youth came home at once, the local
governments had a hard time keeping up job demand. All we
could do was hang around at home until we got our notice.

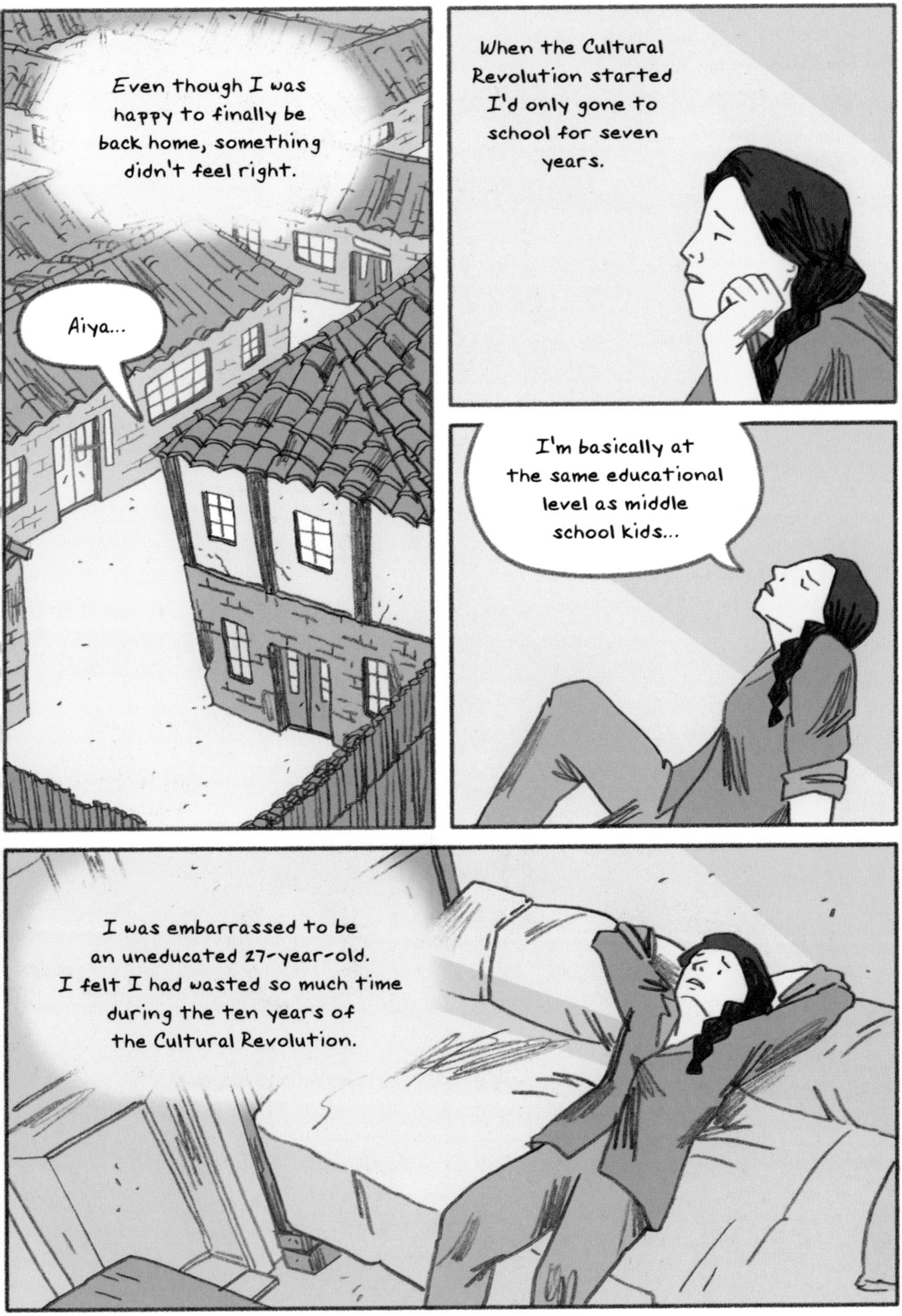
Even though I was happy to finally be back home, something didn't feel right.
Aiya...
When the Cultural Revolution started I'd only gone to school for seven years.
I'm basically at the same educational level as middle school kids...
I was embarrassed to be an uneducated 27-year-old. I felt I had wasted so much time during the ten years of the Cultural Revolution.

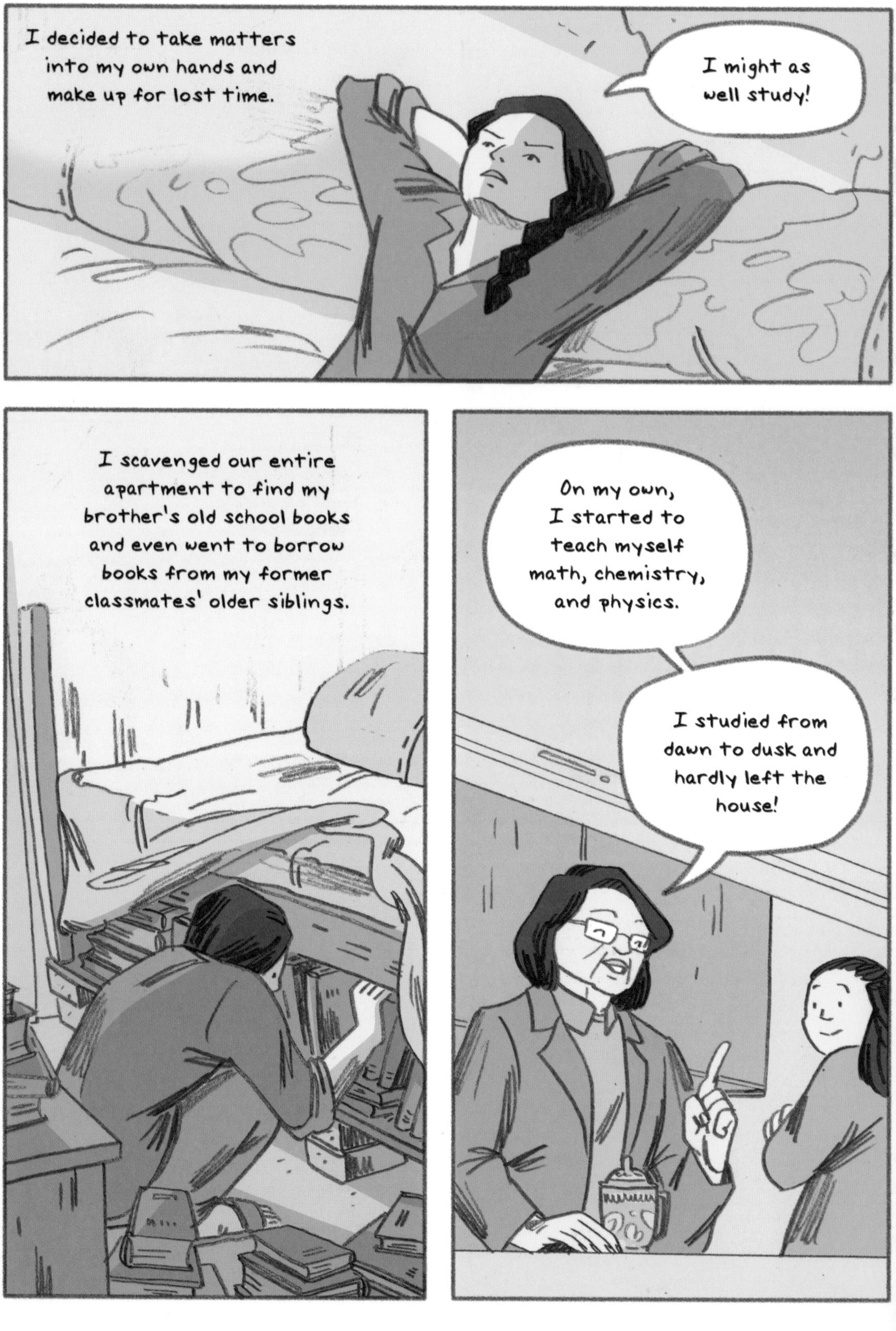
I decided to take matters into my own hands and make up for lost time.
I might as well study!
I scavenged our entire apartment to find my brother's old school books and even went to borrow books from my former classmates' older siblings.
On my own, I started to teach myself math, chemistry, and physics.
I studied from dawn to dusk and hardly left the house!

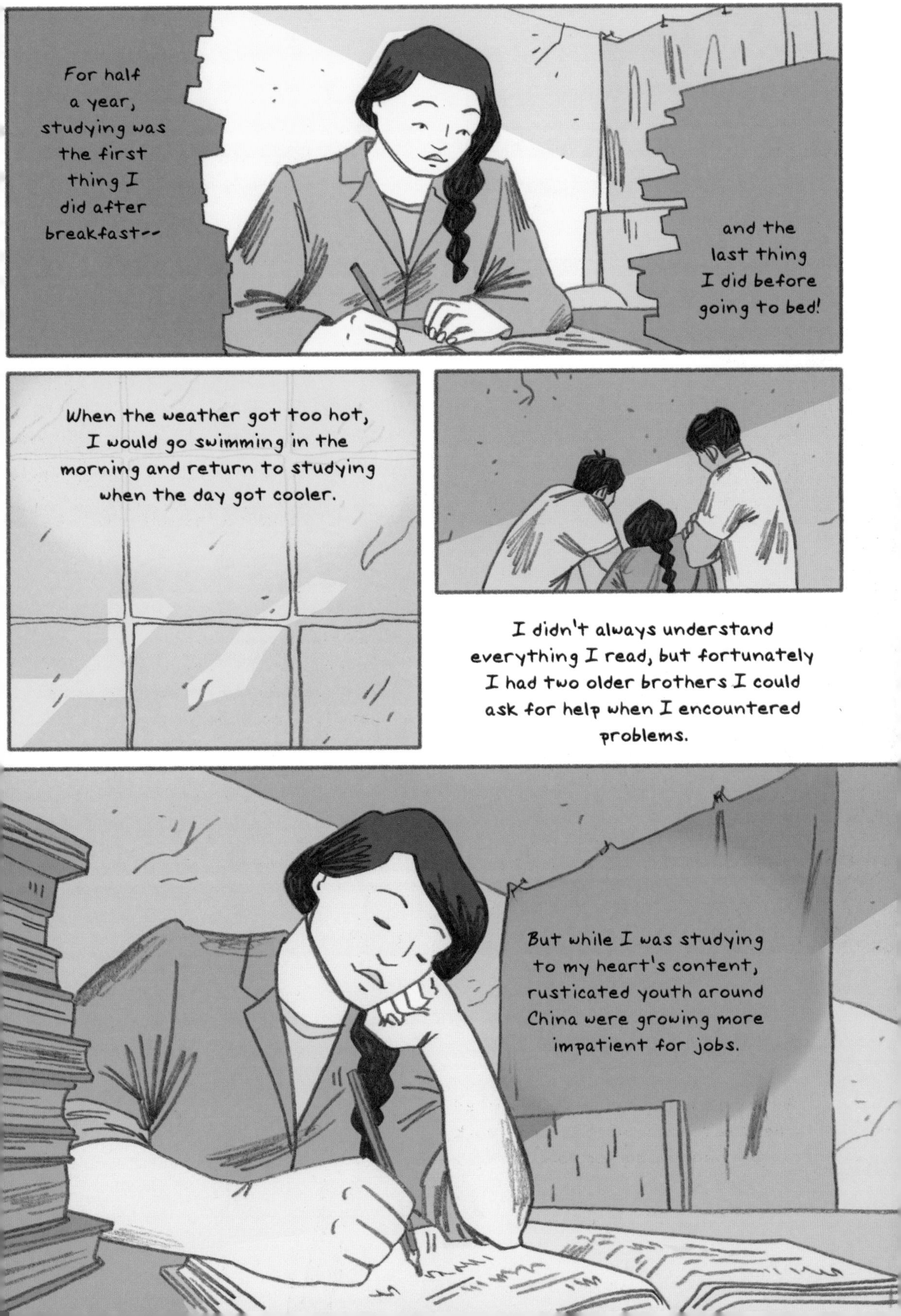
For half a year, studying was the first thing I did after breakfast--
and the last thing I did before going to bed!
When the weather got too hot, I would go swimming in the morning and return to studying when the day got cooler.
I didn't always understand everything I read, but fortunately I had two older brothers I could ask for help when I encountered problems.
But while I was studying to my heart's content, rusticated youth around China were growing more impatient for jobs.

This was especially true in Shanghai
--home for most of the rusticated youth--
where trouble started brewing after half a year of
idleness. Hundreds of thousands of them took
to the streets to demonstrate.

They demanded that the government
arrange jobs for them immediately.

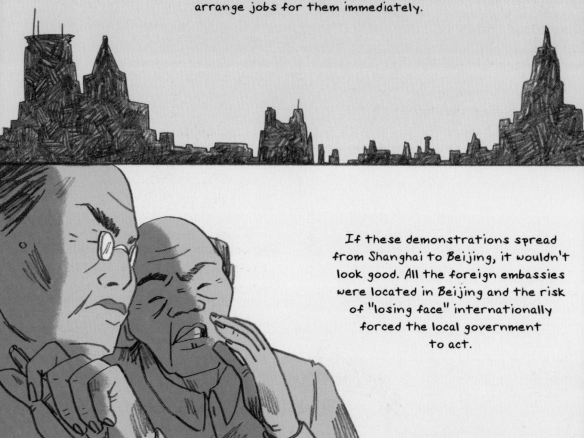

If these demonstrations spread
from Shanghai to Beijing, it wouldn't
look good. All the foreign embassies
were located in Beijing and the risk
of "losing face" internationally
forced the local government
to act.

"Placement tests" were implemented
to best determine what level of work
we were suited for.

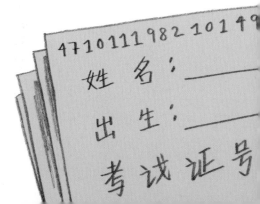

There were two different
placement tests:

1) Aimed at those who'd interrupted
their education in junior high

2) Aimed at those who'd interrupted
their education in high school

Depending on if we passed or failed the exam, we'd be assigned to
one of three different levels of state employment.
But there were major differences between the three
types of employment:

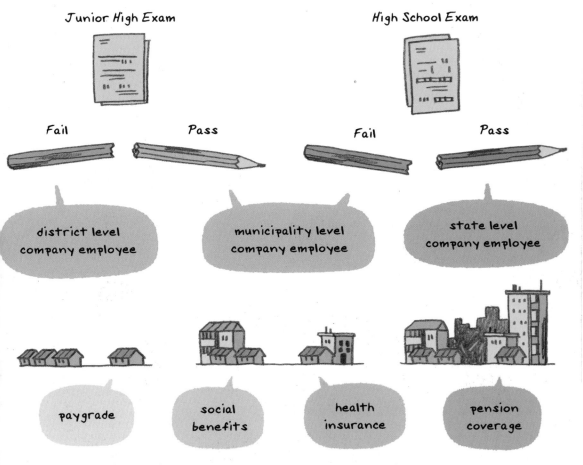

Junior High Exam

High School Exam

Fail

Pass

Fail

Pass

district level
company employee

municipality level
company employee

state level
company employee

paygrade

social
benefits

health
insurance

pension
coverage

You didn't really want to end up on the district level as
they were at the lower end of all these benefits.

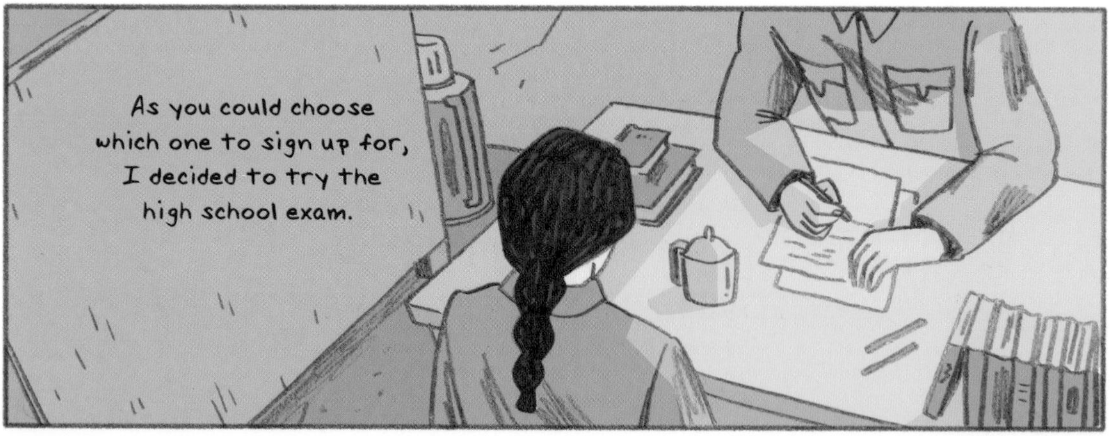
As you could choose which one to sign up for, I decided to try the high school exam.

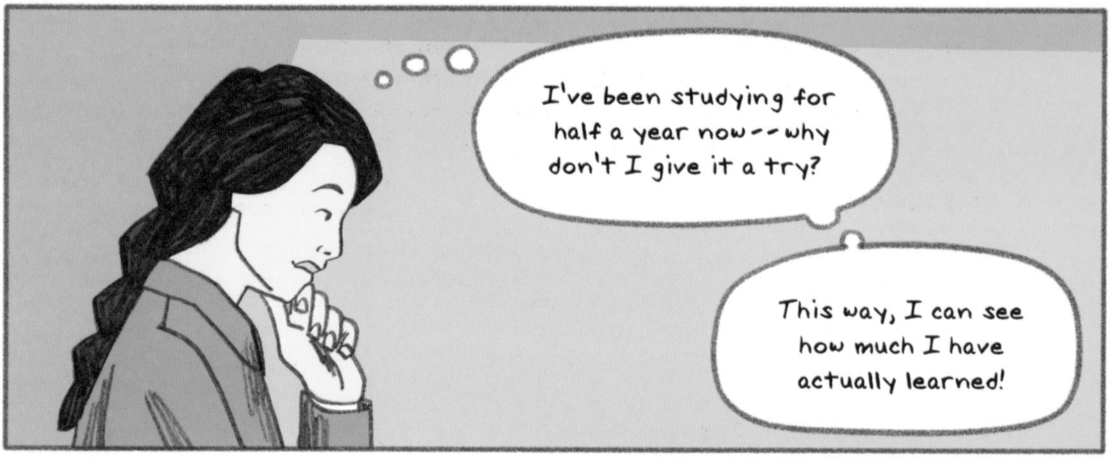
I've been studying for half a year now--why don't I give it a try?
This way, I can see how much I have actually learned!

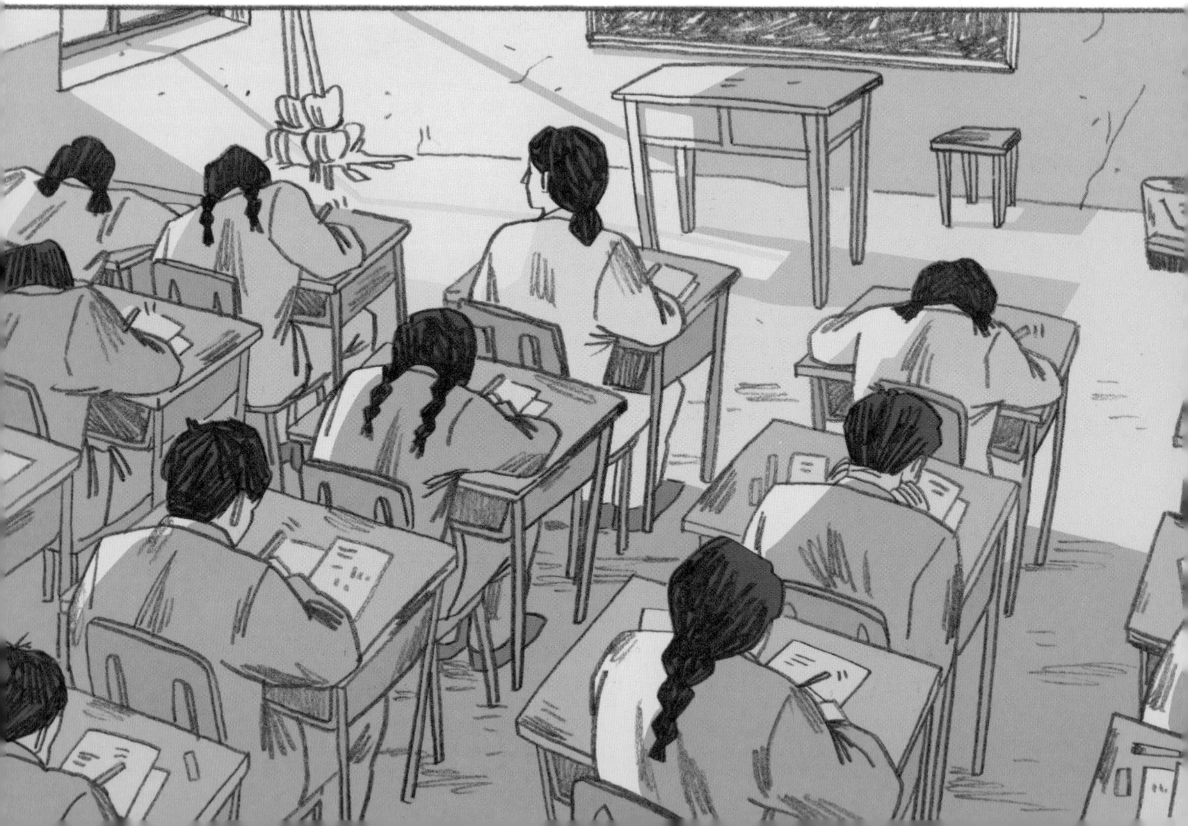

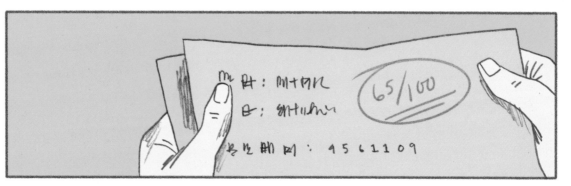

It seemed like my self-study came to fruition after all!

But even with these placement tests, I still had to wait around for almost two months before getting a job. The city of Beijing was arranging work for around 200,000 of us at the same time.

I actually passed the high school exam! And I even did pretty well!

I was so proud!

In September of '79, I finally received notice that I was to work on the driver's team for one of Beijing's medical universities.

I was placed on the preparation team for the construction of their new affiliated hospital--it was to be used as a practice hospital for students.

But as the construction of the hospital was still in its early stages the prep team didn't have much to do...

We were 10 people on the prep team.
But everyone was just sitting around waiting for the construction of the hospital to begin.

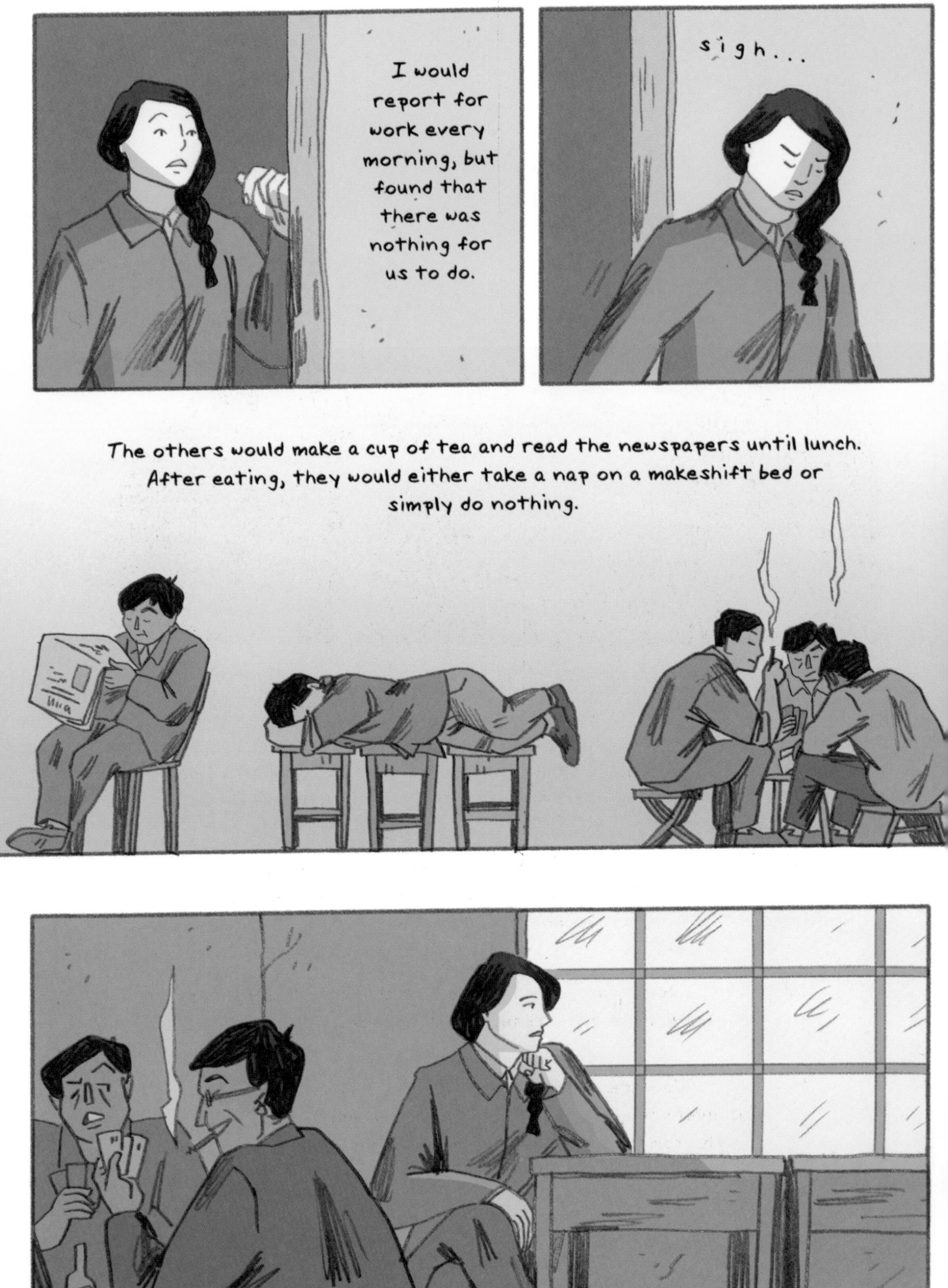
I would report for work every morning, but found that there was nothing for us to do.
sigh...
The others would make a cup of tea and read the newspapers until lunch. After eating, they would either take a nap on a makeshift bed or simply do nothing.

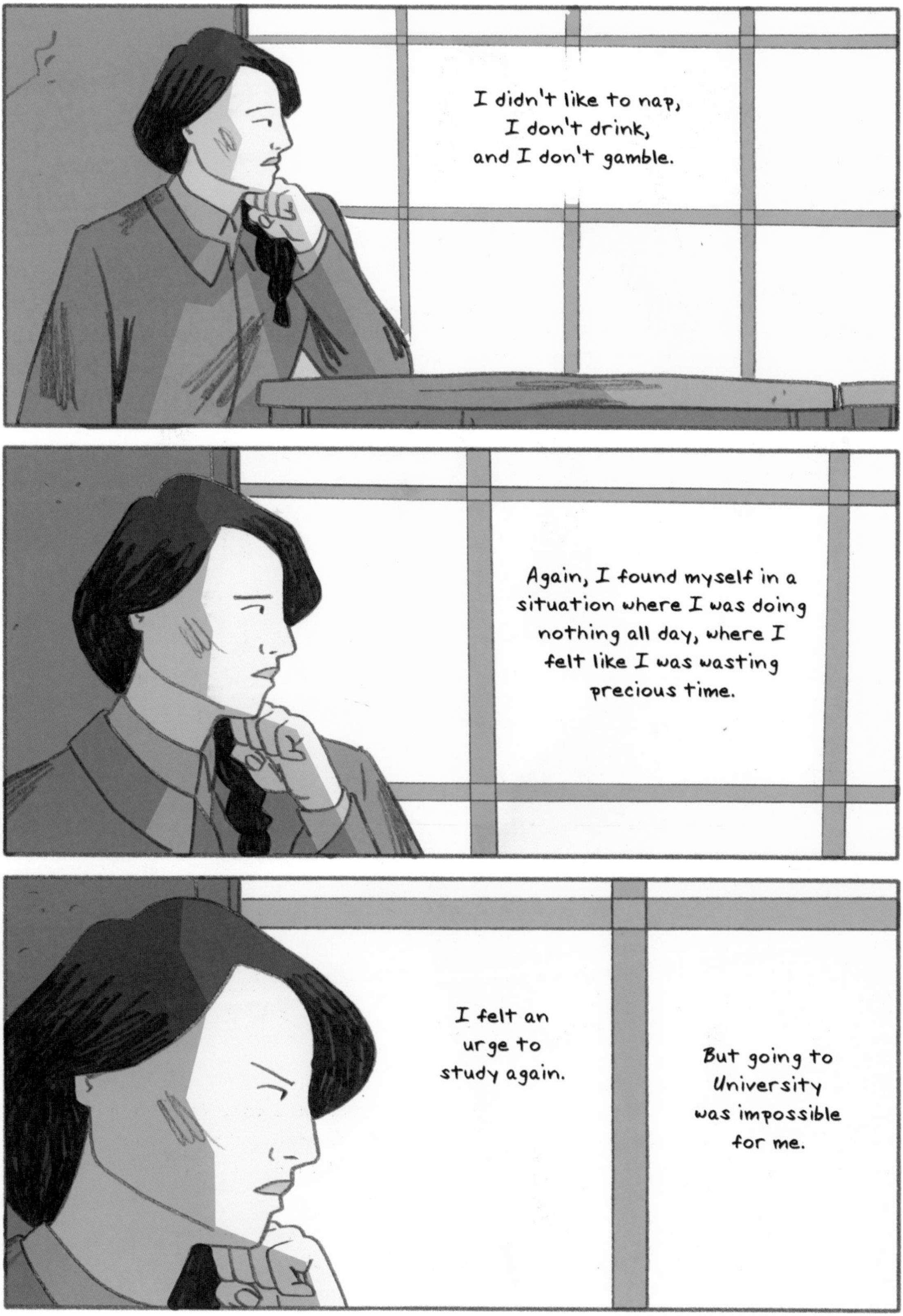
I didn't like to nap,
I don't drink,
and I don't gamble.
Again, I found myself in a situation where I was doing nothing all day, where I felt like I was wasting precious time.
I felt an urge to study again.
But going to University was impossible for me.

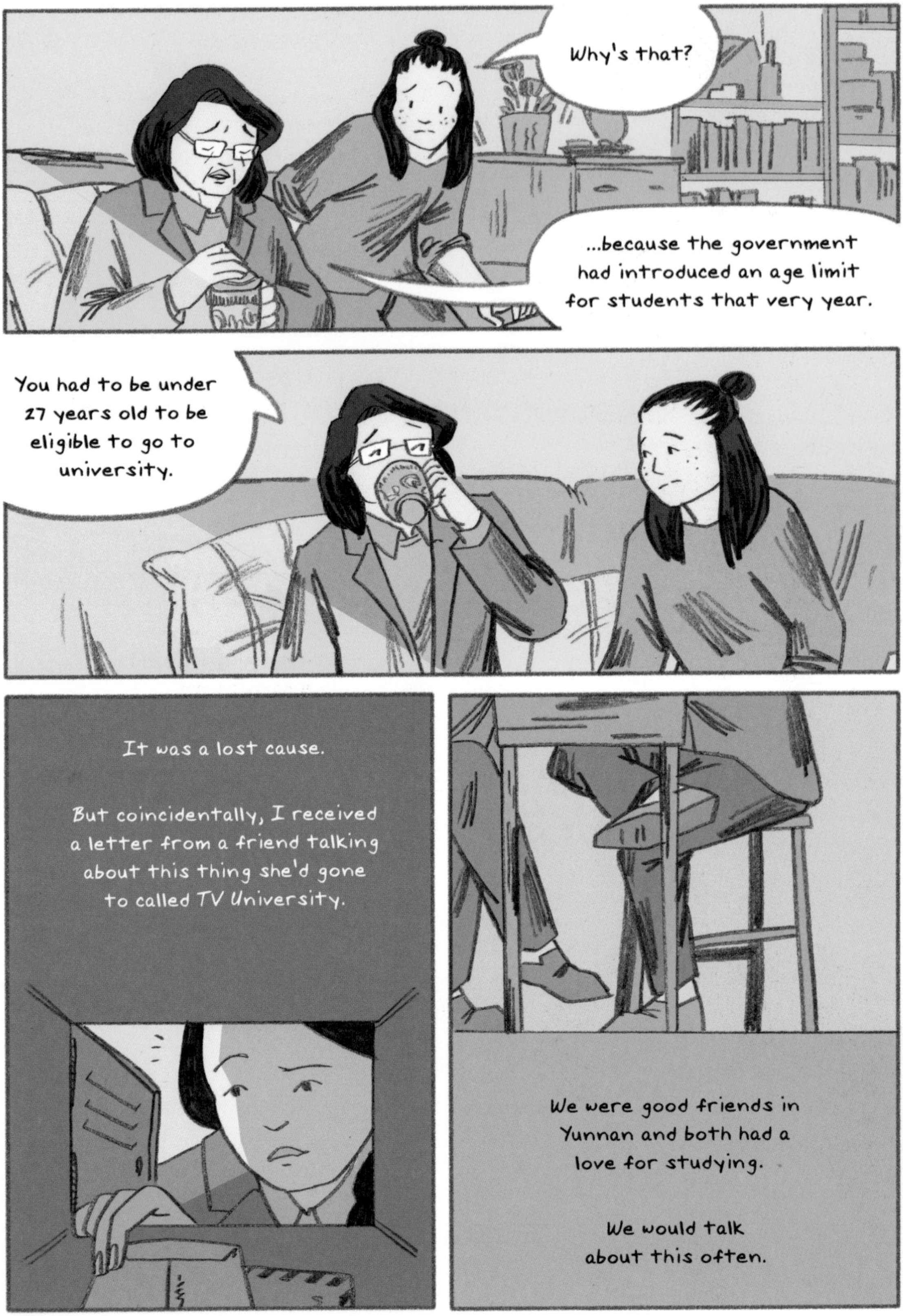
Why's that?
...because the government had introduced an age limit for students that very year.
You had to be under 27 years old to be eligible to go to university.
It was a lost cause.
But coincidentally, I received a letter from a friend talking about this thing she'd gone to called *TV University*.
We were good friends in Yunnan and both had a love for studying.
We would talk about this often.

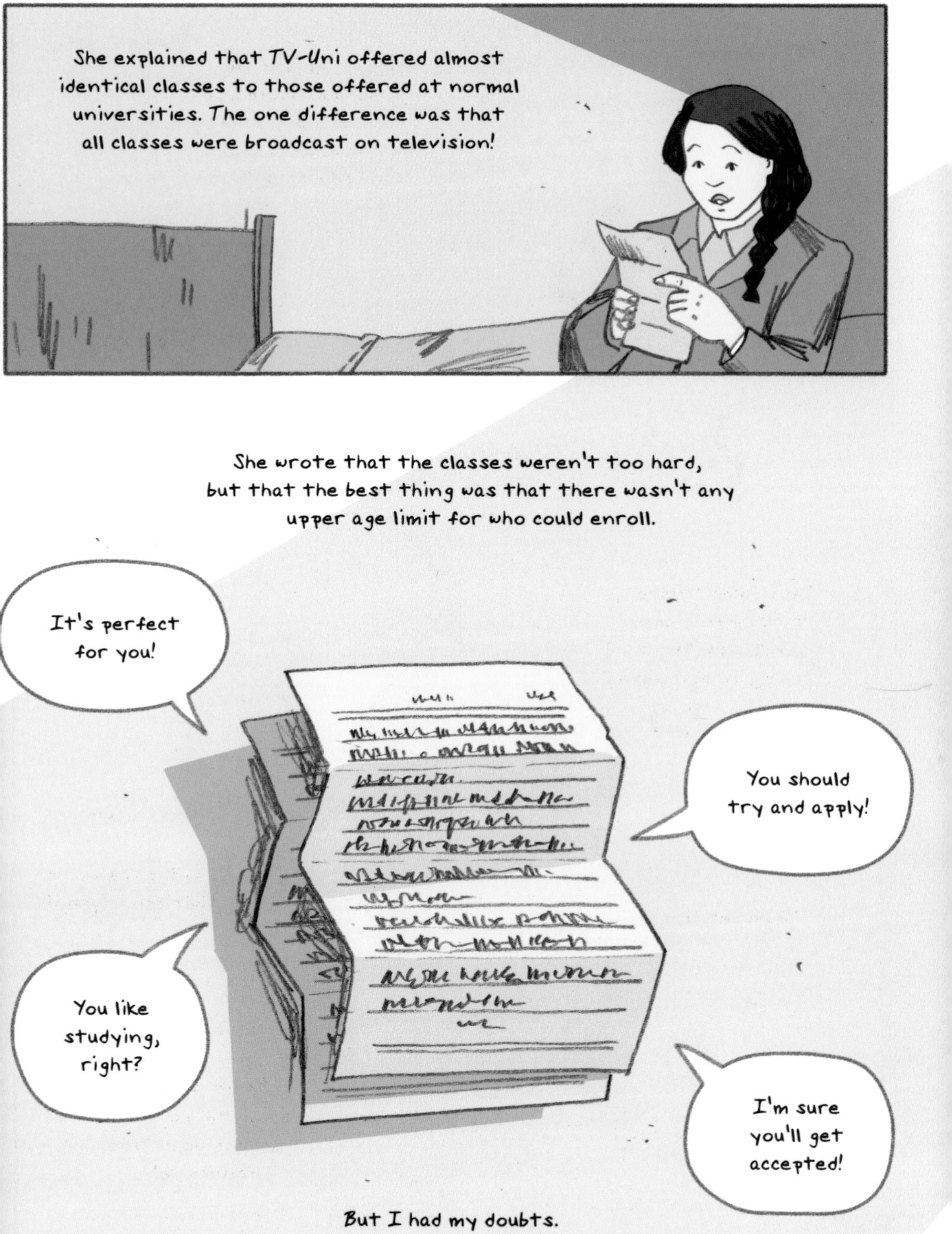
She explained that TV-Uni offered almost identical classes to those offered at normal universities. The one difference was that all classes were broadcast on television!
She wrote that the classes weren't too hard, but that the best thing was that there wasn't any upper age limit for who could enroll.
It's perfect for you!
You should try and apply!
You like studying, right?
I'm sure you'll get accepted!
But I had my doubts.

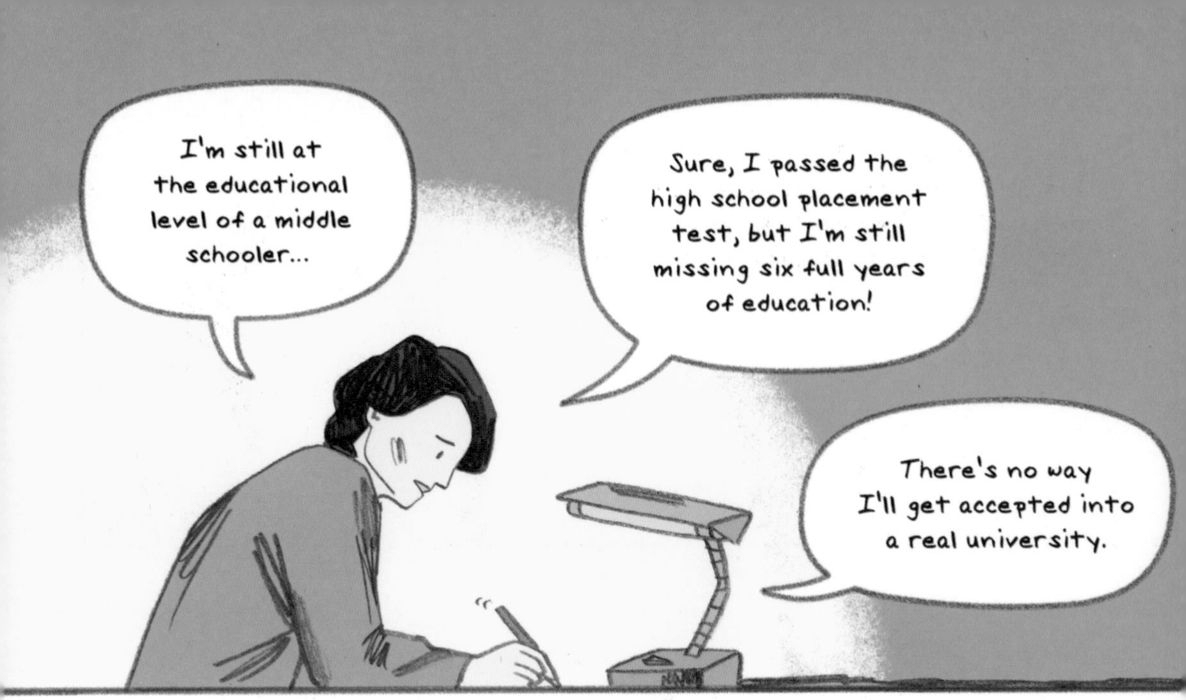
I'm still at the educational level of a middle schooler...
Sure, I passed the high school placement test, but I'm still missing six full years of education!
There's no way I'll get accepted into a real university.

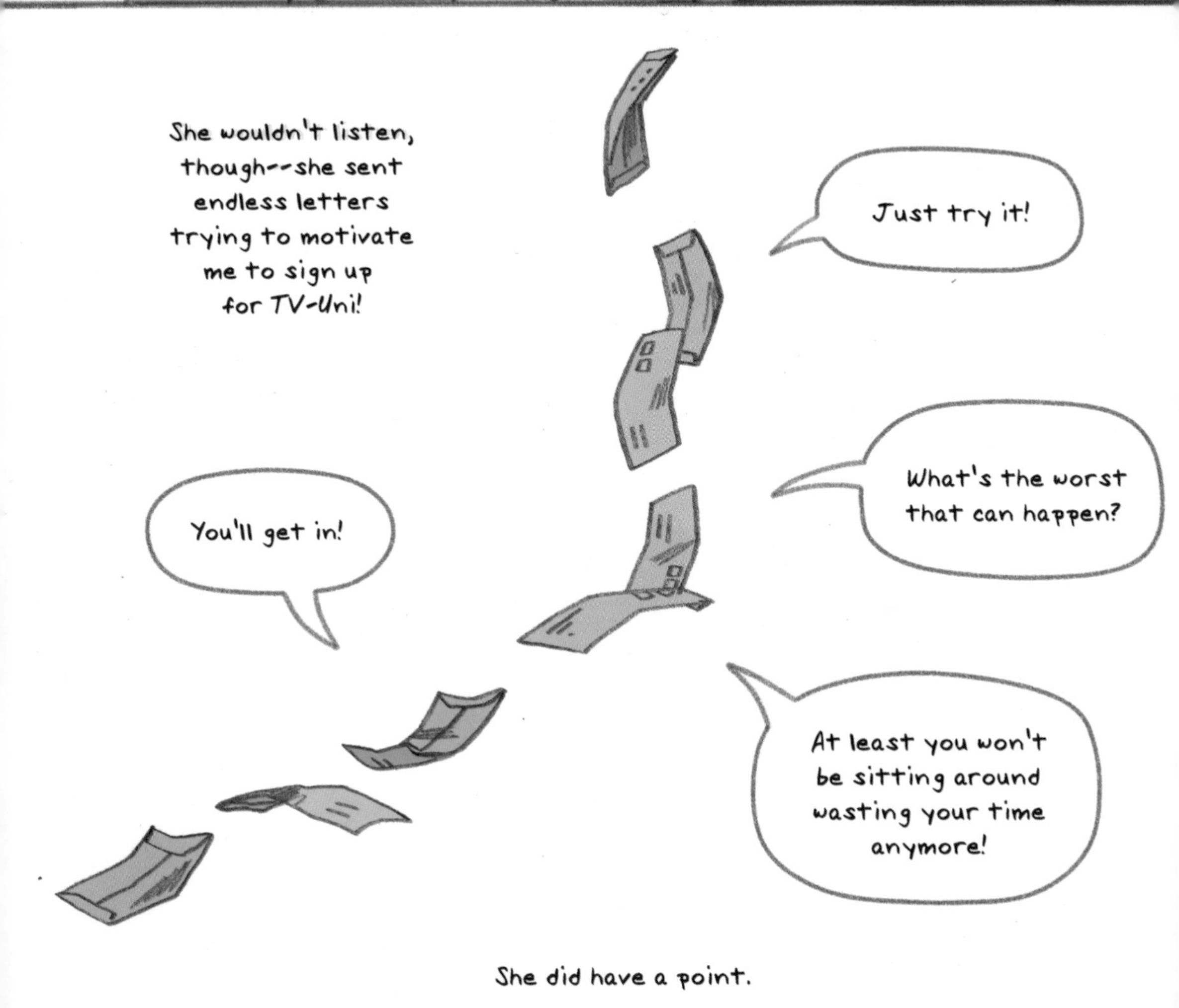
She wouldn't listen, though--she sent endless letters trying to motivate me to sign up for TV-Uni!
Just try it!
What's the worst that can happen?
You'll get in!
At least you won't be sitting around wasting your time anymore!
She did have a point.

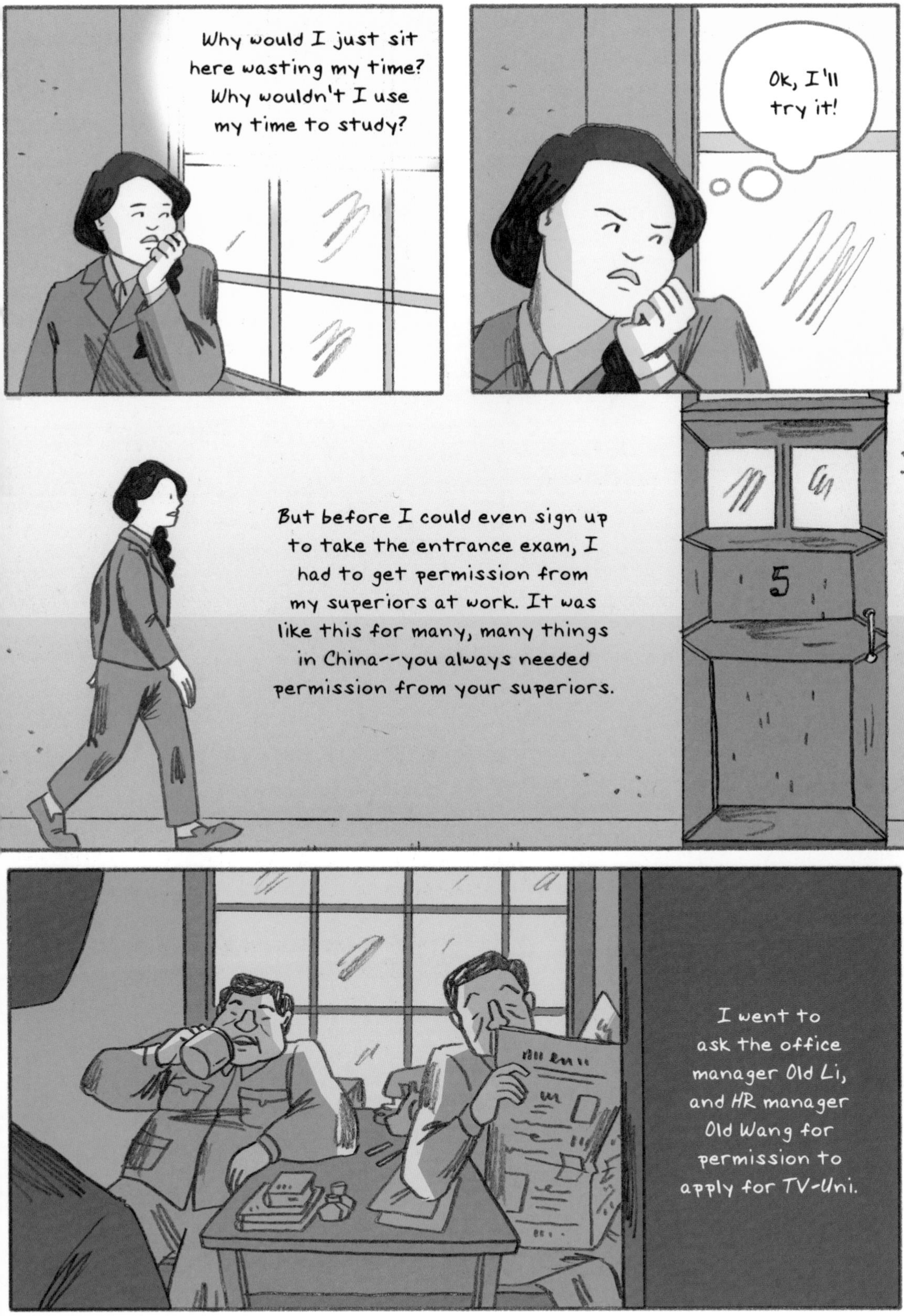
Why would I just sit here wasting my time? Why wouldn't I use my time to study?
Ok, I'll try it!
But before I could even sign up to take the entrance exam, I had to get permission from my superiors at work. It was like this for many, many things in China--you always needed permission from your superiors.
5
I went to ask the office manager Old Li, and HR manager Old Wang for permission to apply for TV-Uni.

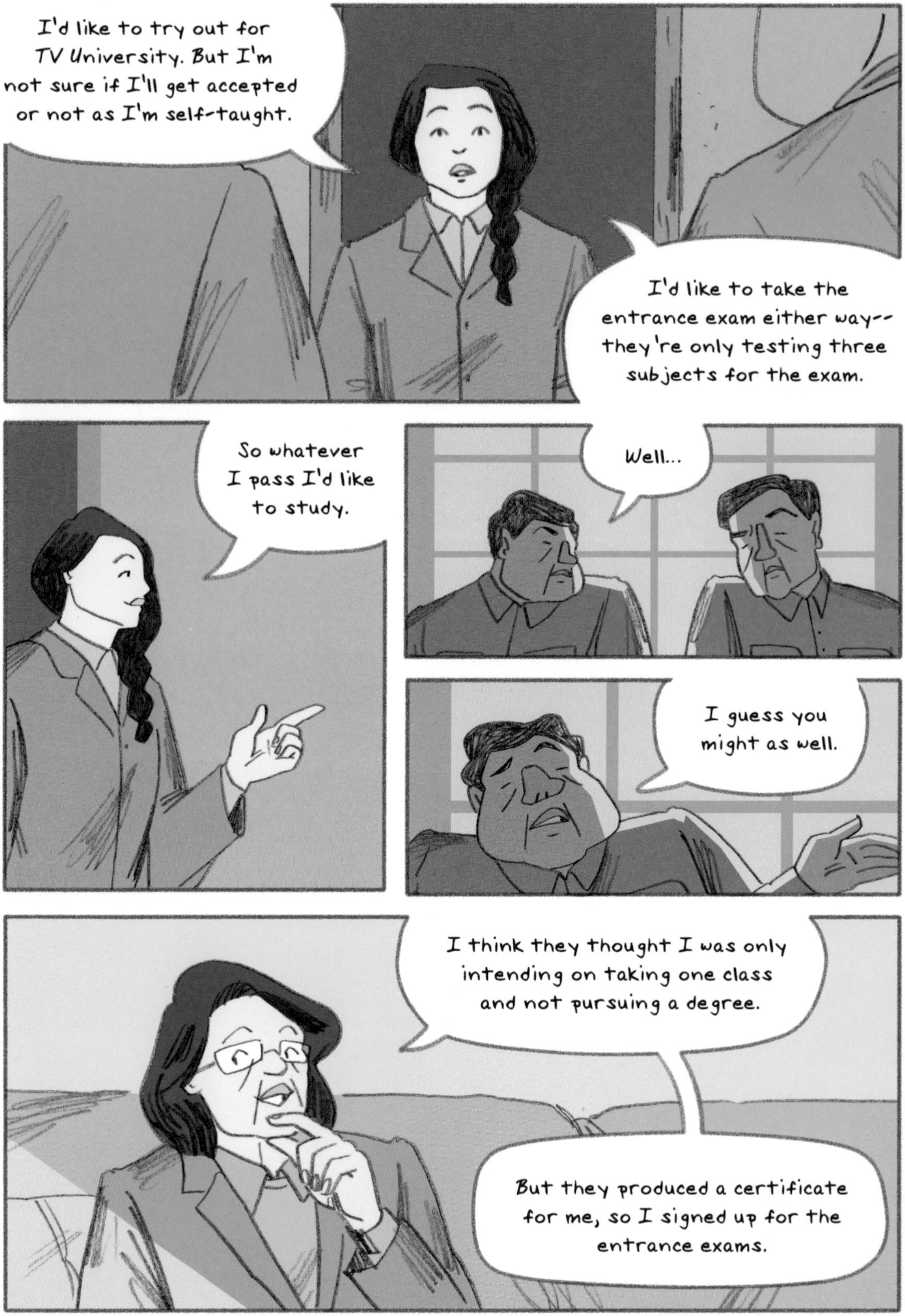
I'd like to try out for TV University. But I'm not sure if I'll get accepted or not as I'm self-taught.
I'd like to take the entrance exam either way--they're only testing three subjects for the exam.
So whatever I pass I'd like to study.
Well...
I guess you might as well.
I think they thought I was only intending on taking one class and not pursuing a degree.
But they produced a certificate for me, so I signed up for the entrance exams.

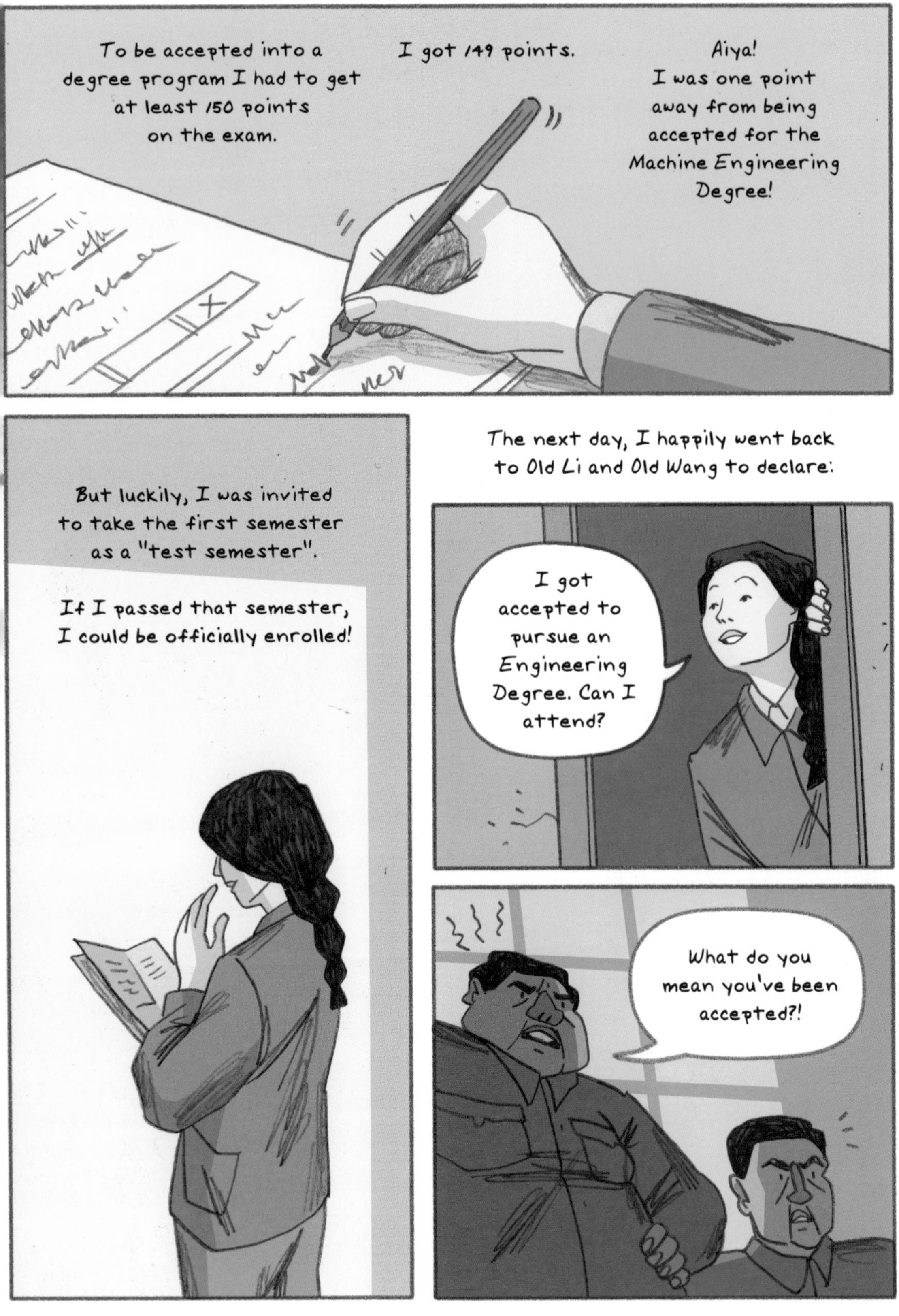
To be accepted into a degree program I had to get at least 150 points on the exam.
I got 149 points.
Aiya! I was one point away from being accepted for the Machine Engineering Degree!
But luckily, I was invited to take the first semester as a "test semester".
If I passed that semester, I could be officially enrolled!
The next day, I happily went back to Old Li and Old Wang to declare:
I got accepted to pursue an Engineering Degree. Can I attend?
What do you mean you've been accepted?!

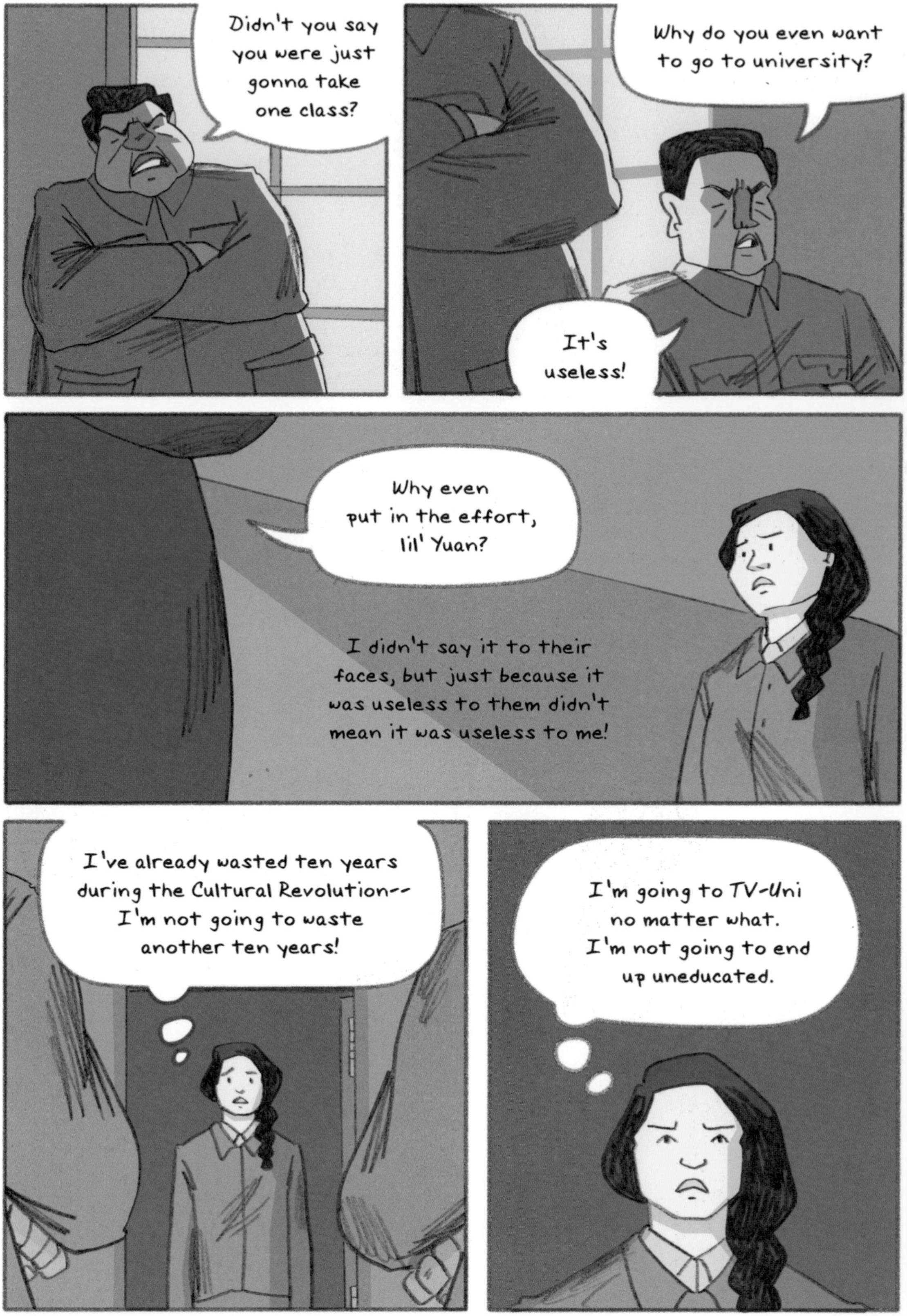
Didn't you say you were just gonna take one class?
Why do you even want to go to university?
It's useless!
Why even put in the effort, lil' Yuan?
I didn't say it to their faces, but just because it was useless to them didn't mean it was useless to me!
I've already wasted ten years during the Cultural Revolution-- I'm not going to waste another ten years!
I'm going to TV-Uni no matter what. I'm not going to end up uneducated.

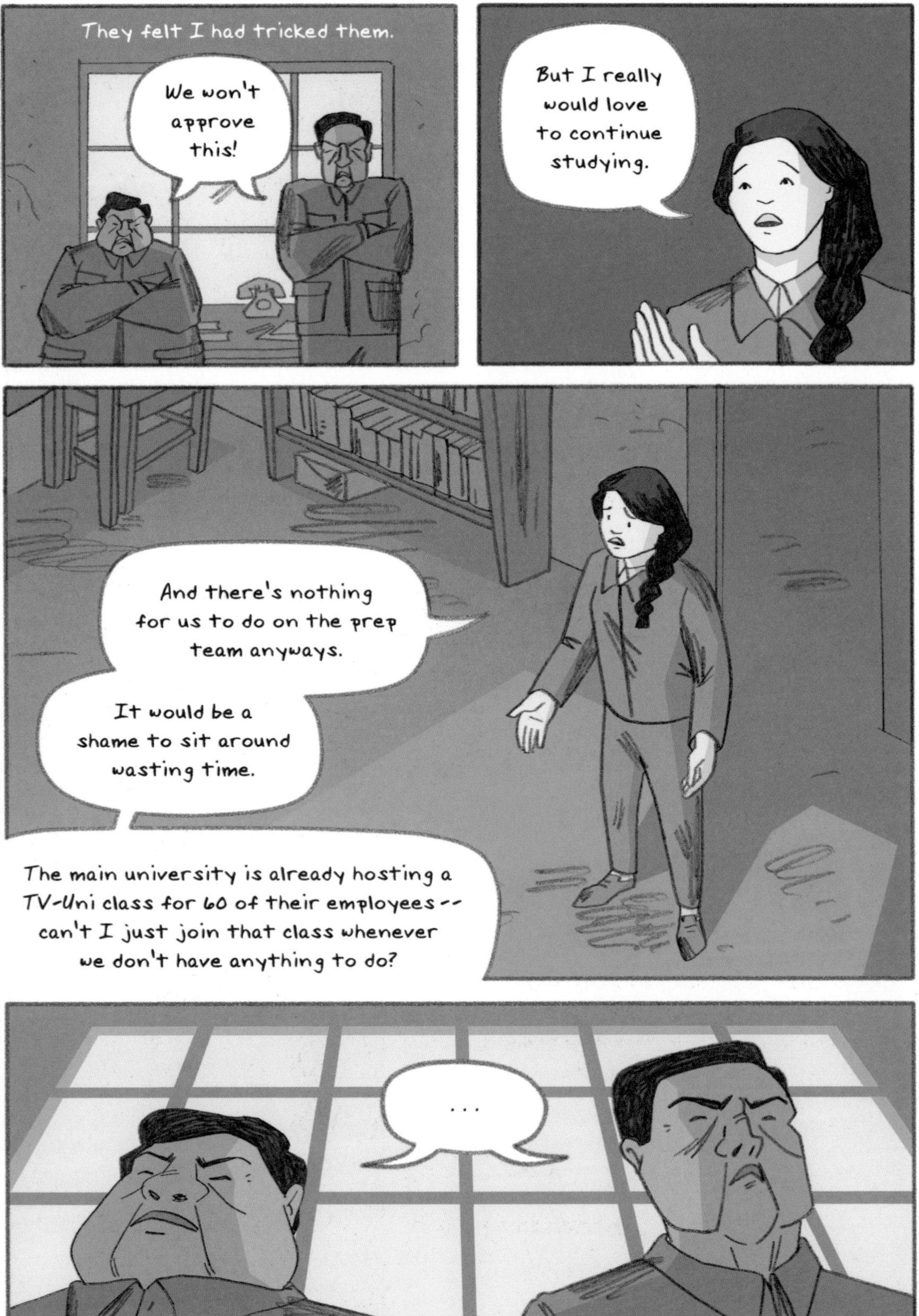
They felt I had tricked them.
We won't approve this!
But I really would love to continue studying.
And there's nothing for us to do on the prep team anyways.
It would be a shame to sit around wasting time.
The main university is already hosting a TV-Uni class for 60 of their employees -- can't I just join that class whenever we don't have anything to do?
...

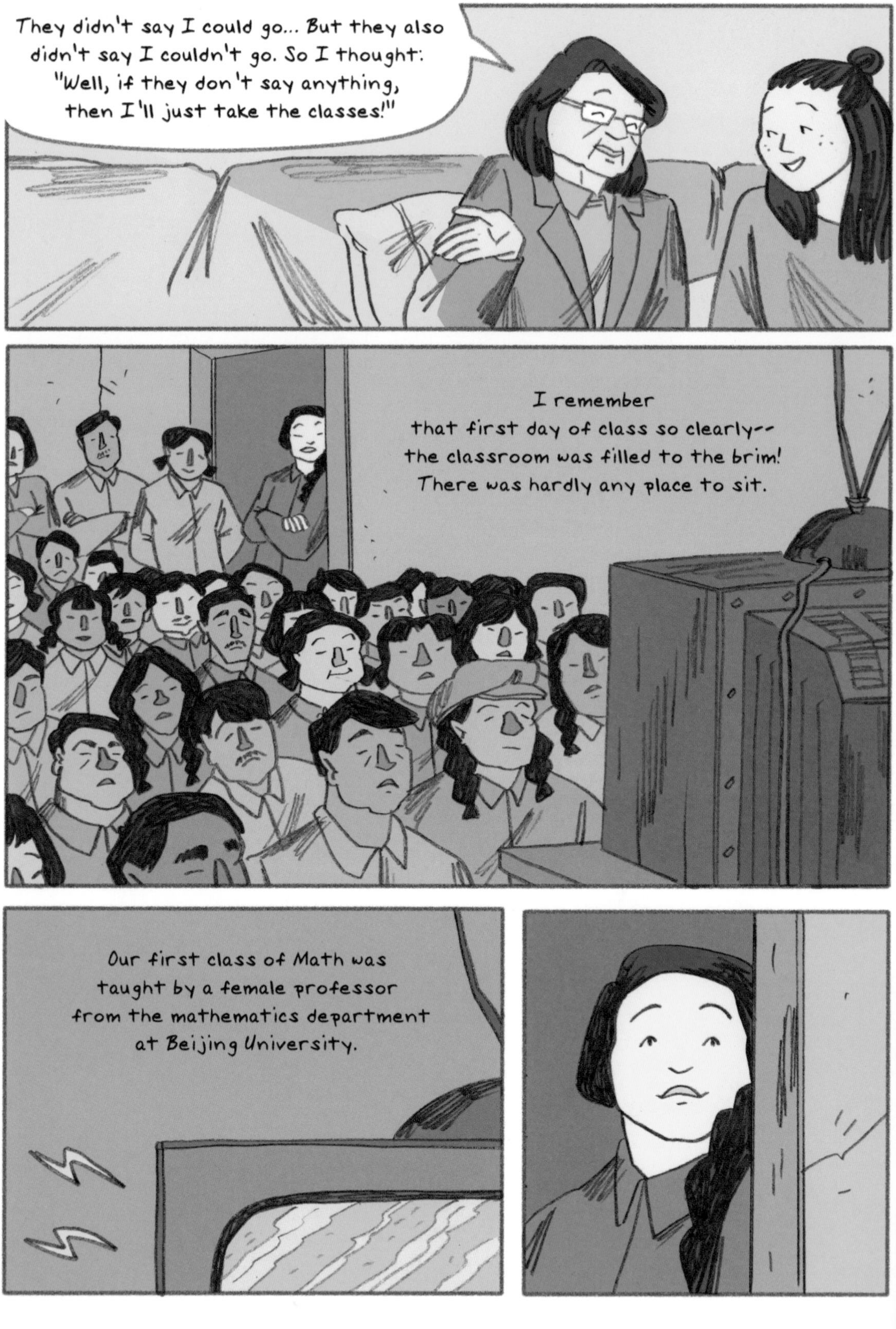
They didn't say I could go... But they also didn't say I couldn't go. So I thought: "Well, if they don't say anything, then I'll just take the classes!"
I remember that first day of class so clearly-- the classroom was filled to the brim! There was hardly any place to sit.
Our first class of Math was taught by a female professor from the mathematics department at Beijing University.

I chose a degree in Machine Engineering at TV-University
because of a talk my father had with one of my older brothers.
This was before the Cultural Revolution had even started and
father was advising him on what to study.

He said:
"Certain things can be dangerous to study.
If you kids want to continue studying, it's
for the better if you study engineering.

"One plus one will always equal two."

This left such a deep impression in my mind, so when it came time
to choose, my gut told me it was safest to go with engineering.

北京四相 1970

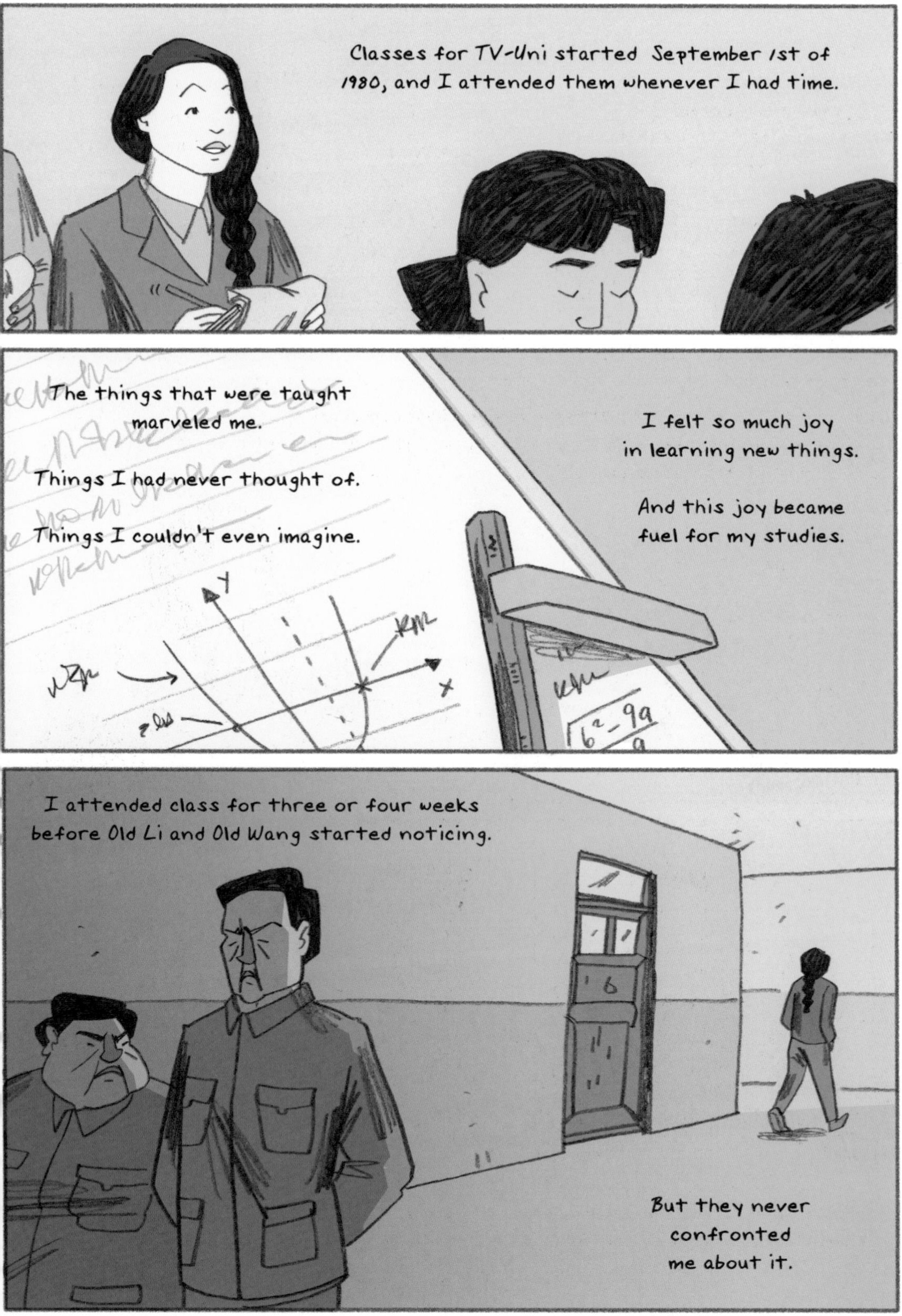
Classes for TV-Uni started September 1st of 1980, and I attended them whenever I had time.
The things that were taught marveled me.
Things I had never thought of.
Things I couldn't even imagine.
I felt so much joy in learning new things.
And this joy became fuel for my studies.
I attended class for three or four weeks before Old Li and Old Wang started noticing.
But they never confronted me about it.

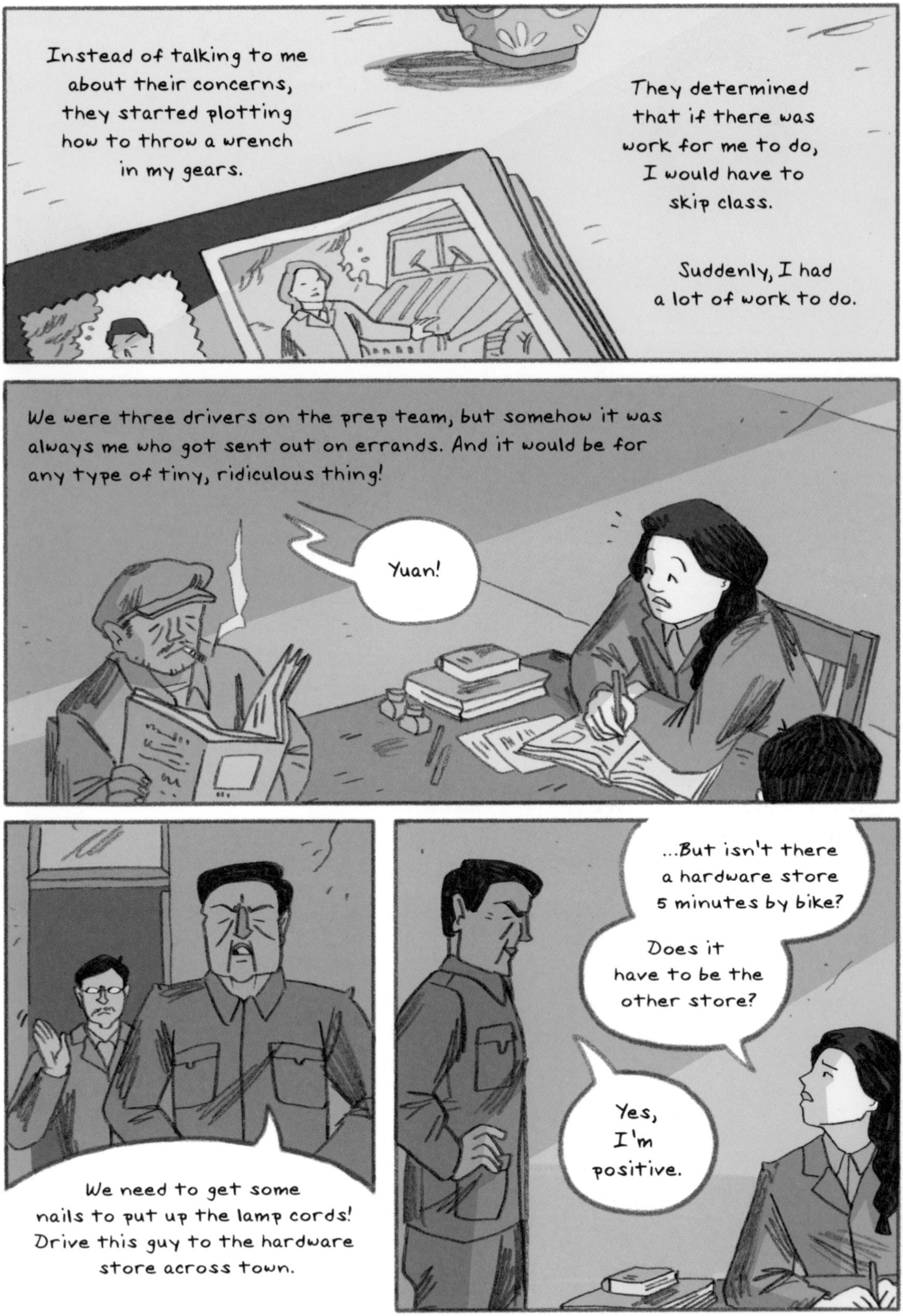
Instead of talking to me about their concerns, they started plotting how to throw a wrench in my gears.
They determined that if there was work for me to do, I would have to skip class.
Suddenly, I had a lot of work to do.
We were three drivers on the prep team, but somehow it was always me who got sent out on errands. And it would be for any type of tiny, ridiculous thing!
Yuan!
We need to get some nails to put up the lamp cords! Drive this guy to the hardware store across town.
...But isn't there a hardware store 5 minutes by bike?
Does it have to be the other store?
Yes, I'm positive.

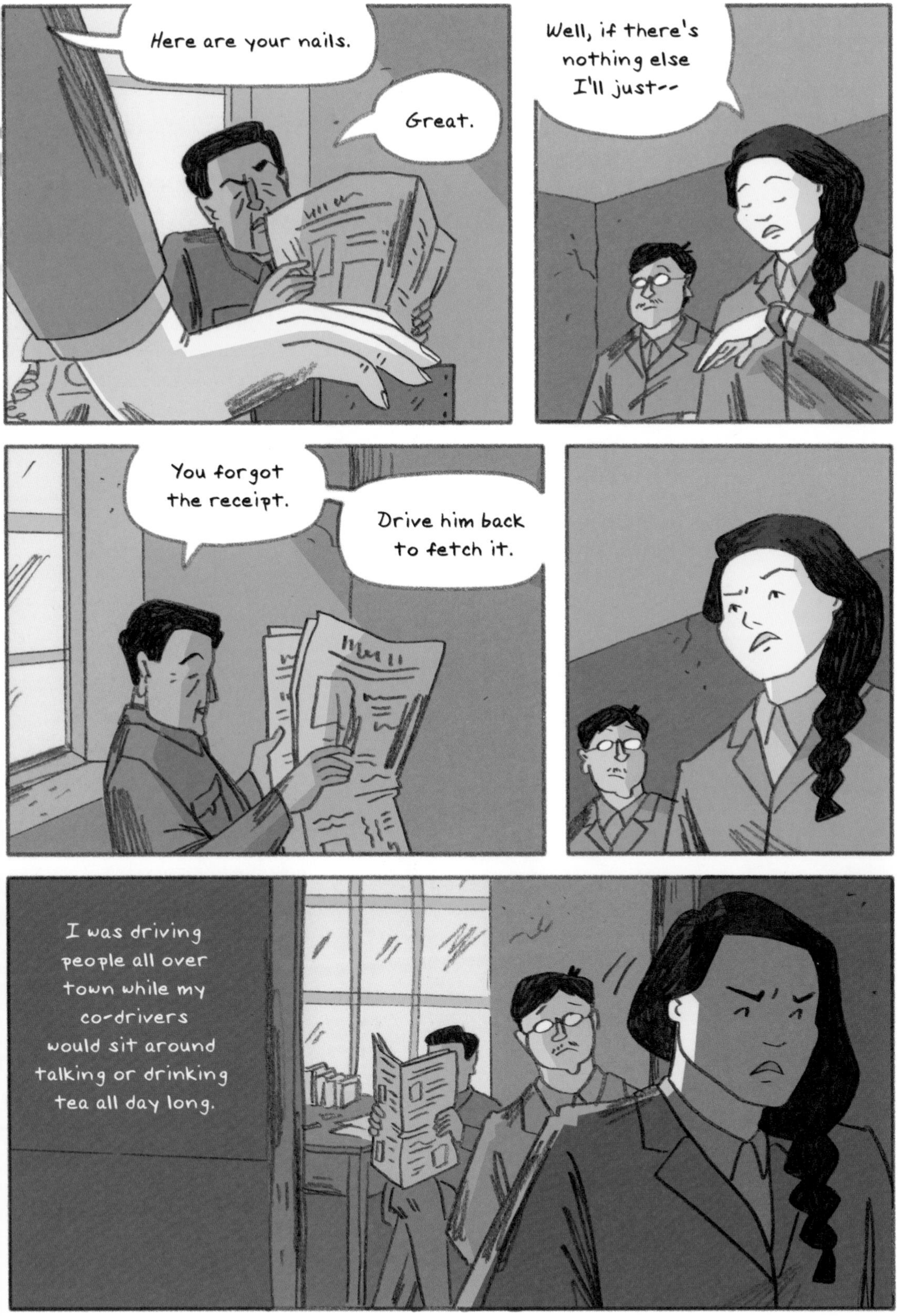
Here are your nails.
Great.
Well, if there's nothing else I'll just--
You forgot the receipt.
Drive him back to fetch it.
I was driving people all over town while my co-drivers would sit around talking or drinking tea all day long.

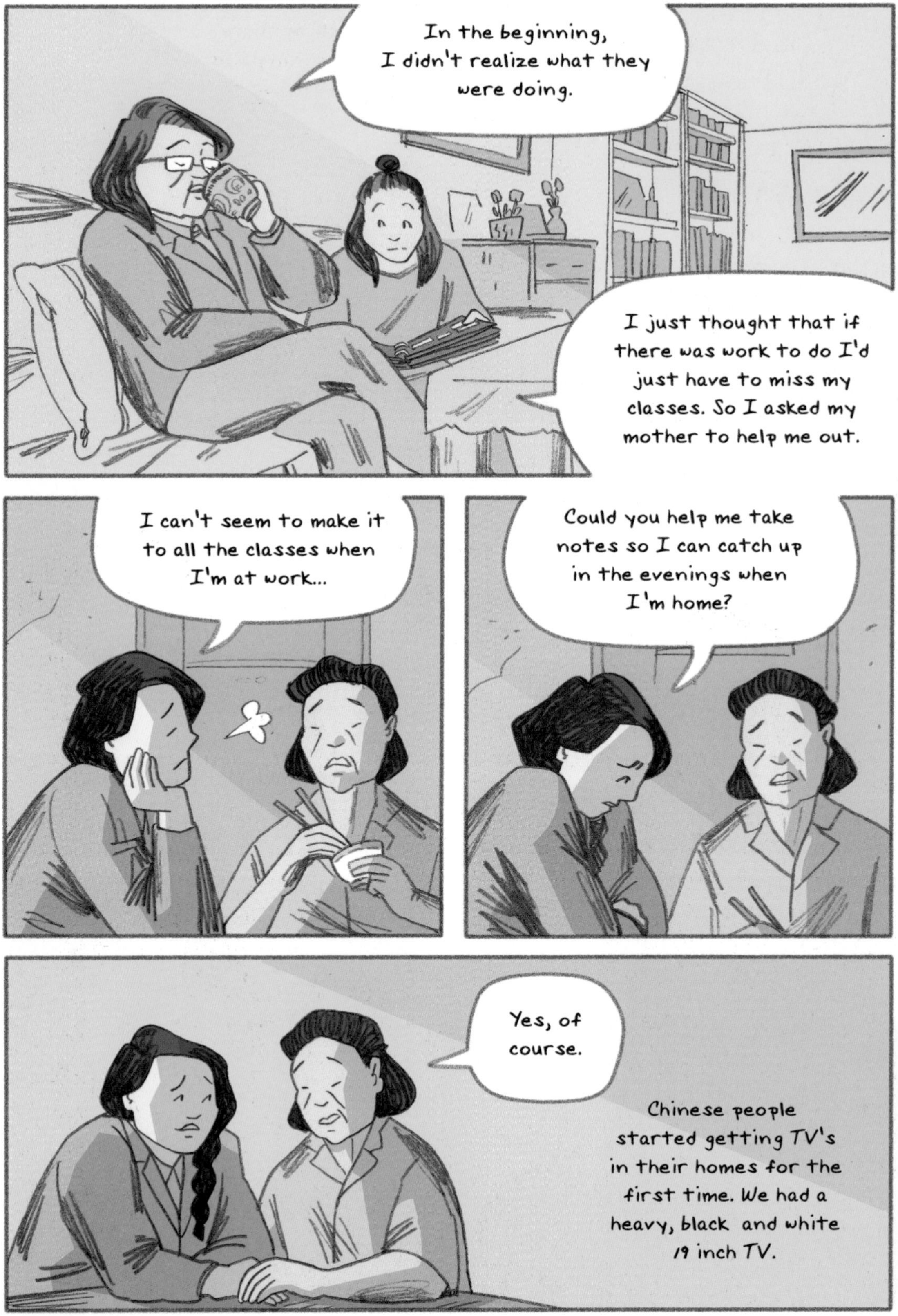
In the beginning, I didn't realize what they were doing.
I just thought that if there was work to do I'd just have to miss my classes. So I asked my mother to help me out.
I can't seem to make it to all the classes when I'm at work...
Could you help me take notes so I can catch up in the evenings when I'm home?
Yes, of course.
Chinese people started getting TV's in their homes for the first time. We had a heavy, black and white 19 inch TV.

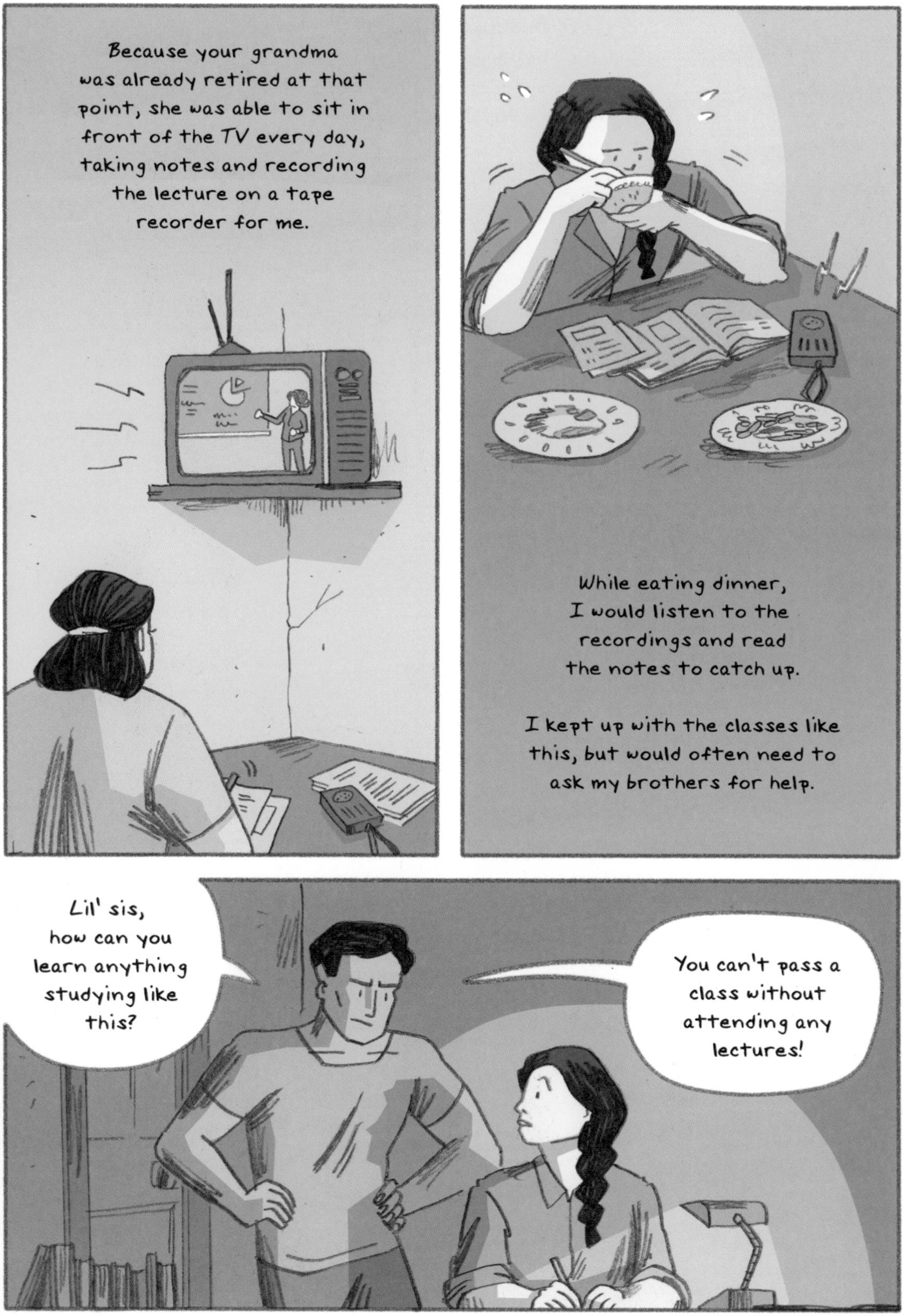
Because your grandma was already retired at that point, she was able to sit in front of the TV every day, taking notes and recording the lecture on a tape recorder for me.
While eating dinner, I would listen to the recordings and read the notes to catch up.
I kept up with the classes like this, but would often need to ask my brothers for help.
Lil' sis, how can you learn anything studying like this?
You can't pass a class without attending any lectures!

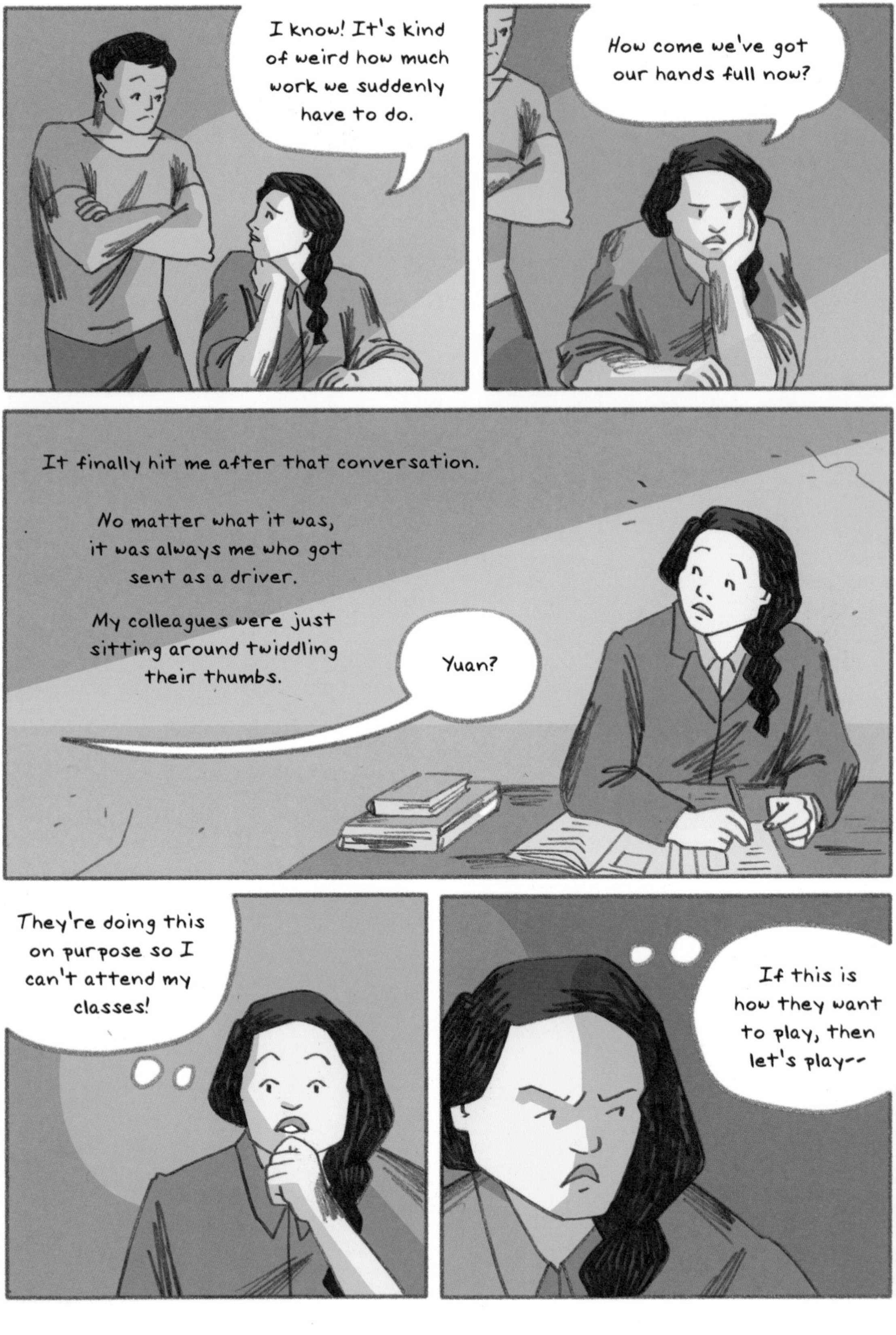
I know! It's kind of weird how much work we suddenly have to do.
How come we've got our hands full now?
It finally hit me after that conversation.
No matter what it was, it was always me who got sent as a driver.
My colleagues were just sitting around twiddling their thumbs.
Yuan?
They're doing this on purpose so I can't attend my classes!
If this is how they want to play, then let's play--

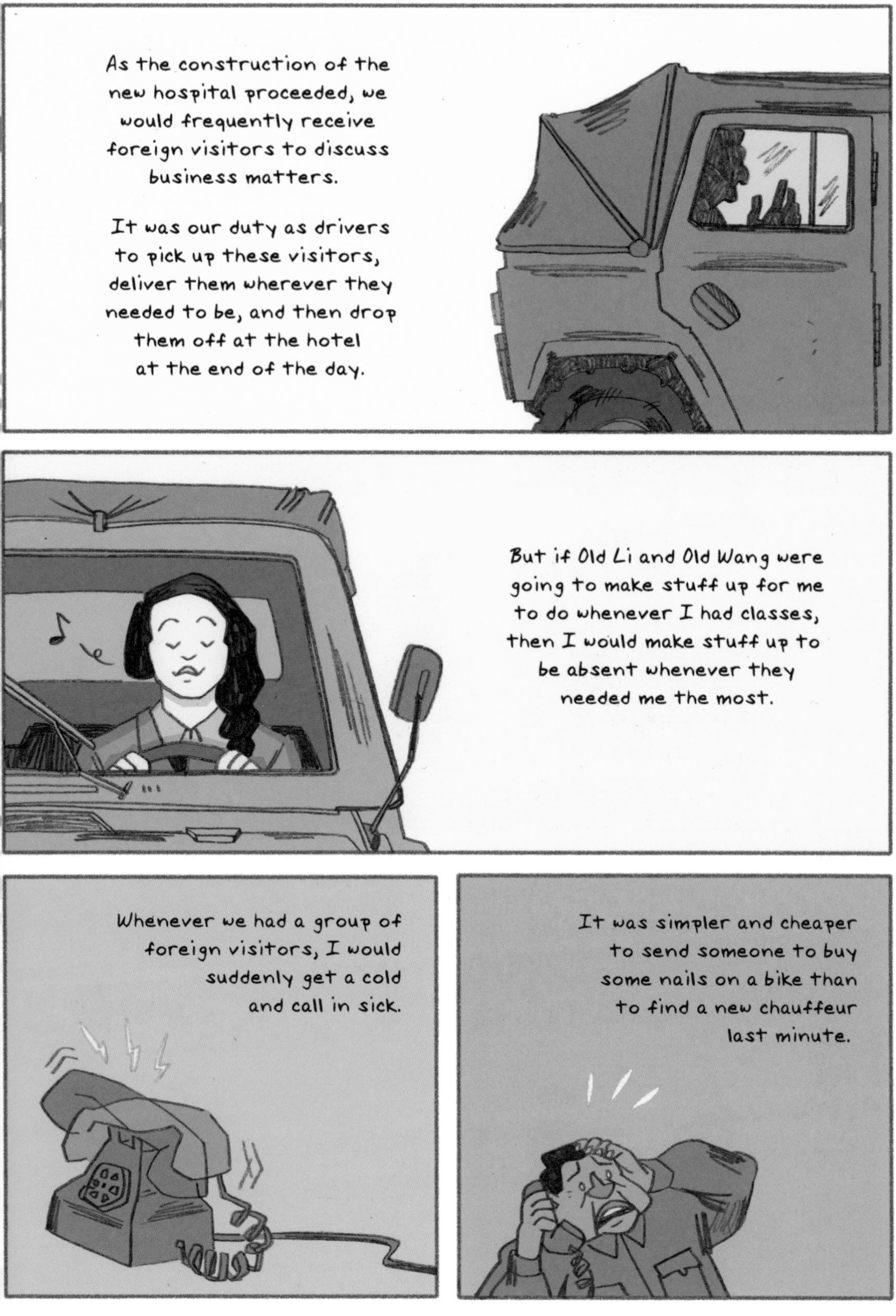
As the construction of the new hospital proceeded, we would frequently receive foreign visitors to discuss business matters.
It was our duty as drivers to pick up these visitors, deliver them wherever they needed to be, and then drop them off at the hotel at the end of the day.
But if Old Li and Old Wang were going to make stuff up for me to do whenever I had classes, then I would make stuff up to be absent whenever they needed me the most.
Whenever we had a group of foreign visitors, I would suddenly get a cold and call in sick.
It was simpler and cheaper to send someone to buy some nails on a bike than to find a new chauffeur last minute.

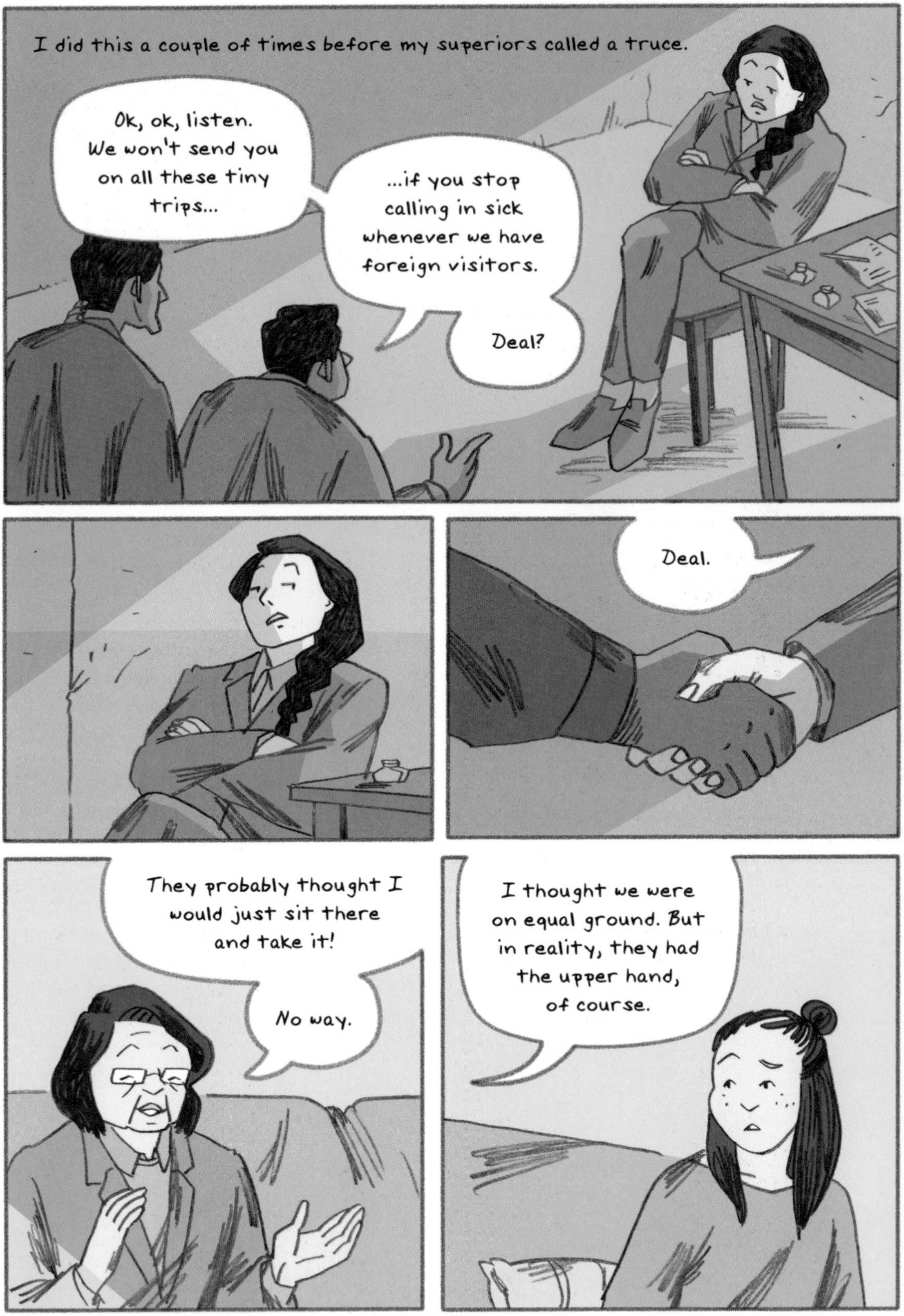
I did this a couple of times before my superiors called a truce.
Ok, ok, listen. We won't send you on all these tiny trips...
...if you stop calling in sick whenever we have foreign visitors.
Deal?
Deal.
They probably thought I would just sit there and take it!
No way.
I thought we were on equal ground. But in reality, they had the upper hand, of course.

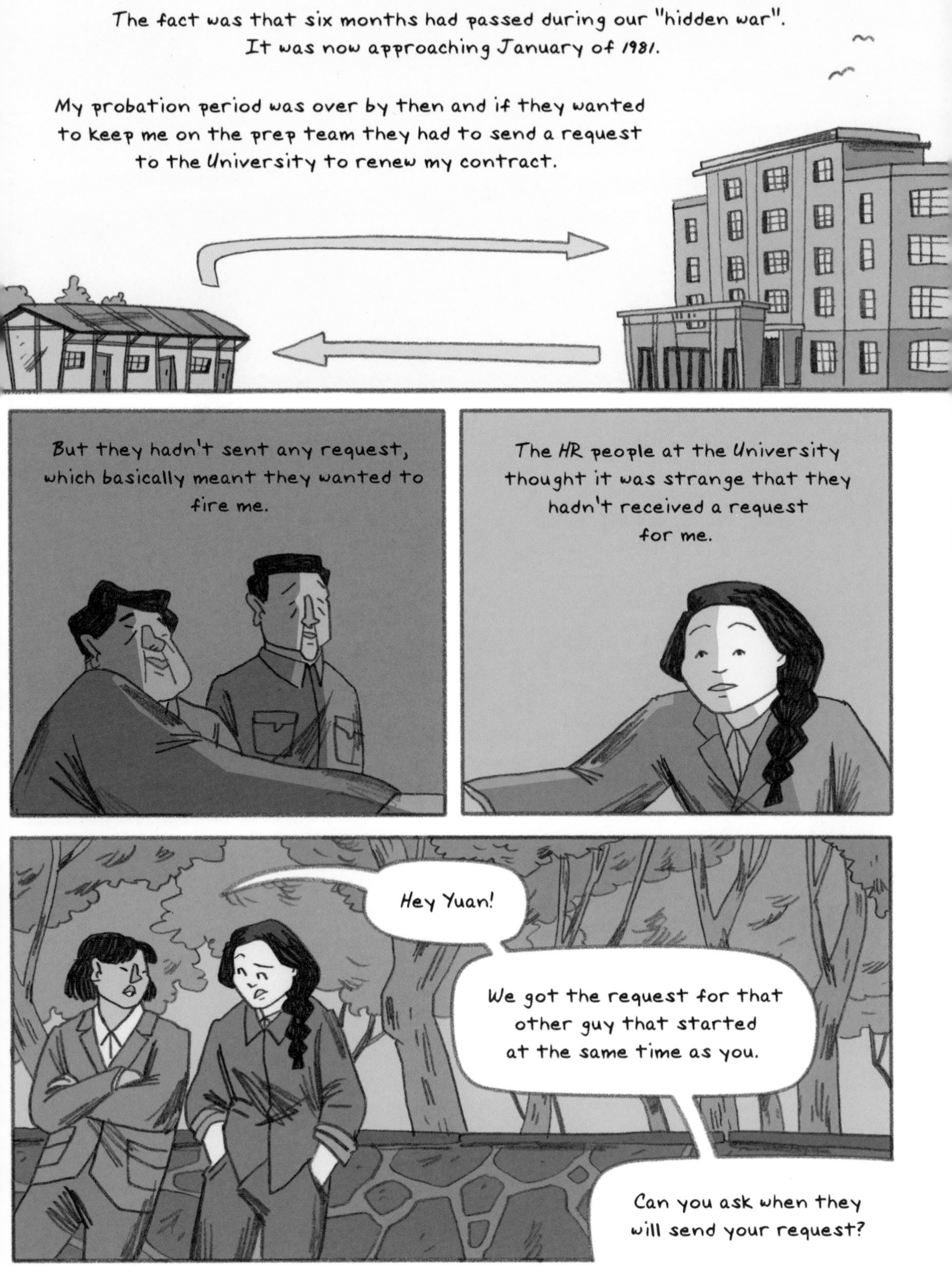
The fact was that six months had passed during our "hidden war".
It was now approaching January of 1981.
My probation period was over by then and if they wanted to keep me on the prep team they had to send a request to the University to renew my contract.
But they hadn't sent any request, which basically meant they wanted to fire me.
The HR people at the University thought it was strange that they hadn't received a request for me.
Hey Yuan!
We got the request for that other guy that started at the same time as you.
Can you ask when they will send your request?

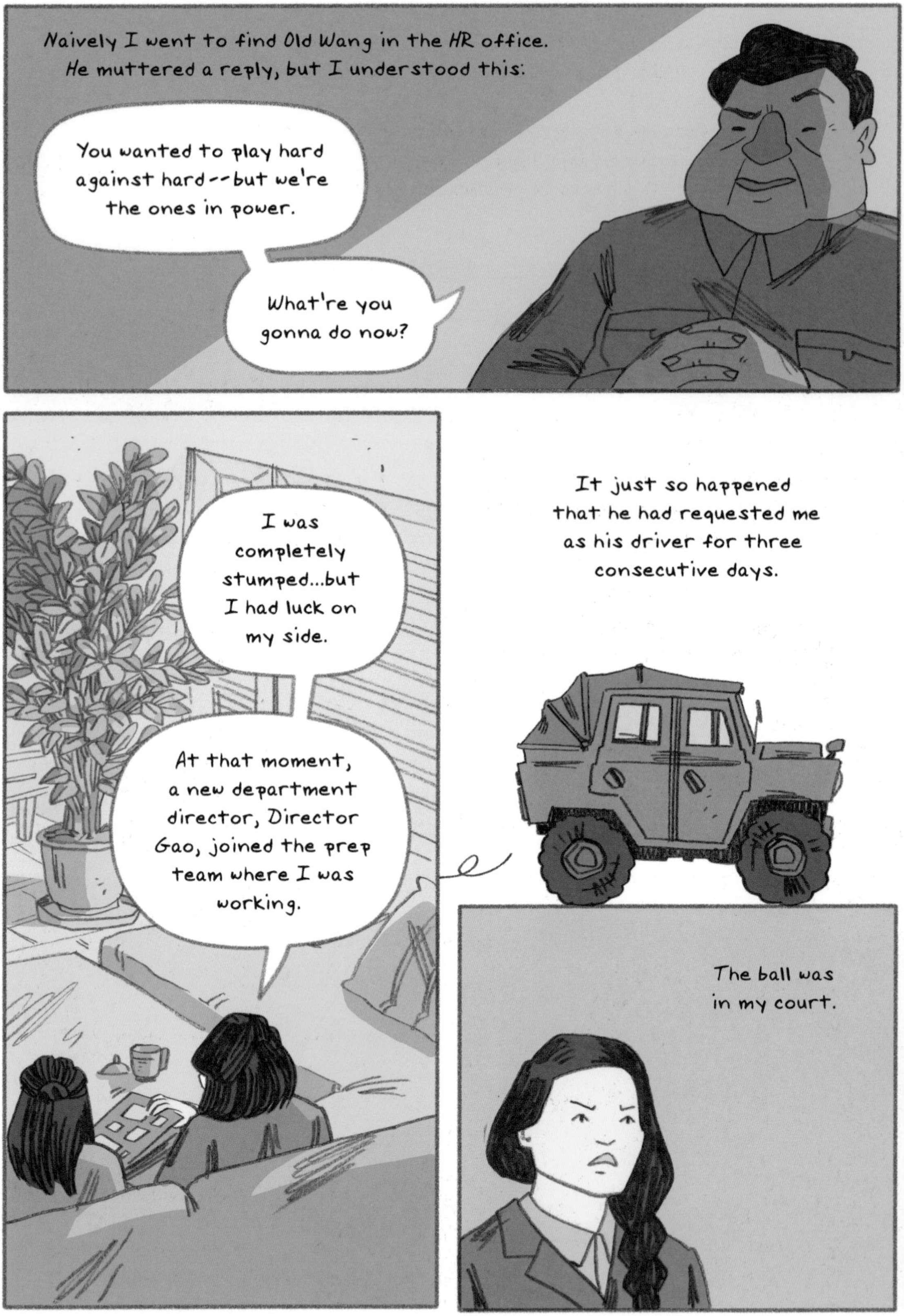
Naively I went to find Old Wang in the HR office. He muttered a reply, but I understood this:
You wanted to play hard against hard--but we're the ones in power.
What're you gonna do now?
I was completely stumped...but I had luck on my side.
At that moment, a new department director, Director Gao, joined the prep team where I was working.
It just so happened that he had requested me as his driver for three consecutive days.
The ball was in my court.

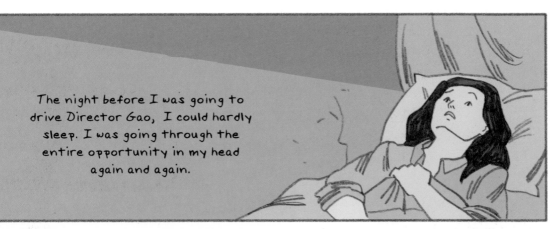

The night before I was going to drive Director Gao, I could hardly sleep. I was going through the entire opportunity in my head again and again.

First thing next morning, I approached him:

Director Gao, I would like to discuss something with you.

Yes?

It's about the renewal of my contract at the preparation team.

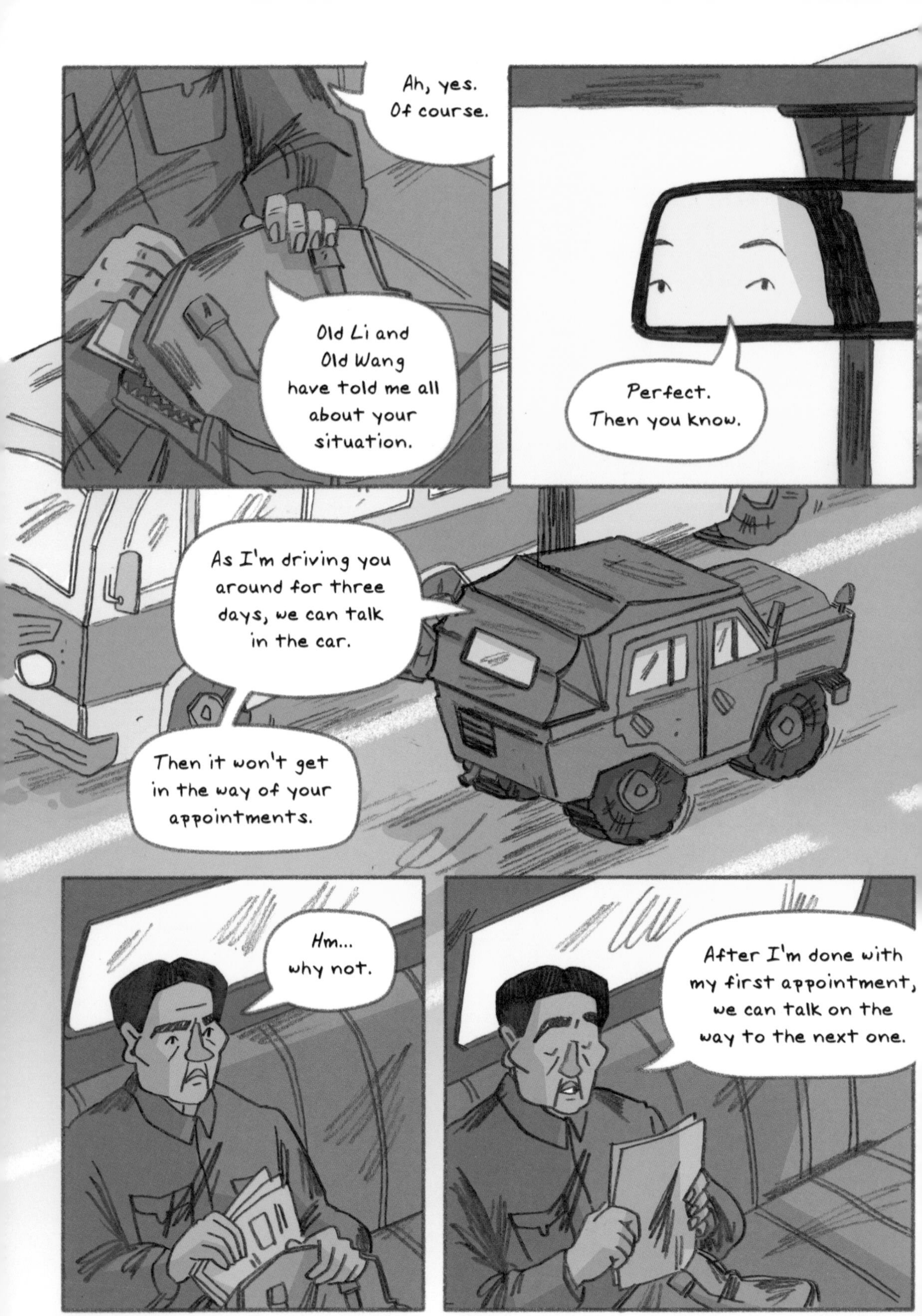
Ah, yes. Of course.
Old Li and Old Wang have told me all about your situation.
Perfect. Then you know.
As I'm driving you around for three days, we can talk in the car.
Then it won't get in the way of your appointments.
Hm... why not.
After I'm done with my first appointment, we can talk on the way to the next one.

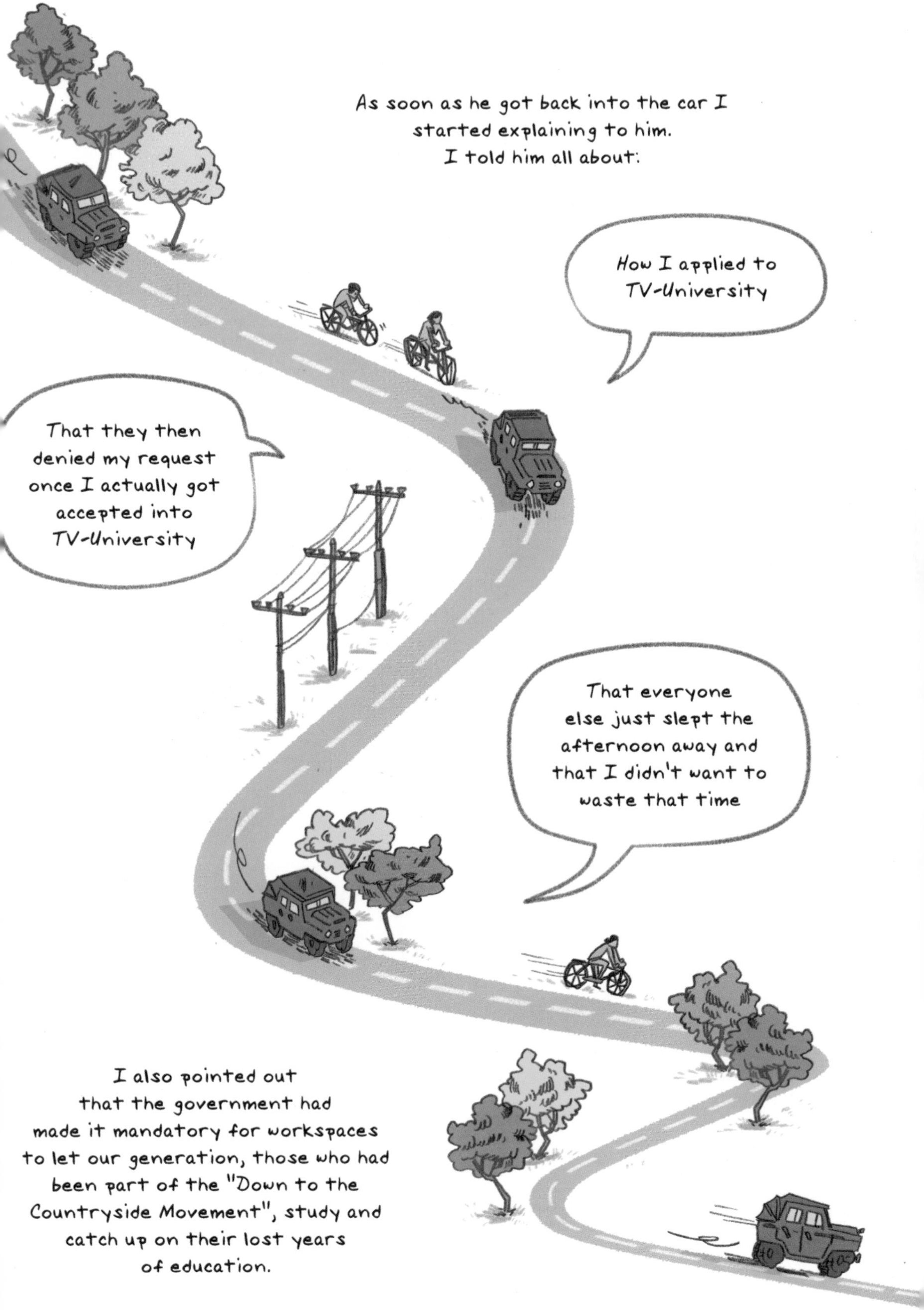
As soon as he got back into the car I started explaining to him. I told him all about:
How I applied to TV-University
That they then denied my request once I actually got accepted into TV-University
That everyone else just slept the afternoon away and that I didn't want to waste that time
I also pointed out that the government had made it mandatory for workspaces to let our generation, those who had been part of the "Down to the Countryside Movement", study and catch up on their lost years of education.

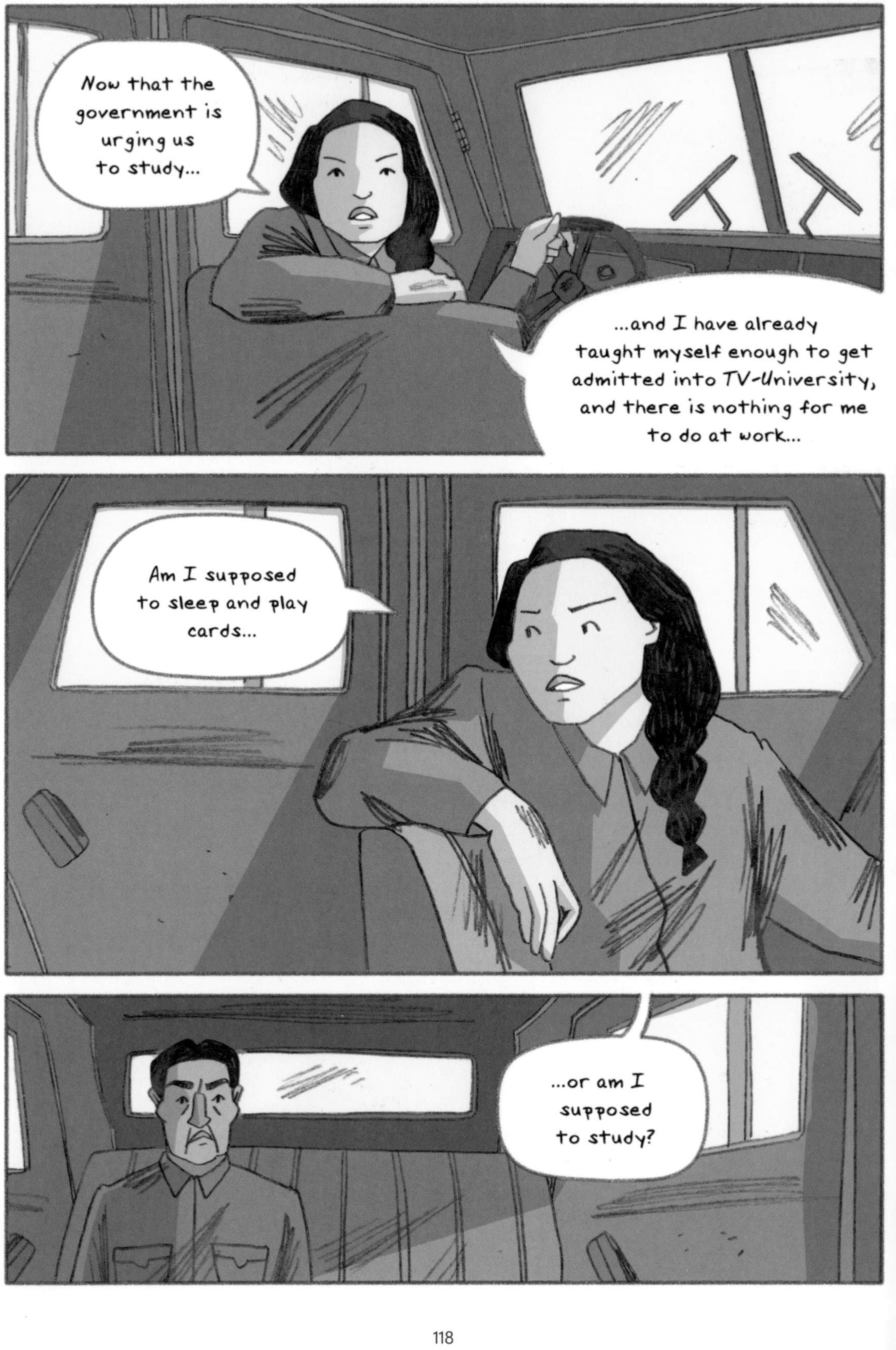
Now that the government is urging us to study...
...and I have already taught myself enough to get admitted into TV-University, and there is nothing for me to do at work...
Am I supposed to sleep and play cards...
...or am I supposed to study?

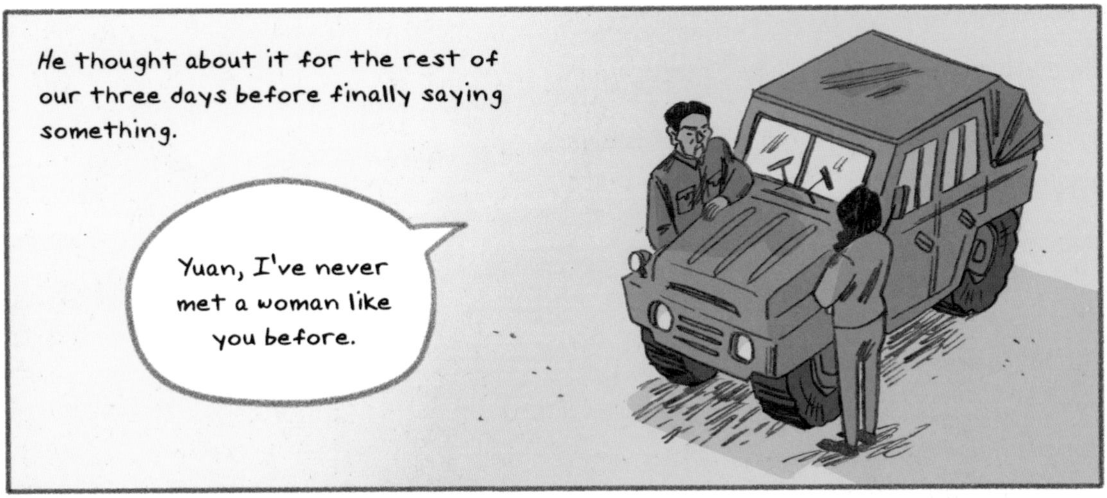
He thought about it for the rest of our three days before finally saying something.
Yuan, I've never met a woman like you before.

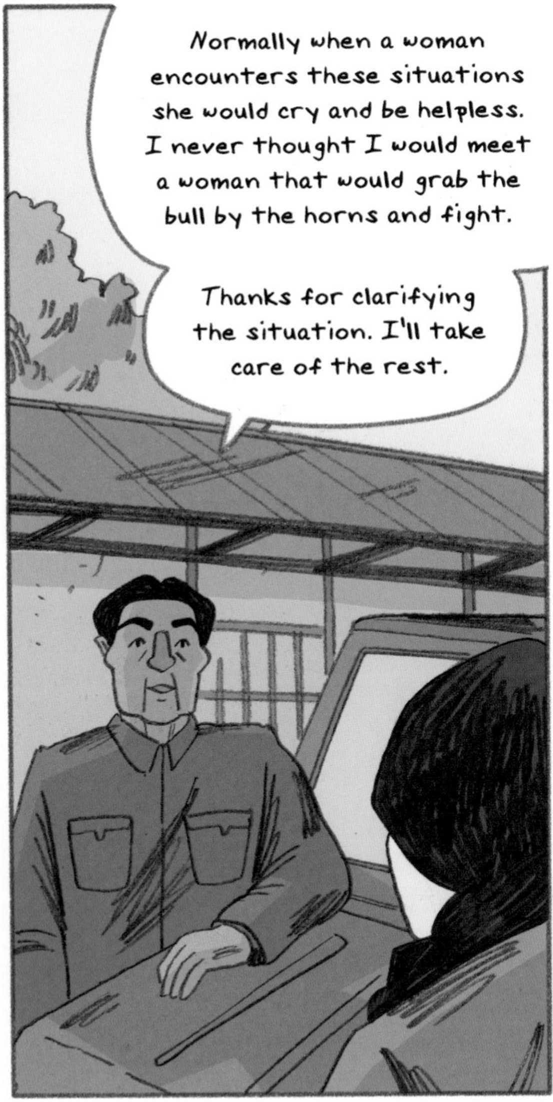
Normally when a woman encounters these situations she would cry and be helpless. I never thought I would meet a woman that would grab the bull by the horns and fight.
Thanks for clarifying the situation. I'll take care of the rest.

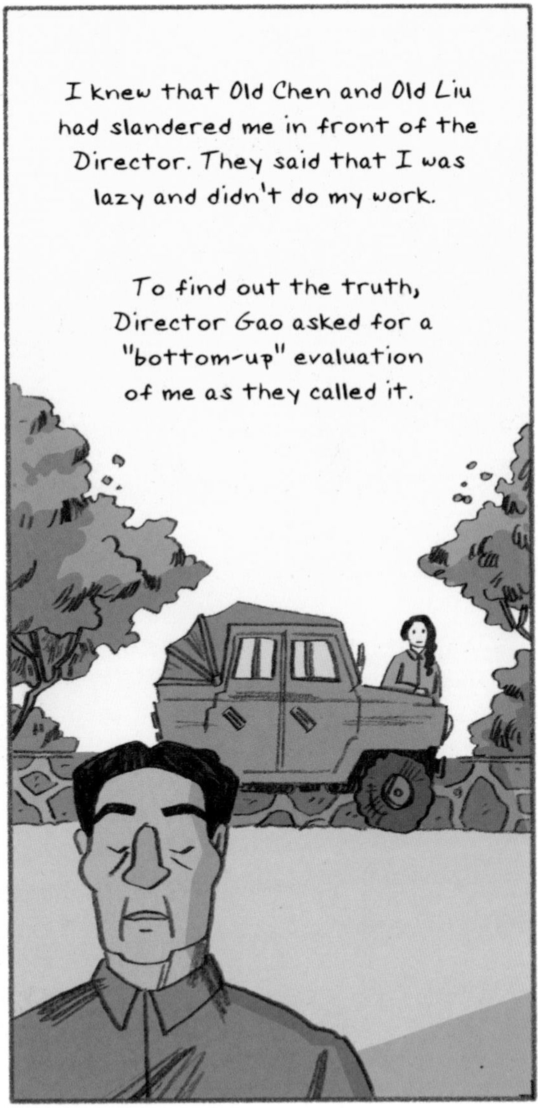
I knew that Old Chen and Old Liu had slandered me in front of the Director. They said that I was lazy and didn't do my work.
To find out the truth, Director Gao asked for a "bottom-up" evaluation of me as they called it.

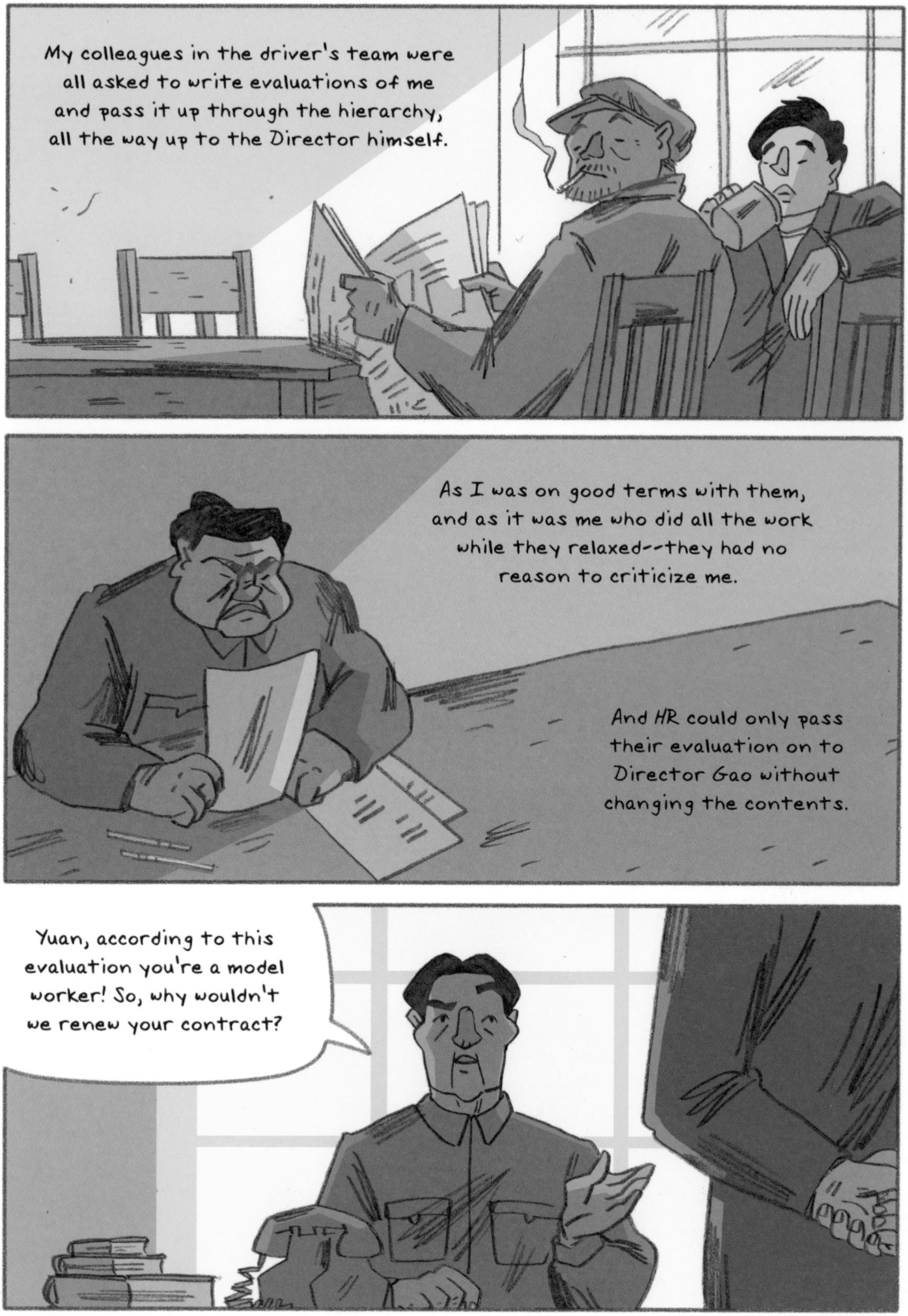
My colleagues in the driver's team were all asked to write evaluations of me and pass it up through the hierarchy, all the way up to the Director himself.
As I was on good terms with them, and as it was me who did all the work while they relaxed--they had no reason to criticize me.
And HR could only pass their evaluation on to Director Gao without changing the contents.
Yuan, according to this evaluation you're a model worker! So, why wouldn't we renew your contract?

Old Li and Old Wang were forced to renew my contract in the end.

But just because I was officially hired didn't mean they couldn't disrupt my studies.

They would send me off on even more errands to stop me from attending classes. And, on top of their sabotaging, the prep team's workload had increased because we were finally in the midst of the new hospital's construction.

In the beginning, I could still make it to around 40% of my classes, but now I made it to maybe 5-10% of them.

I relied completely on the notes and recordings my mother made for me. I would bring my books to work. Whenever I had to wait for passengers to finish a meeting, I would study.

When I was two years into my four year degree we got a new vice director for the preparation team--Vice Director Sun. He was in charge of office management, HR, and our drivers team.

Of course, Old Li and Old Wang went to slander me as soon as Vice Director Sun arrived in our department.

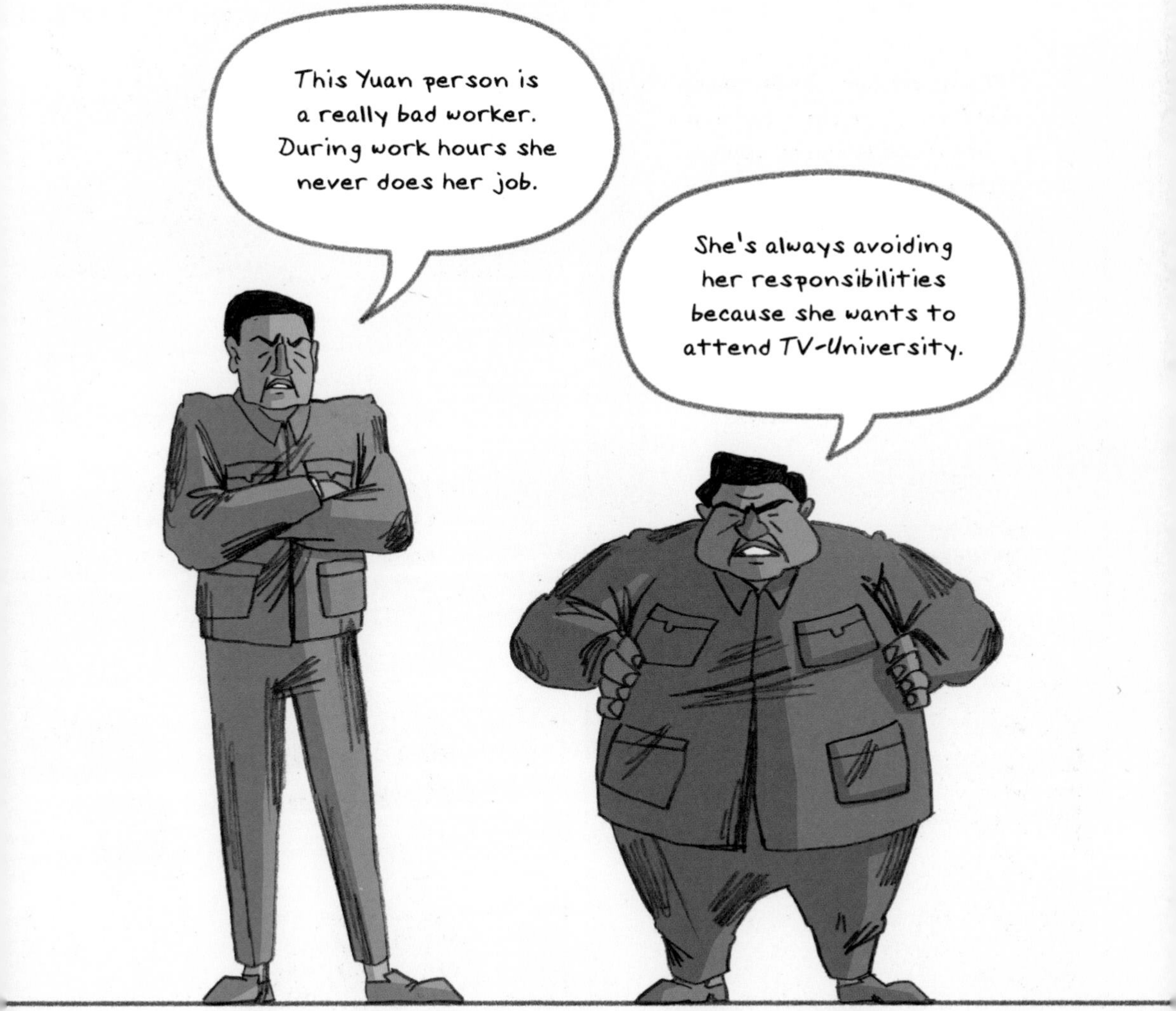
This Yuan person is a really bad worker. During work hours she never does her job.
She's always avoiding her responsibilities because she wants to attend TV-University.

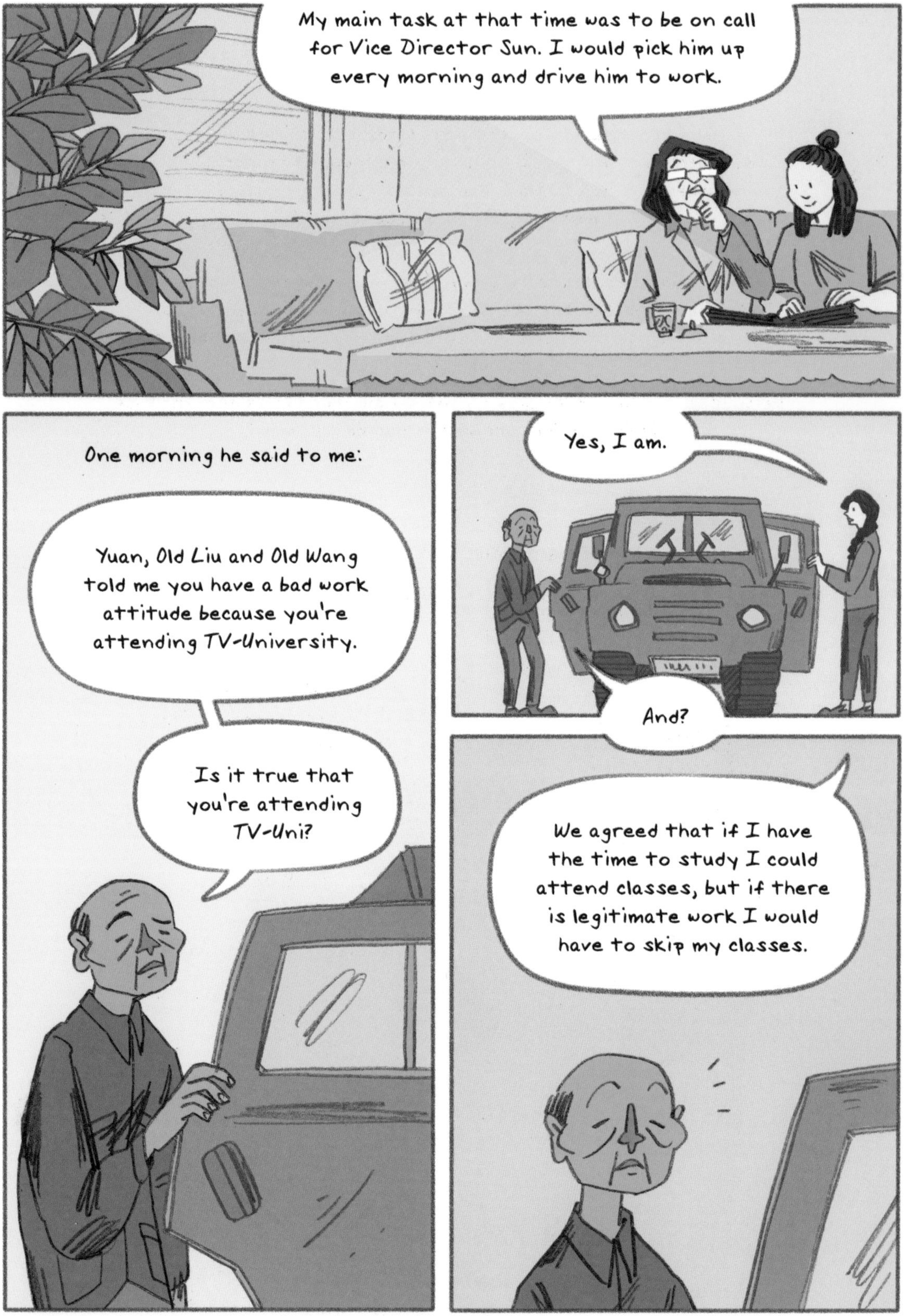

My main task at that time was to be on call for Vice Director Sun. I would pick him up every morning and drive him to work.
One morning he said to me:
Yuan, Old Liu and Old Wang told me you have a bad work attitude because you're attending TV-University.
Is it true that you're attending TV-Uni?
Yes, I am.
And?
We agreed that if I have the time to study I could attend classes, but if there is legitimate work I would have to skip my classes.

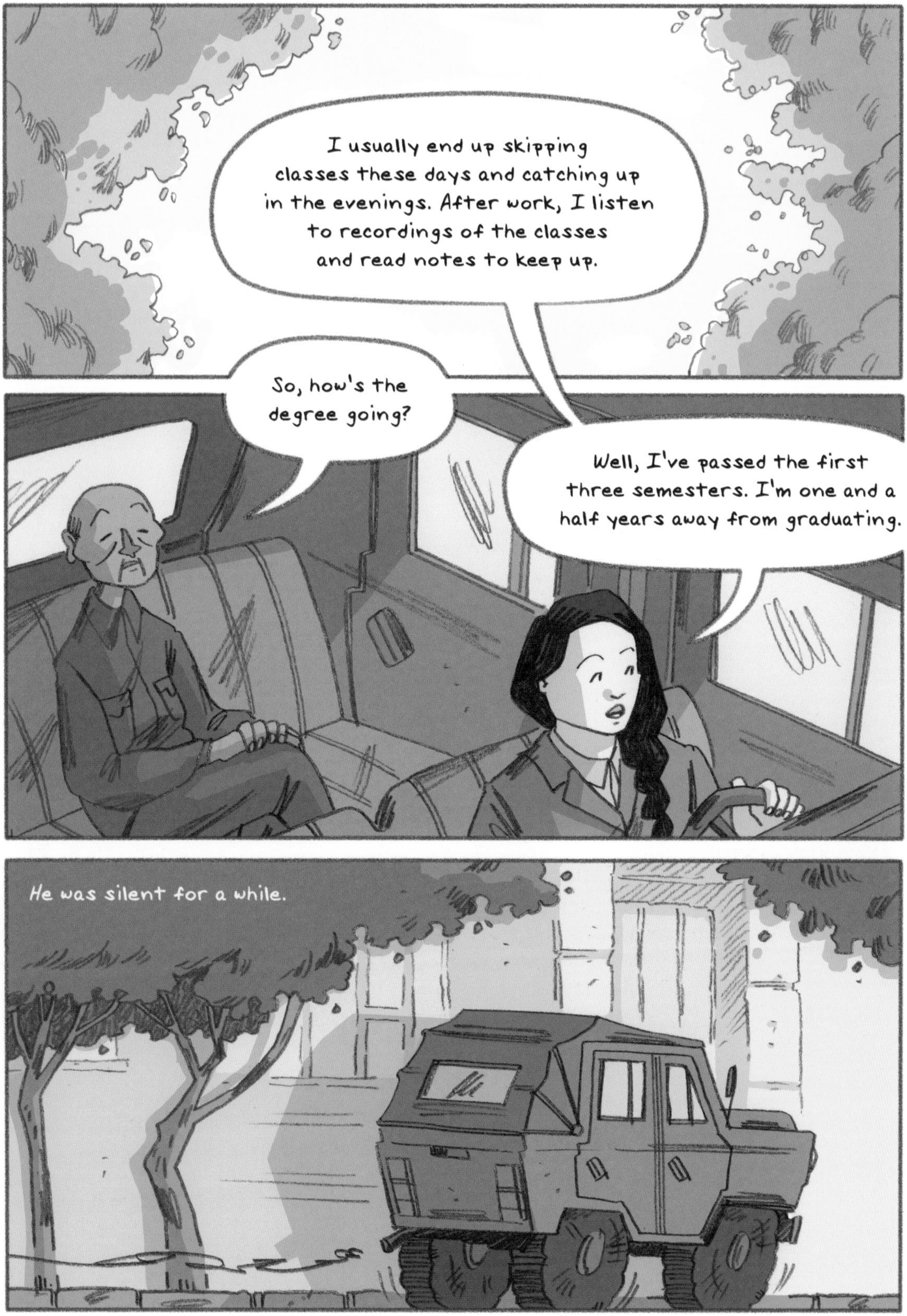

So, how's the degree going?
Well, I've passed the first three semesters. I'm one and a half years away from graduating.
I usually end up skipping classes these days and catching up in the evenings. After work, I listen to recordings of the classes and read notes to keep up.
He was silent for a while.

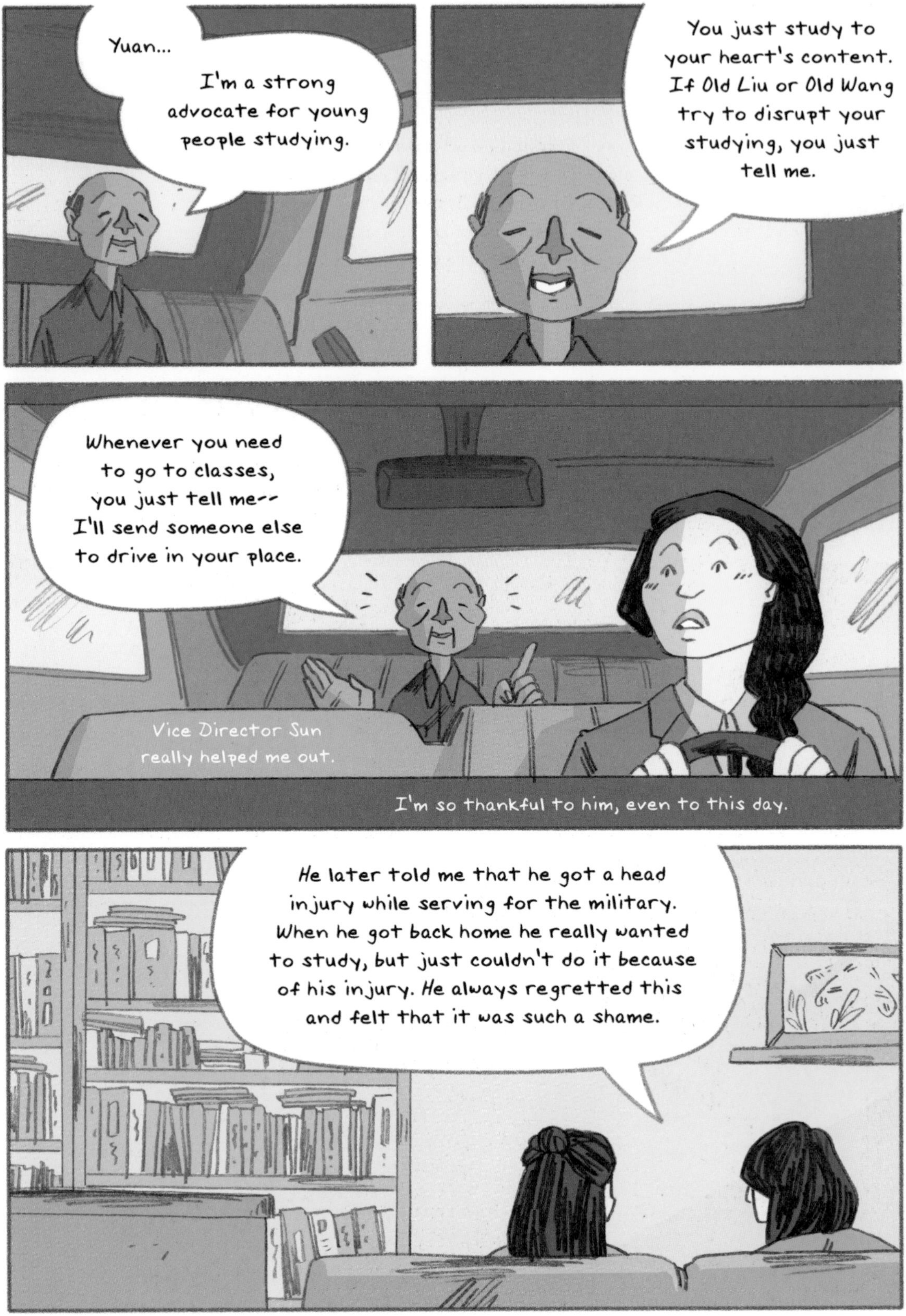
Yuan... I'm a strong advocate for young people studying.
You just study to your heart's content. If Old Liu or Old Wang try to disrupt your studying, you just tell me.
Whenever you need to go to classes, you just tell me-- I'll send someone else to drive in your place.
Vice Director Sun really helped me out.
I'm so thankful to him, even to this day.
He later told me that he got a head injury while serving for the military. When he got back home he really wanted to study, but just couldn't do it because of his injury. He always regretted this and felt that it was such a shame.

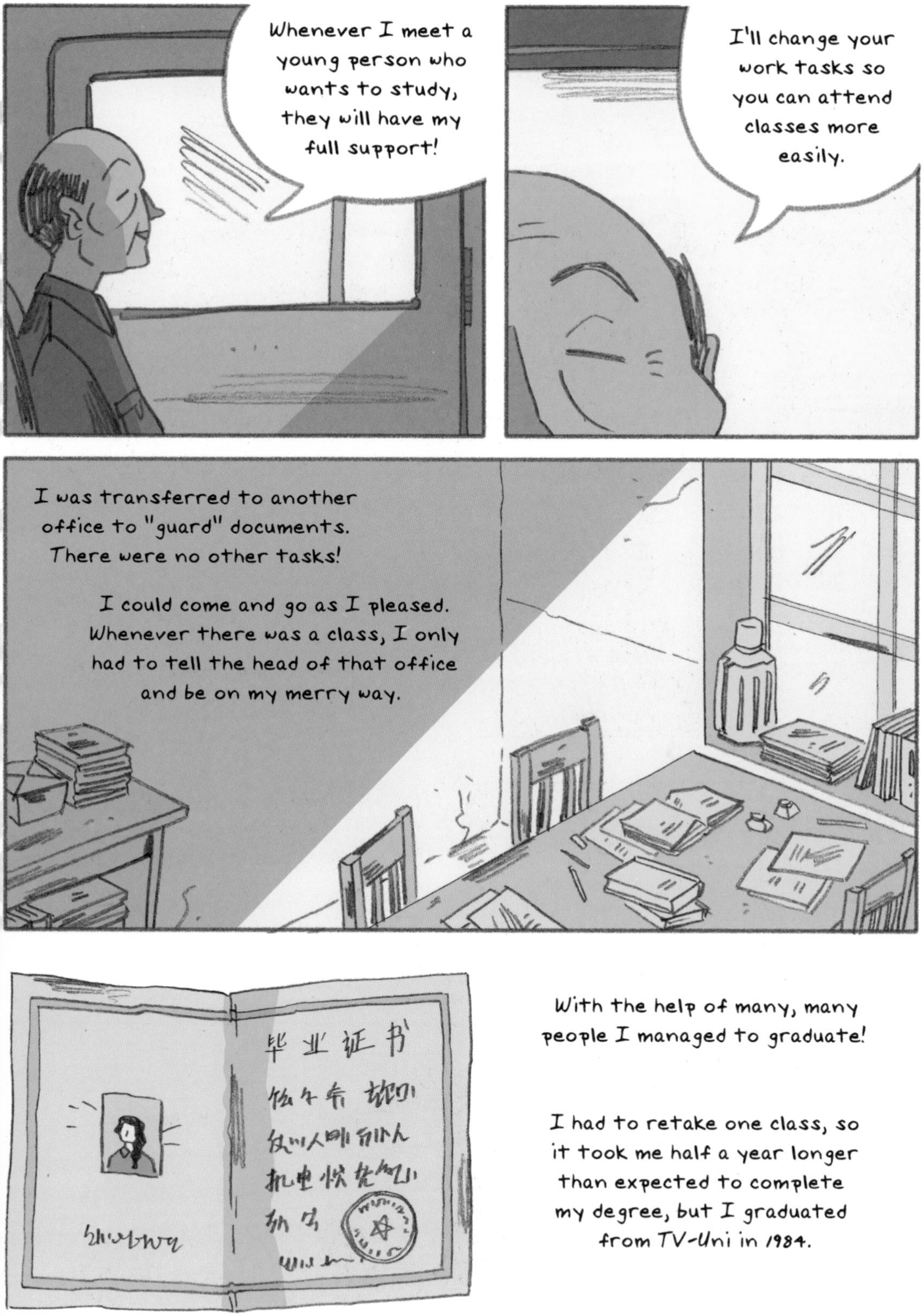
Whenever I meet a young person who wants to study, they will have my full support!
I'll change your work tasks so you can attend classes more easily.
I was transferred to another office to "guard" documents. There were no other tasks!
I could come and go as I pleased. Whenever there was a class, I only had to tell the head of that office and be on my merry way.
毕业证书
With the help of many, many people I managed to graduate!
I had to retake one class, so it took me half a year longer than expected to complete my degree, but I graduated from TV-Uni in 1984.

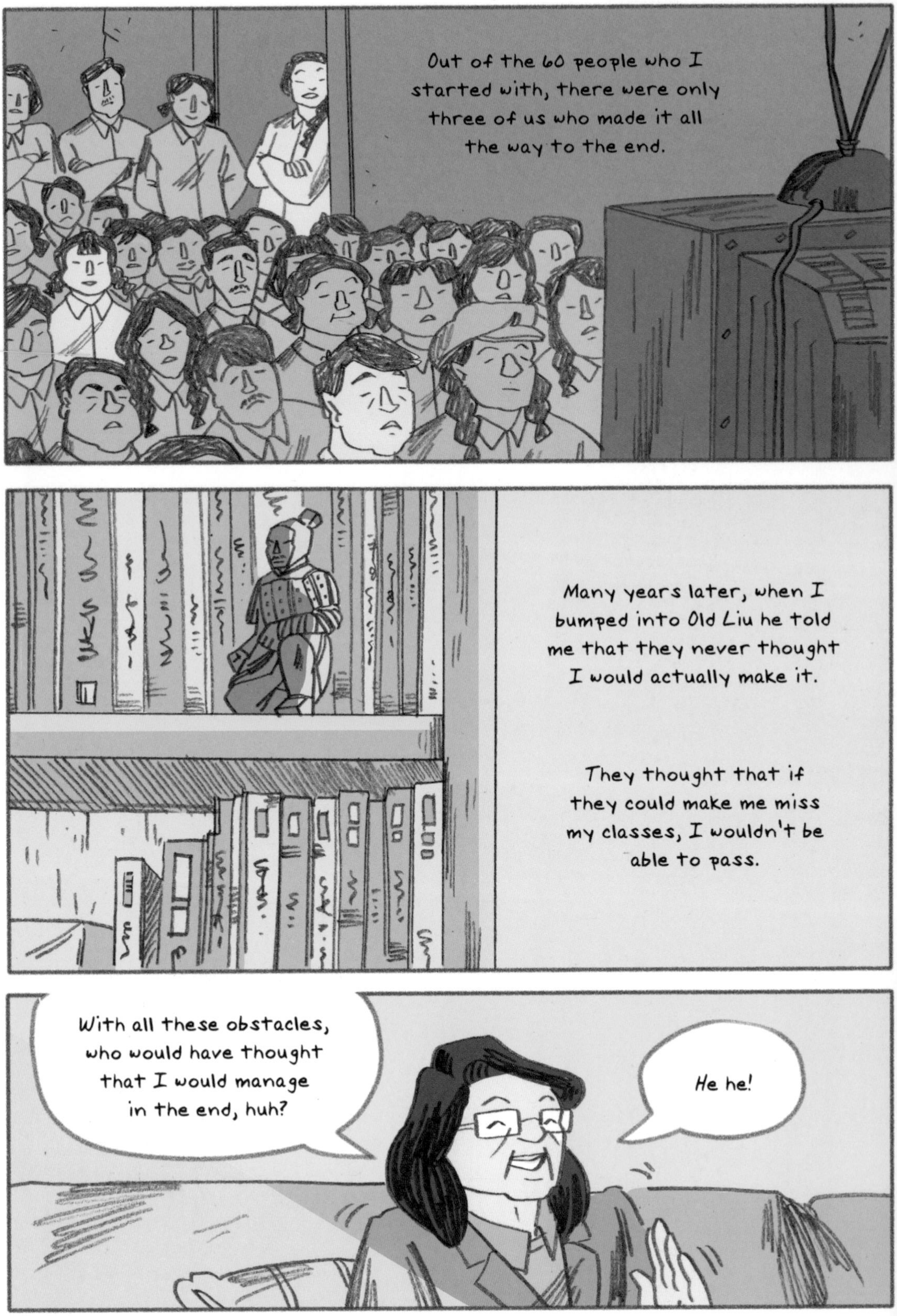
Out of the 60 people who I started with, there were only three of us who made it all the way to the end.
Many years later, when I bumped into Old Liu he told me that they never thought I would actually make it.
They thought that if they could make me miss my classes, I wouldn't be able to pass.
With all these obstacles, who would have thought that I would manage in the end, huh?
He he!

I worked my way up, and after two years I
was promoted from technician to engineer.

But something still bothered me.

Even though I had the title of an engineer,
I wanted a proper bachelor's degree.
And since I couldn't get one in China,
I started thinking about moving abroad.

Back in 1977, my mother had gotten in touch with my uncles in the
United States and in Sweden to determine if this was possible
with their help.

My uncle in the US said that he didn't have the financial
stability to help out, but my uncle in Sweden said that he
could look into it. Maybe I could get a short-term visa
and take some exams to be eligible for Swedish universities?

At that point I knew very little of Sweden, I didn't even have a clue where it
was or what is was like to live there. All I knew was that it was very far away.
The only countries we ever heard about were Japan, England, France,
the Soviet Union, and the United States. I hardly knew the names
for the rest of the countries in the world.

And getting a visa to travel was not without complication.

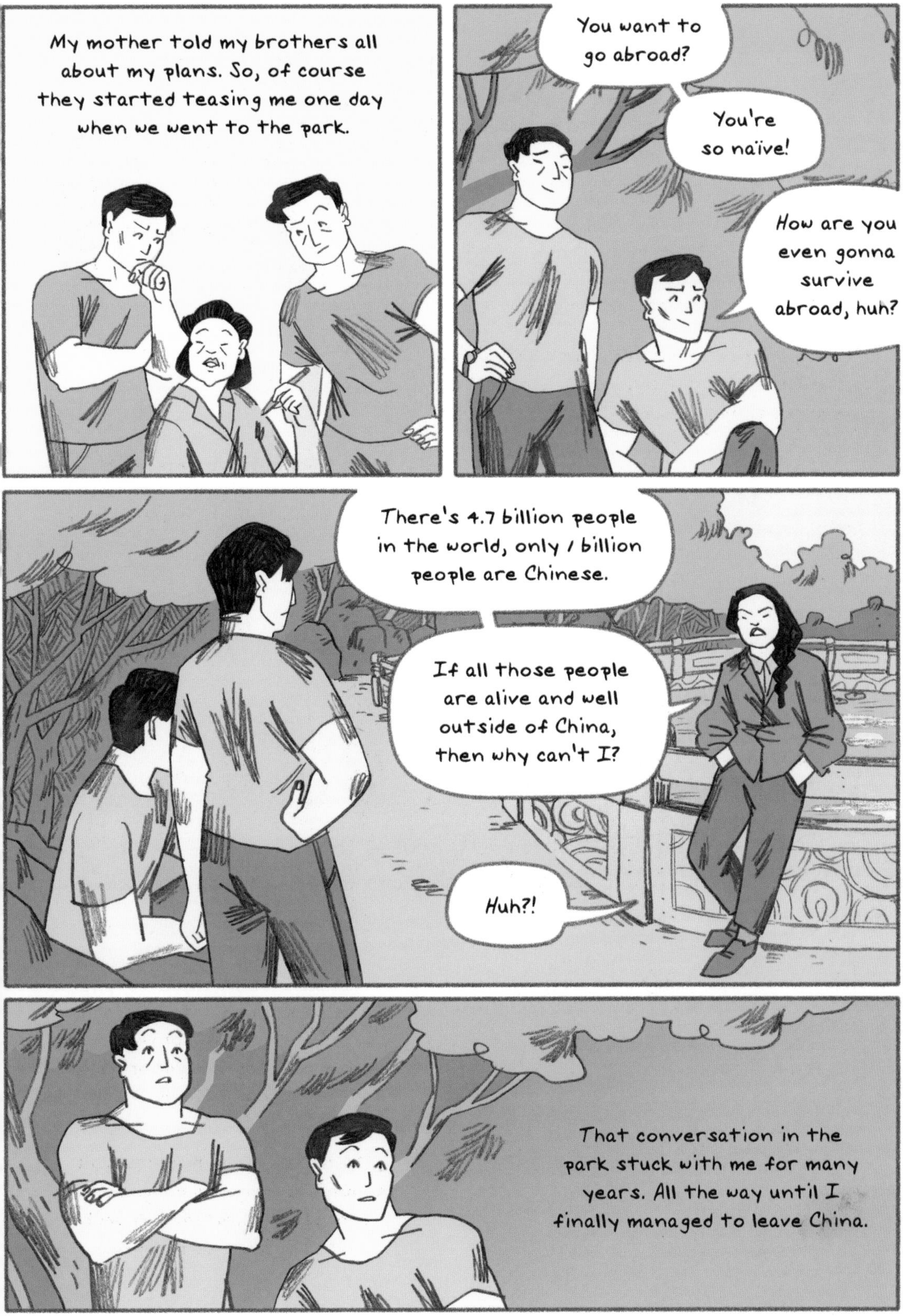

My mother told my brothers all about my plans. So, of course they started teasing me one day when we went to the park.
You want to go abroad?
You're so naïve!
How are you even gonna survive abroad, huh?
There's 4.7 billion people in the world, only 1 billion people are Chinese.
If all those people are alive and well outside of China, then why can't I?
Huh?!
That conversation in the park stuck with me for many years. All the way until I finally managed to leave China.

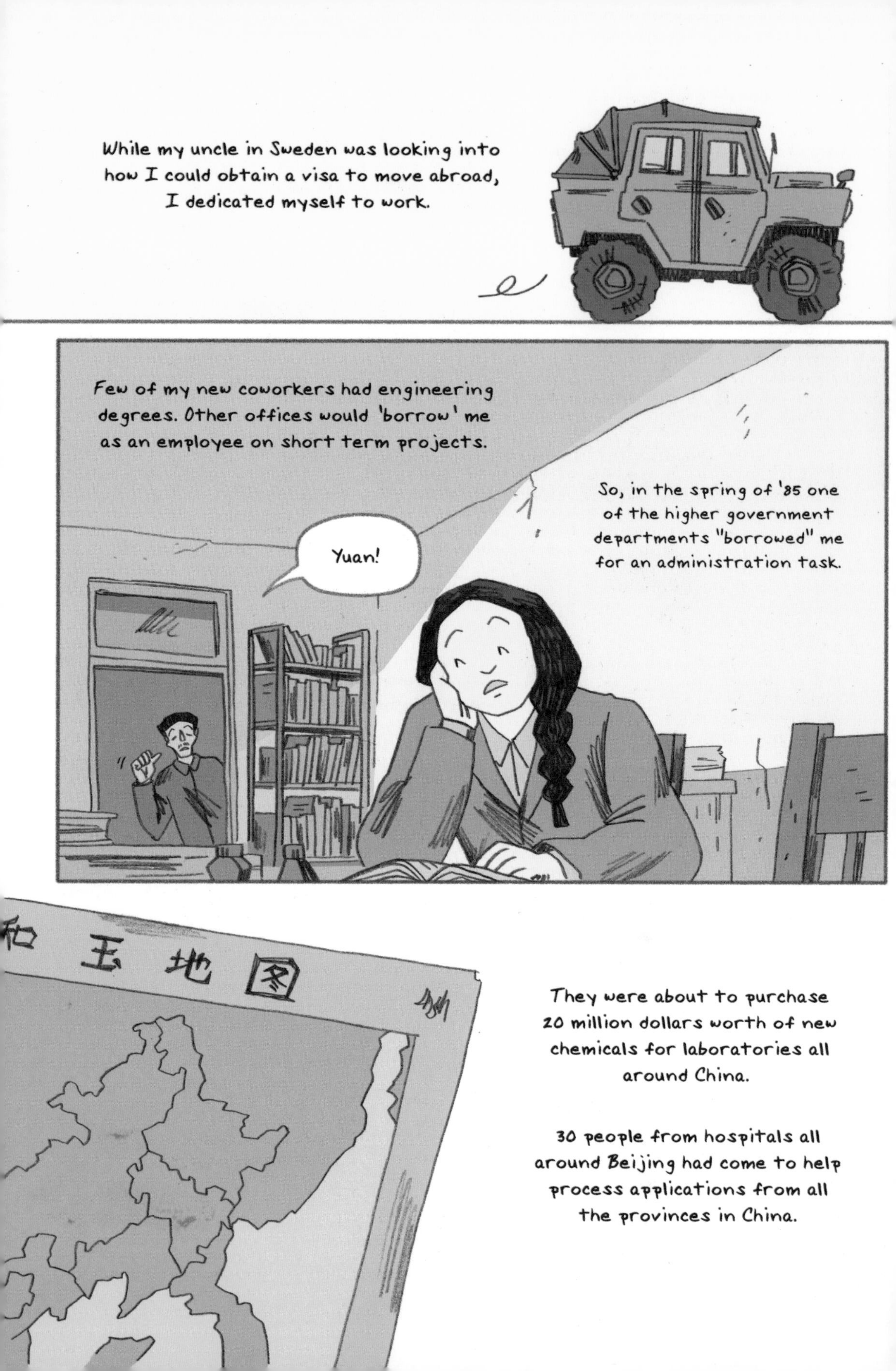
While my uncle in Sweden was looking into how I could obtain a visa to move abroad, I dedicated myself to work.
Few of my new coworkers had engineering degrees. Other offices would 'borrow' me as an employee on short term projects.
So, in the spring of '85 one of the higher government departments "borrowed" me for an administration task.
Yuan!
和玉地图
They were about to purchase 20 million dollars worth of new chemicals for laboratories all around China.
30 people from hospitals all around Beijing had come to help process applications from all the provinces in China.

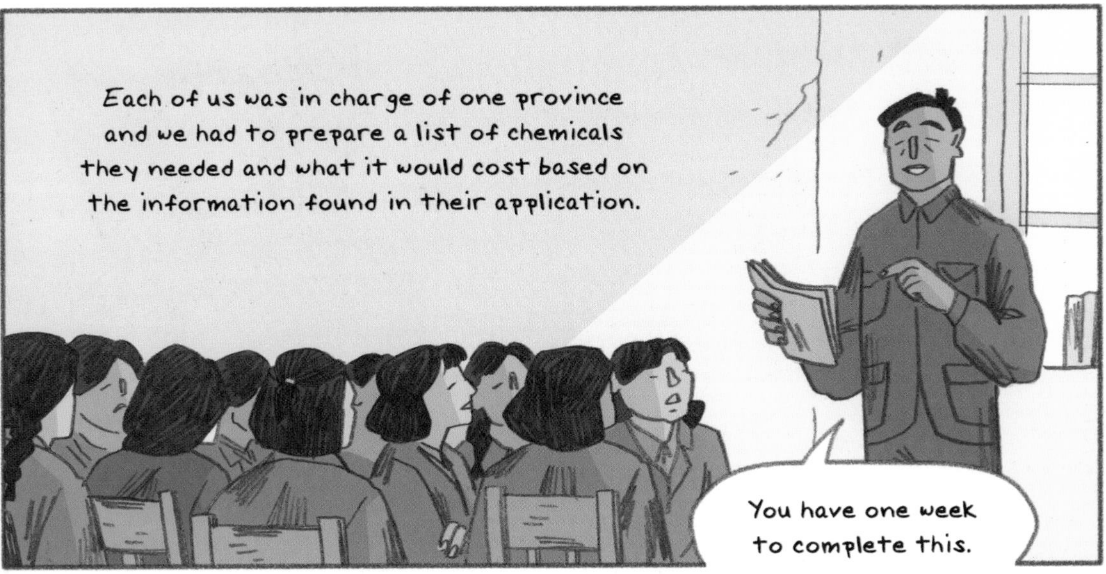
Each of us was in charge of one province and we had to prepare a list of chemicals they needed and what it would cost based on the information found in their application.
You have one week to complete this.

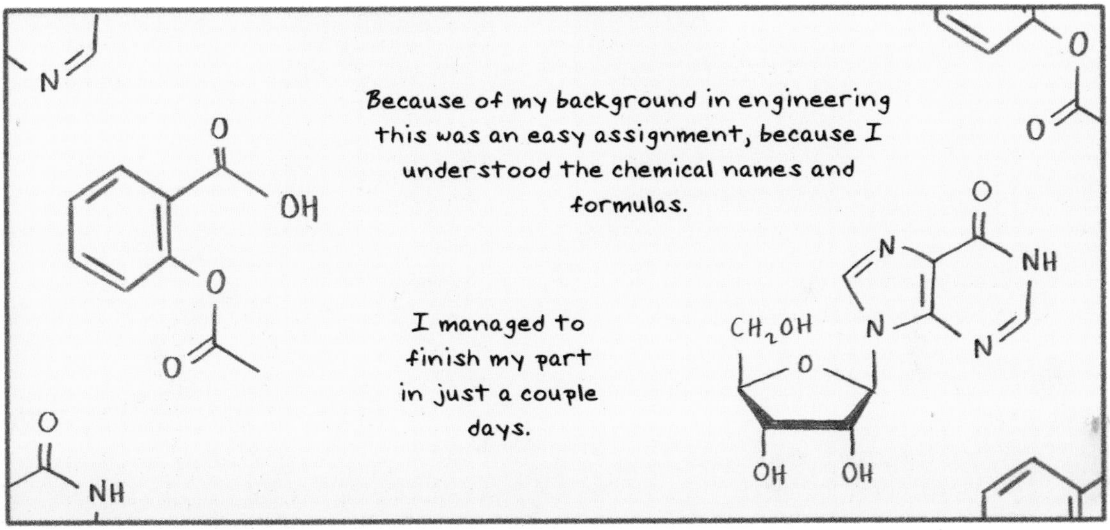
Because of my background in engineering this was an easy assignment, because I understood the chemical names and formulas.
I managed to finish my part in just a couple days.

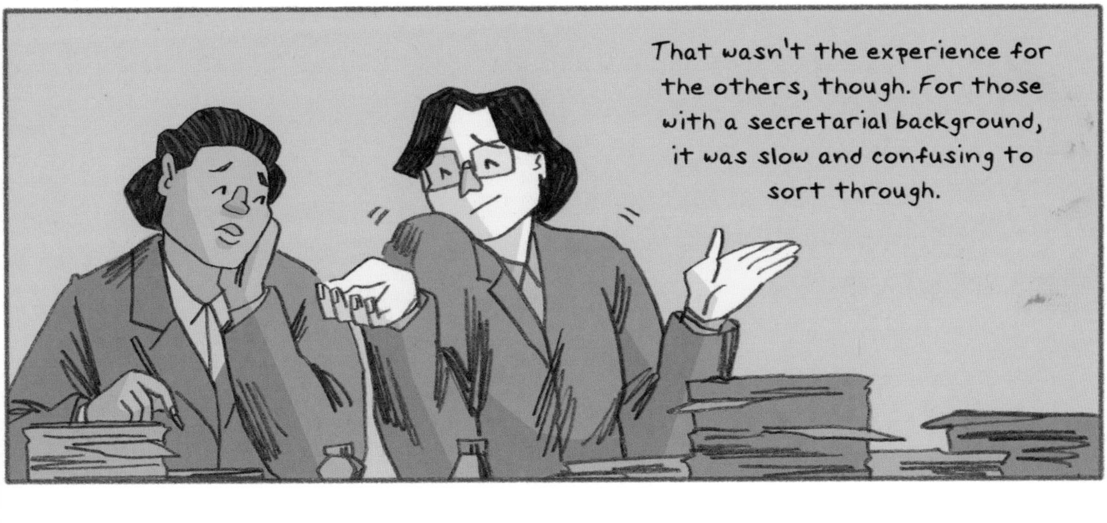
That wasn't the experience for the others, though. For those with a secretarial background, it was slow and confusing to sort through.

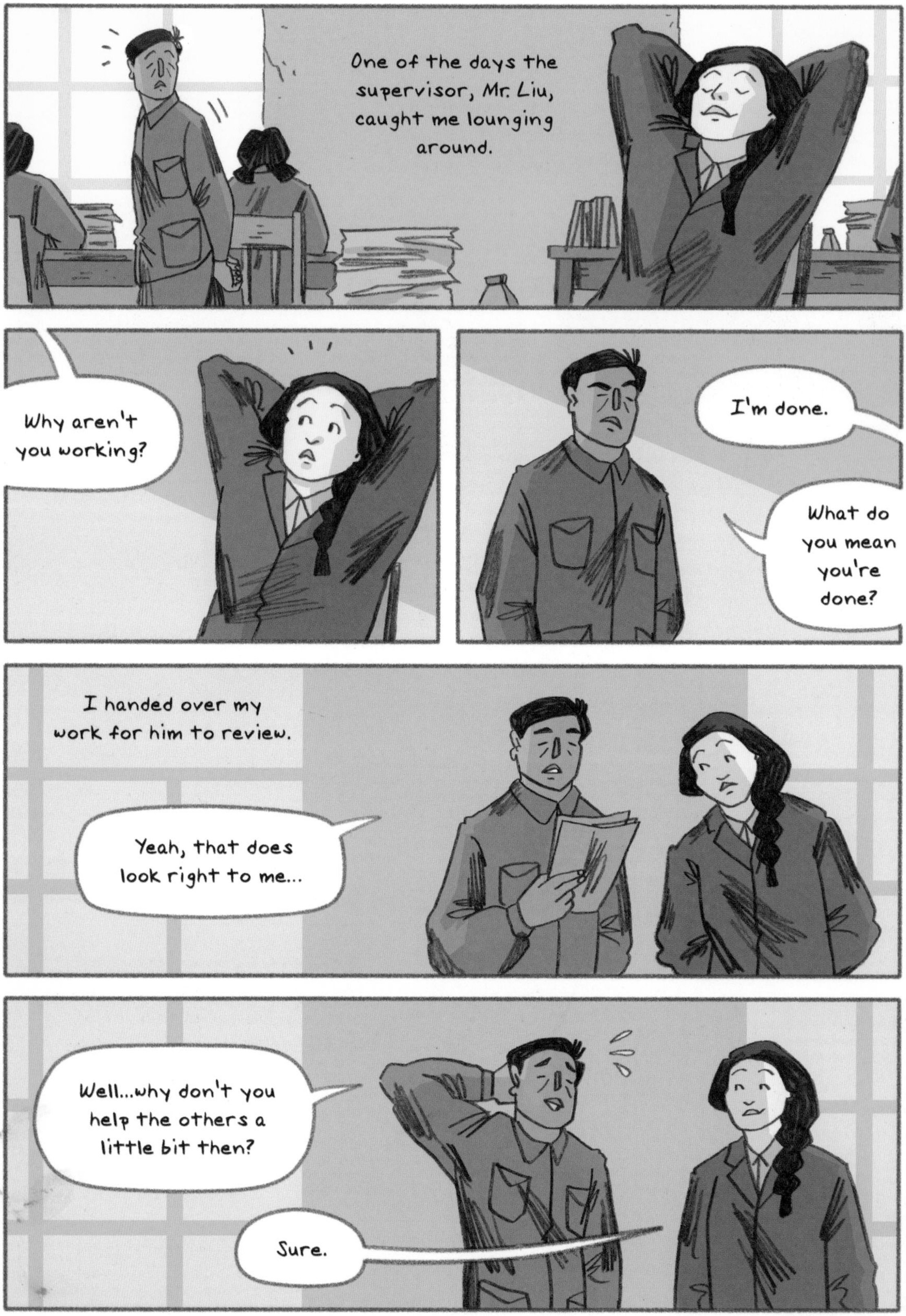
One of the days the supervisor, Mr. Liu, caught me lounging around.
Why aren't you working?
I'm done.
What do you mean you're done?
I handed over my work for him to review.
Yeah, that does look right to me...
Well...why don't you help the others a little bit then?
Sure.

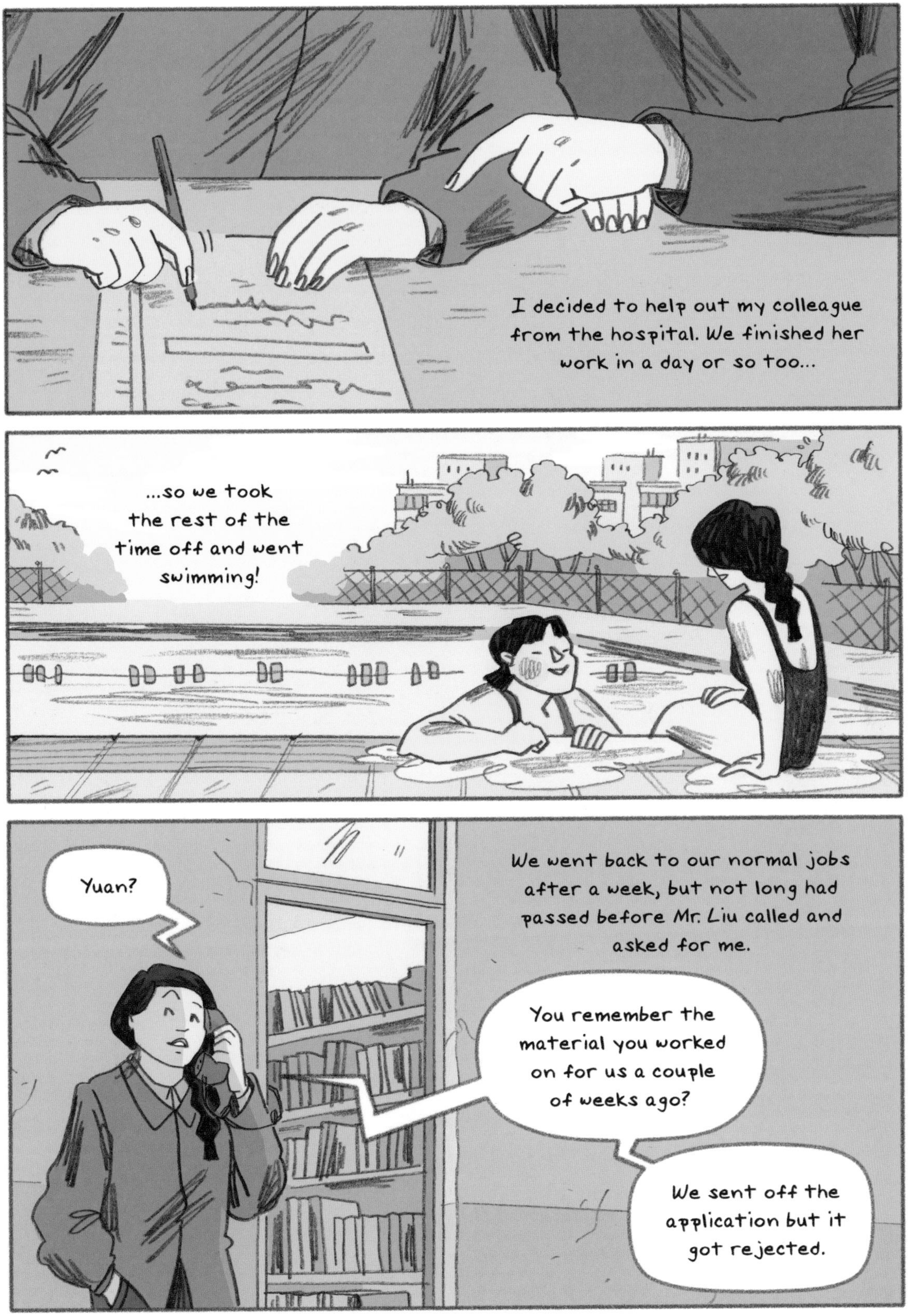
I decided to help out my colleague from the hospital. We finished her work in a day or so too...
...so we took the rest of the time off and went swimming!
We went back to our normal jobs after a week, but not long had passed before Mr. Liu called and asked for me.
Yuan?
You remember the material you worked on for us a couple of weeks ago?
We sent off the application but it got rejected.

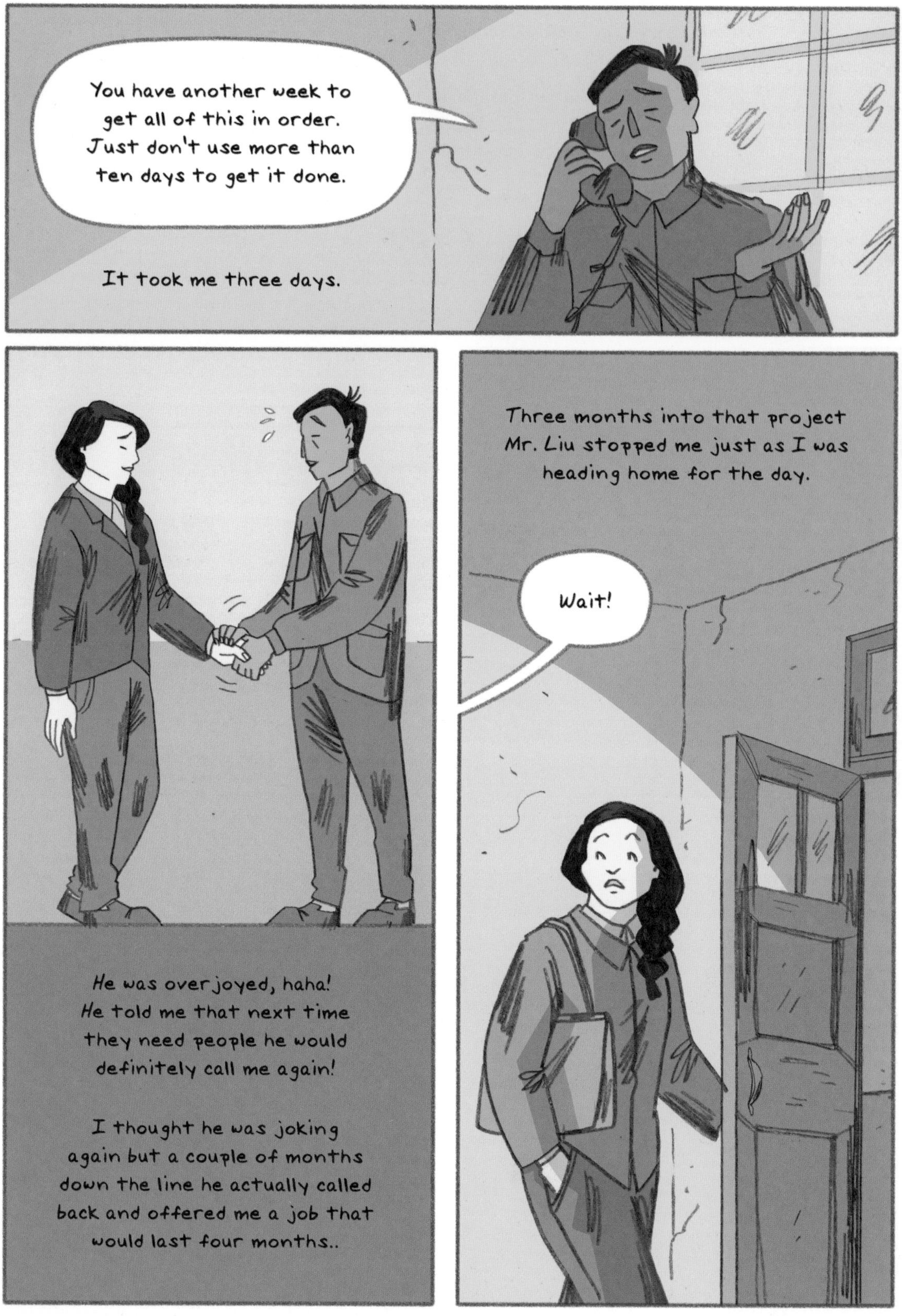
You have another week to get all of this in order. Just don't use more than ten days to get it done.
It took me three days.
He was overjoyed, haha! He told me that next time they need people he would definitely call me again!
I thought he was joking again but a couple of months down the line he actually called back and offered me a job that would last four months..
Three months into that project Mr. Liu stopped me just as I was heading home for the day.
Wait!

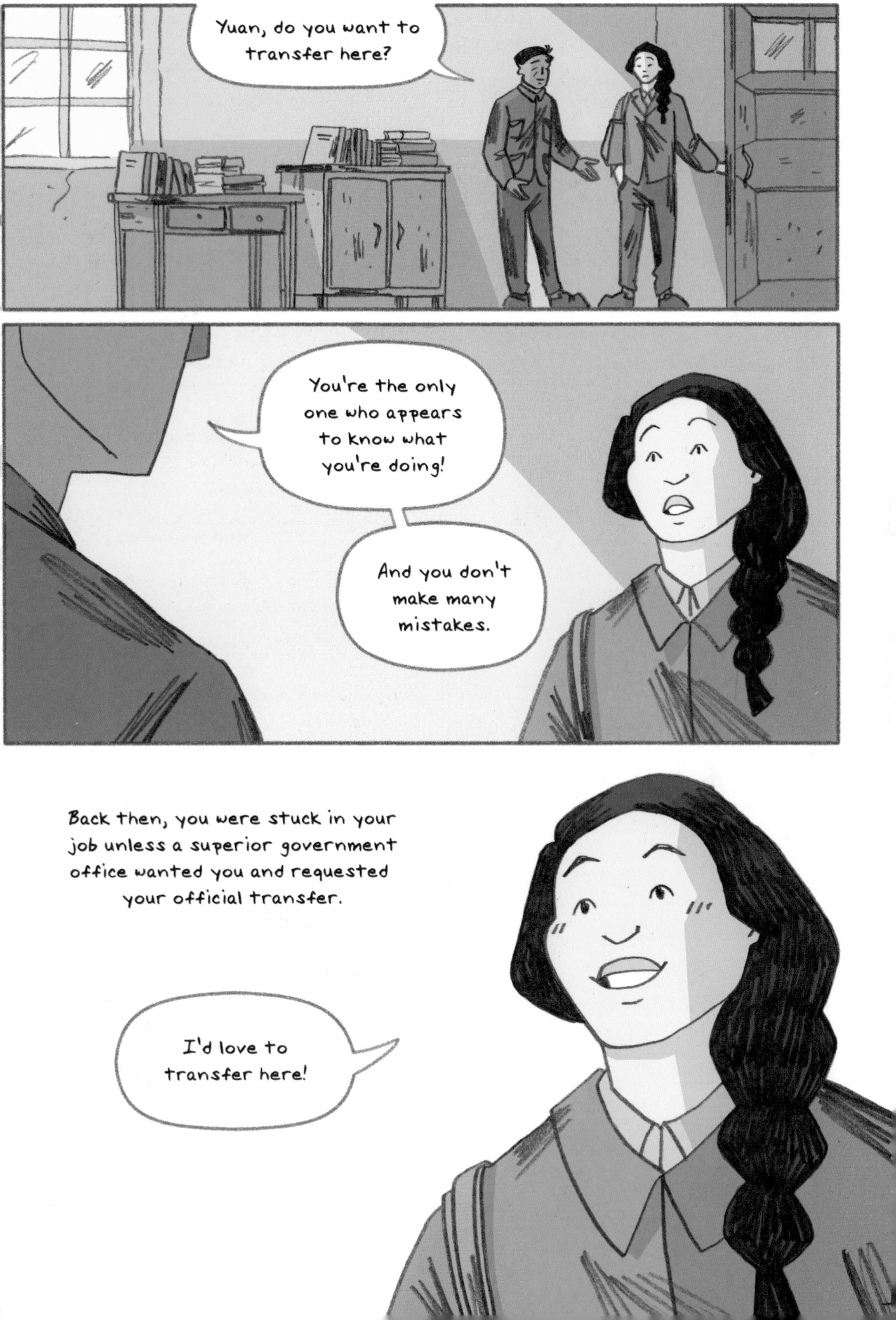
Yuan, do you want to transfer here?
You're the only one who appears to know what you're doing!
And you don't make many mistakes.
Back then, you were stuck in your job unless a superior government office wanted you and requested your official transfer.
I'd love to transfer here!

Just as I was to tell my mother of my great fortune, she revealed she had news for me that evening too.

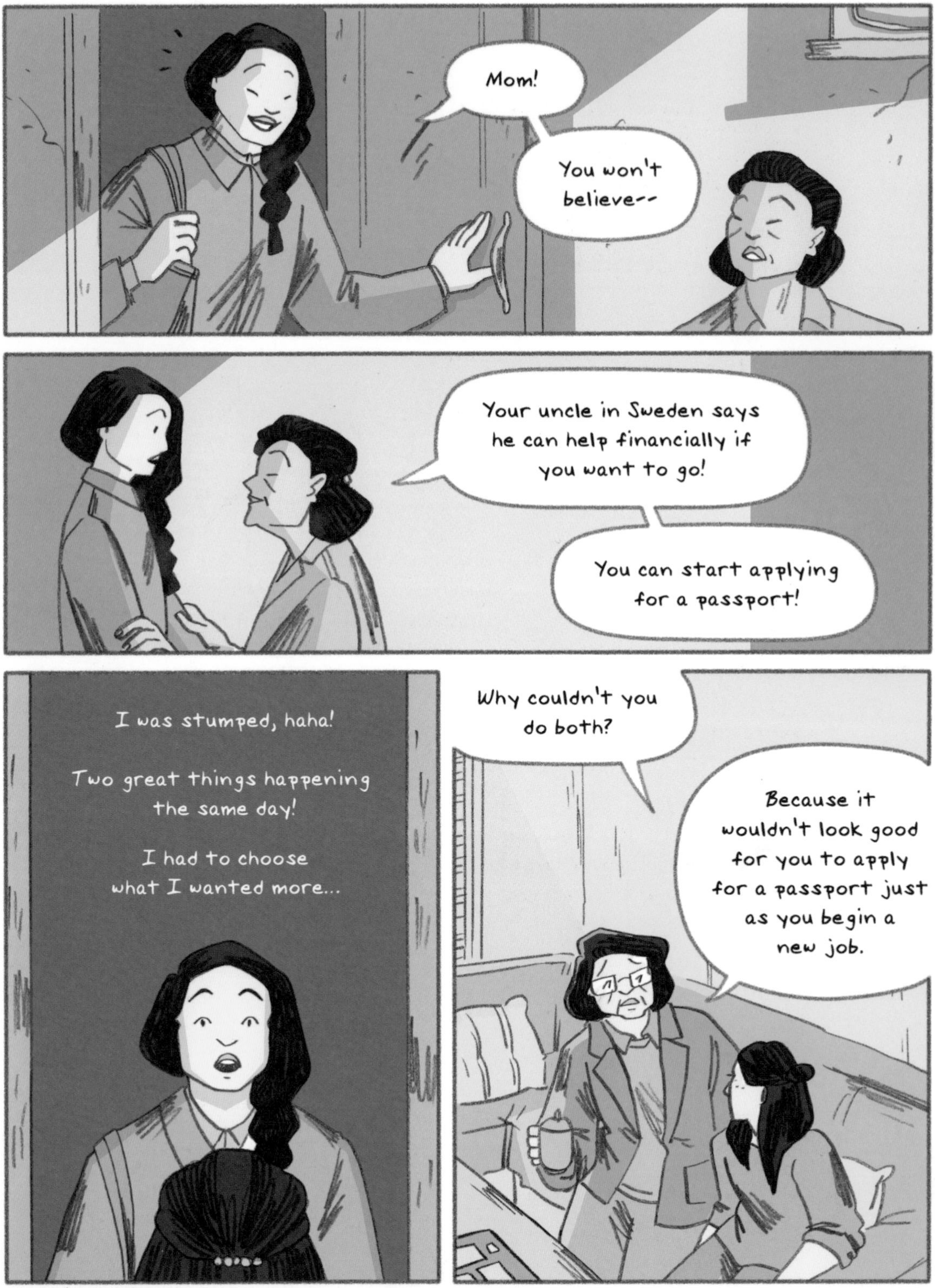
Mom!
You won't believe--
Your uncle in Sweden says he can help financially if you want to go!
You can start applying for a passport!
I was stumped, haha!
Two great things happening the same day!
I had to choose what I wanted more...
Why couldn't you do both?
Because it wouldn't look good for you to apply for a passport just as you begin a new job.

What in the world was I to do?

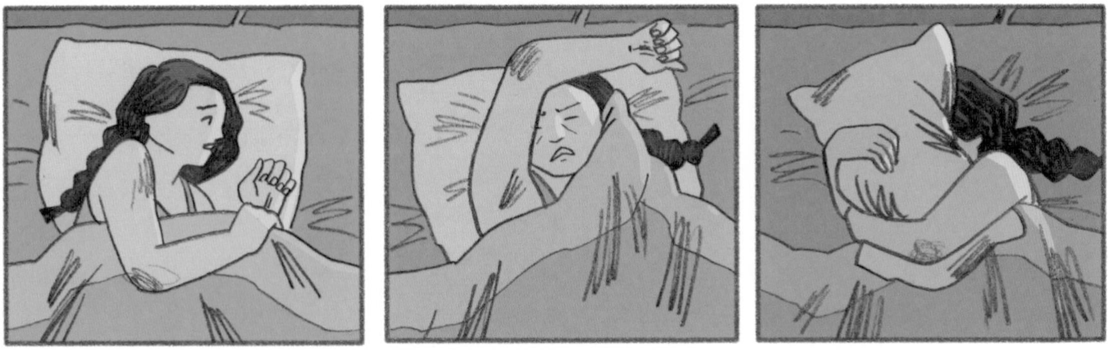

I had been offered a great job, but I really wanted to go to Sweden...
I'd been wanting to go abroad for almost ten years.

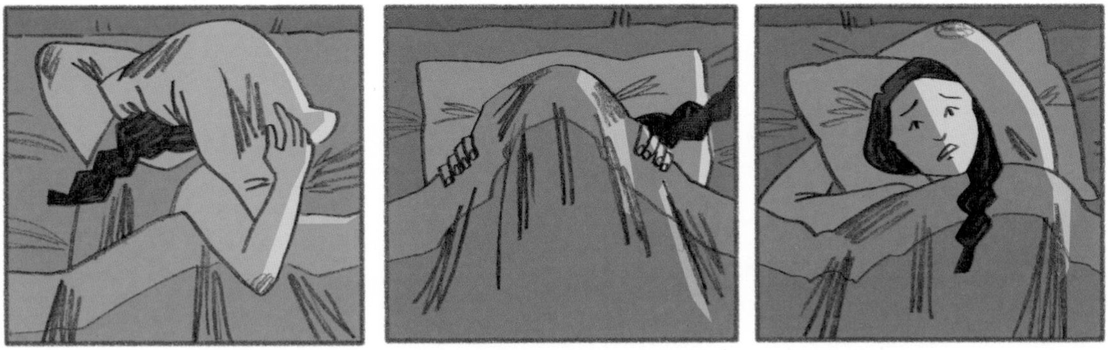

And I wasn't getting younger, I was already 34 years old.

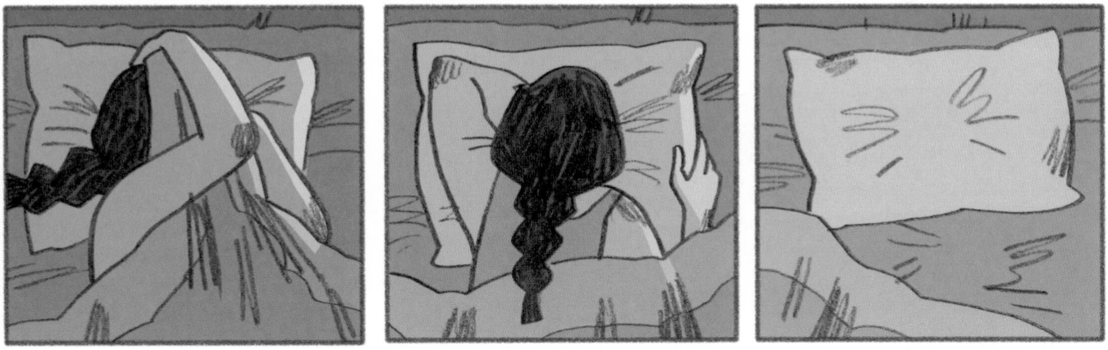

In the end, I told them I
couldn't transfer after all.

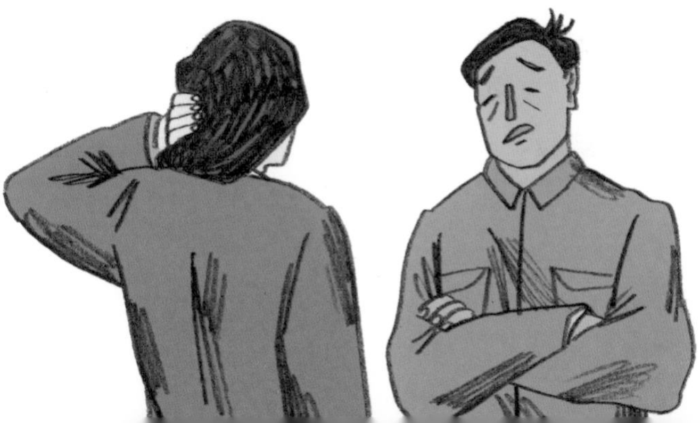

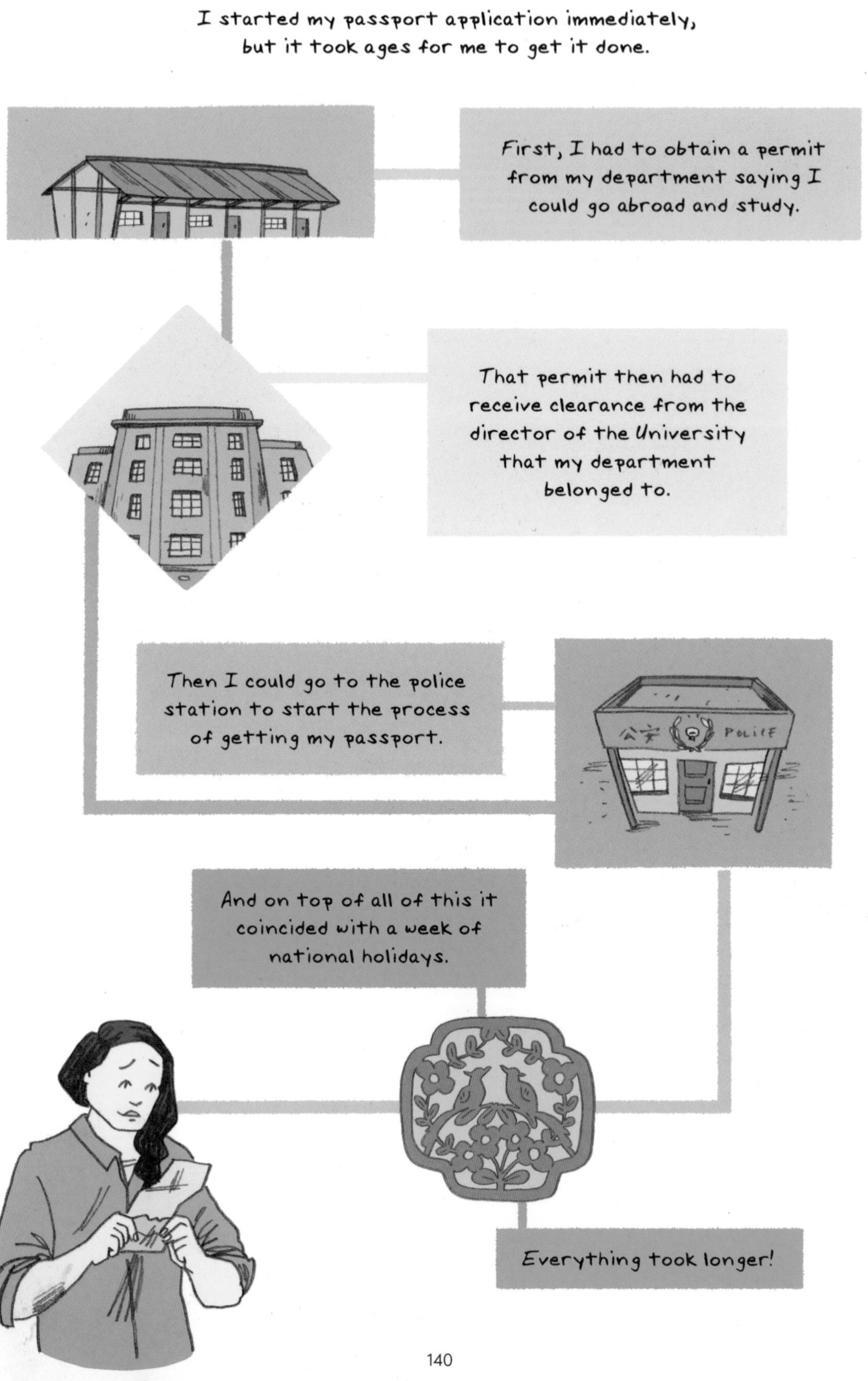
I started my passport application immediately, but it took ages for me to get it done.
First, I had to obtain a permit from my department saying I could go abroad and study.
That permit then had to receive clearance from the director of the University that my department belonged to.
Then I could go to the police station to start the process of getting my passport.
公安
POLICE
And on top of all of this it coincided with a week of national holidays.
Everything took longer!

By November of '85, I could finally go to the Swedish Embassy in Beijing to apply for a student visa.

But my application was denied.

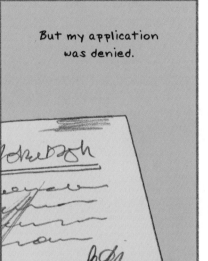

I learned that just one month earlier the universities in Sweden had introduced a requirement that you must pass the *TOEFL* exam to be eligible for a student visa.

TOEFL is an English-language exam for people looking to immigrate or study and work abroad.

What a mess! I had to pass the *TOEFL* test to get my visa--but I had never studied *English!*

So what did you do?

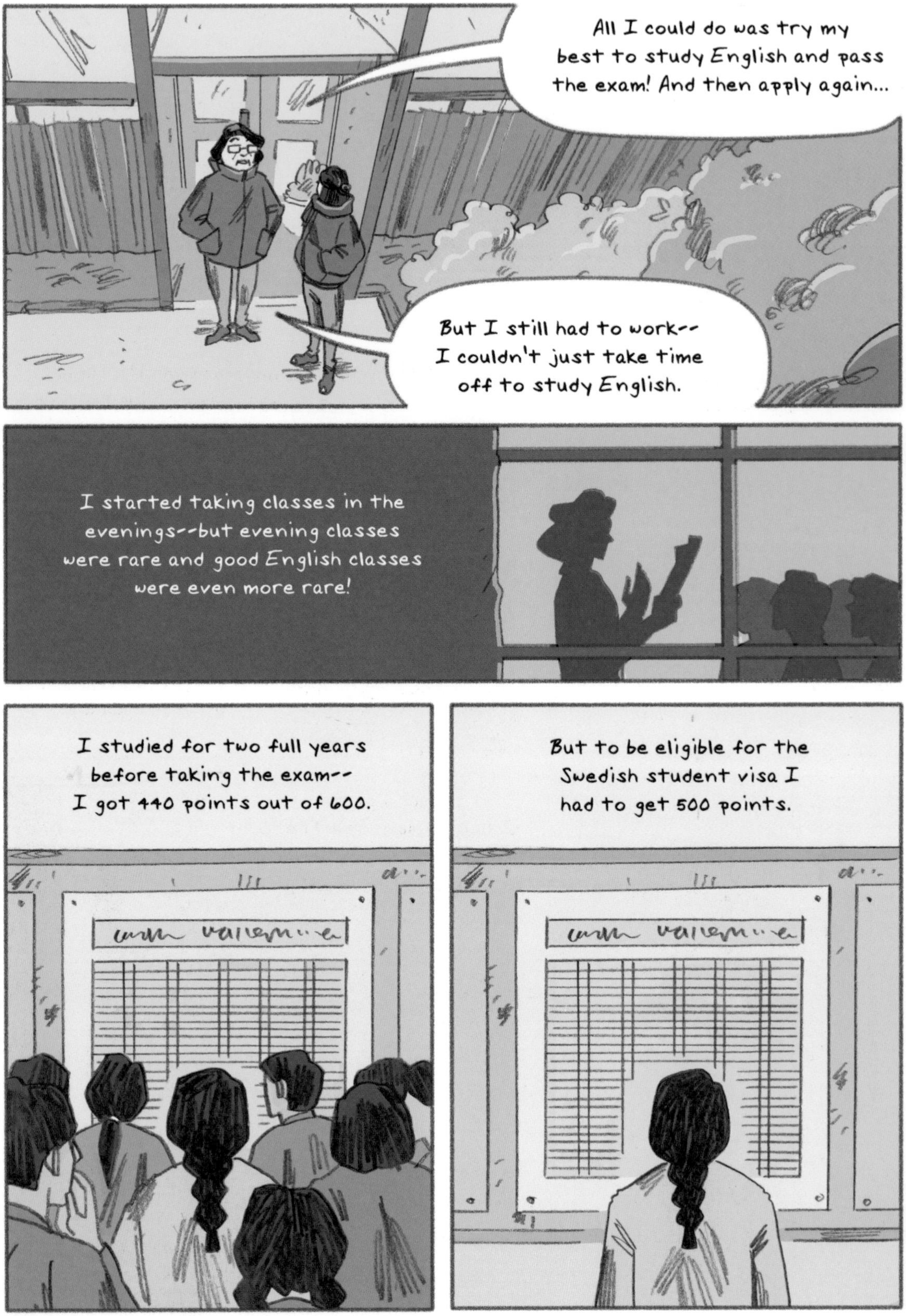
All I could do was try my best to study English and pass the exam! And then apply again...
But I still had to work-- I couldn't just take time off to study English.
I started taking classes in the evenings--but evening classes were rare and good English classes were even more rare!
I studied for two full years before taking the exam-- I got 440 points out of 600.
But to be eligible for the Swedish student visa I had to get 500 points.

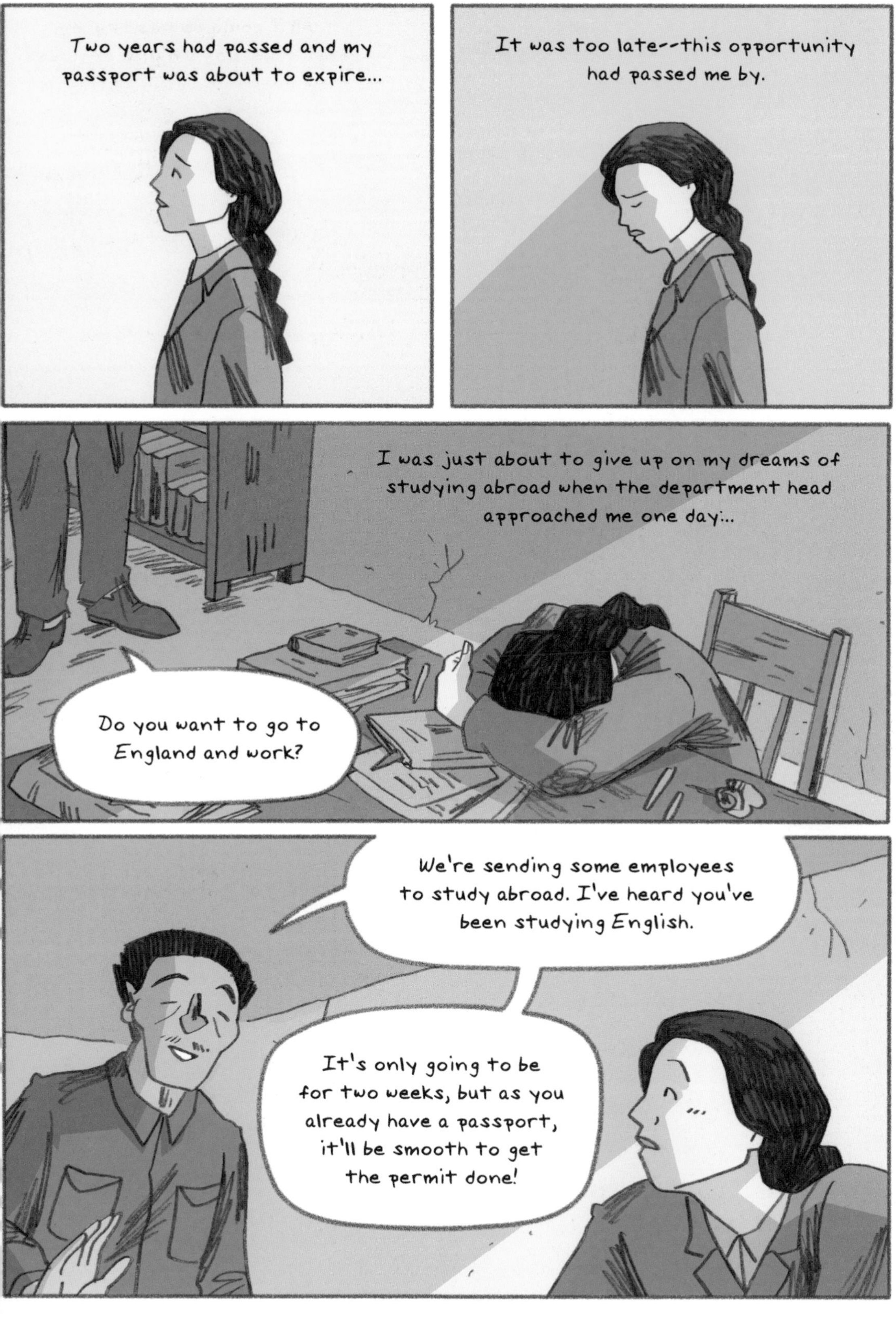
Two years had passed and my passport was about to expire...
It was too late--this opportunity had passed me by.
I was just about to give up on my dreams of studying abroad when the department head approached me one day:...
Do you want to go to England and work?
We're sending some employees to study abroad. I've heard you've been studying English.
It's only going to be for two weeks, but as you already have a passport, it'll be smooth to get the permit done!

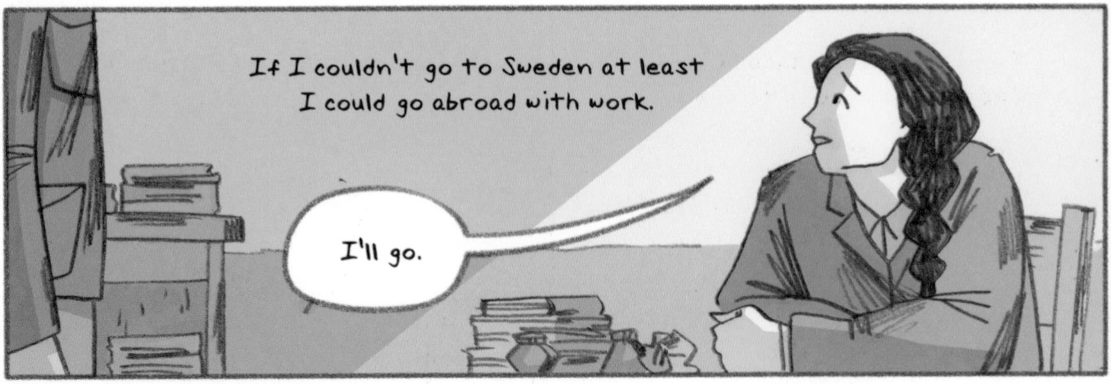
If I couldn't go to Sweden at least
I could go abroad with work.
I'll go.

And not unlike before, that very same evening, my mother said to me:

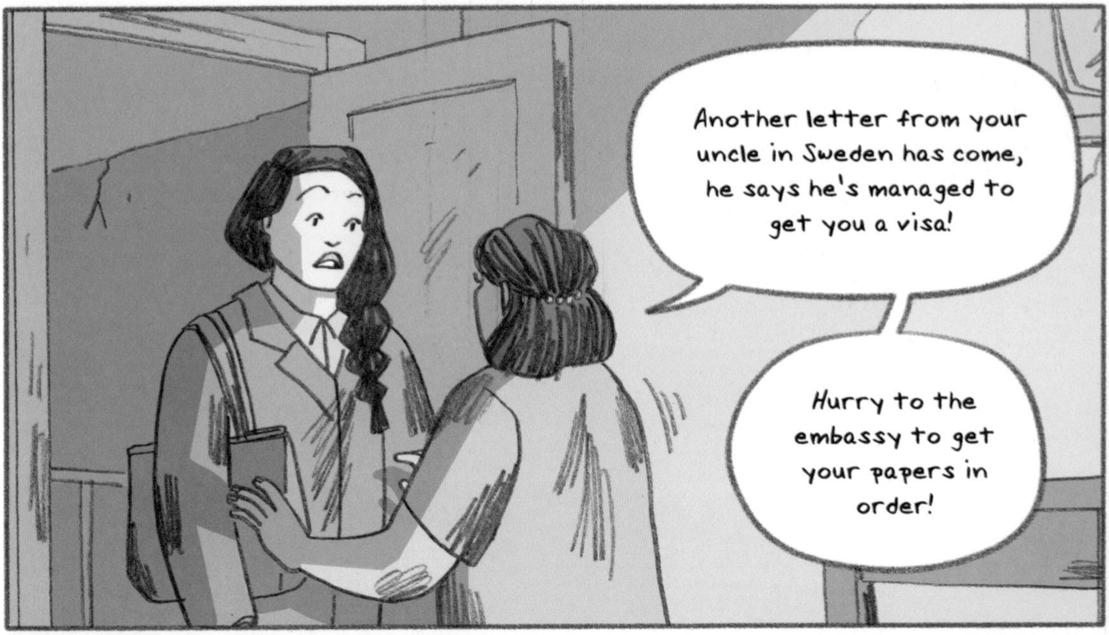
Another letter from your uncle in Sweden has come, he says he's managed to get you a visa!
Hurry to the embassy to get your papers in order!

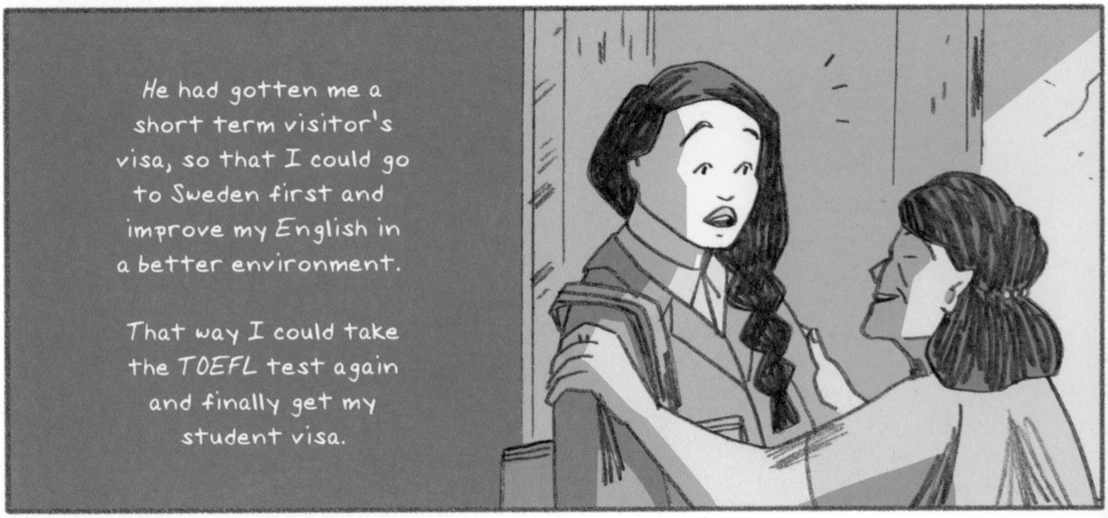
He had gotten me a short term visitor's visa, so that I could go to Sweden first and improve my English in a better environment.
That way I could take the TOEFL test again and finally get my student visa.

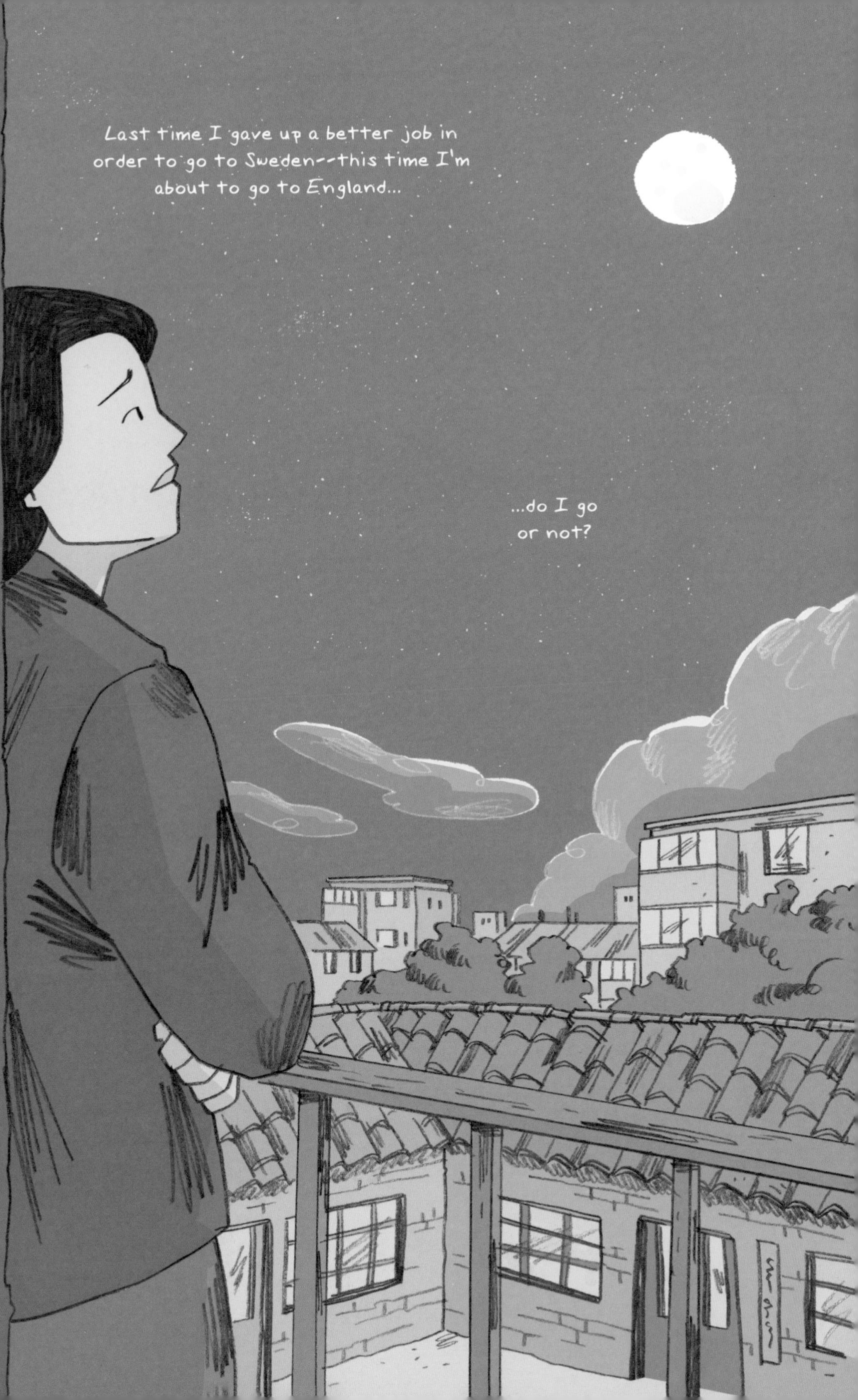
Last time I gave up a better job in order to go to Sweden--this time I'm about to go to England...
...do I go or not?

After nearly a decade of carrying this dream in my heart it suddenly all worked out.

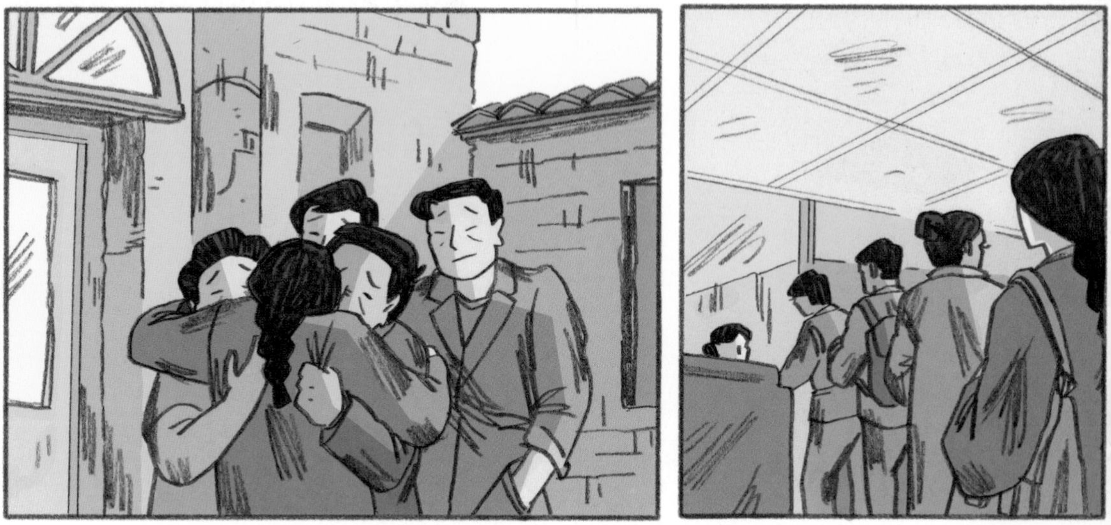

I finally encountered an opportunity which, with the love and help of my family, I could pursue.

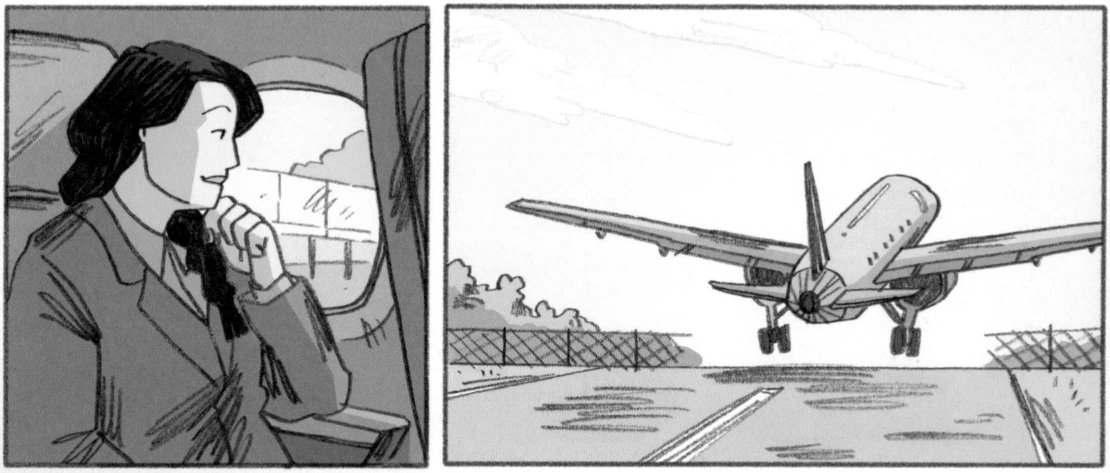

I left on a plane for Sweden on September 1st, 1987.

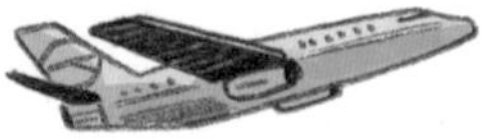

It's now almost 50 years after the Cultural Revolution ended.

Some of the Rusticated youth have looked back on the Down to the Countryside movement and expressed that they look back on these "lost years of youth" with no regrets.

But the majority of the rest of us who had to live through it feel that one should not forget all the hardships and suffering — and most of all not glorify it.

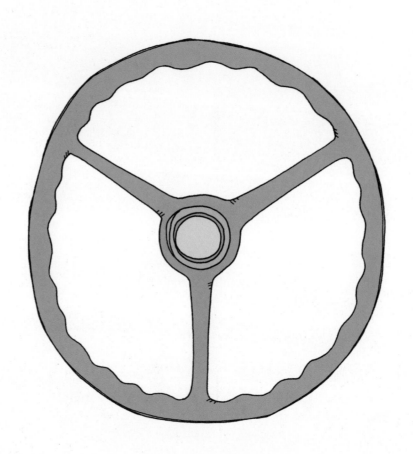

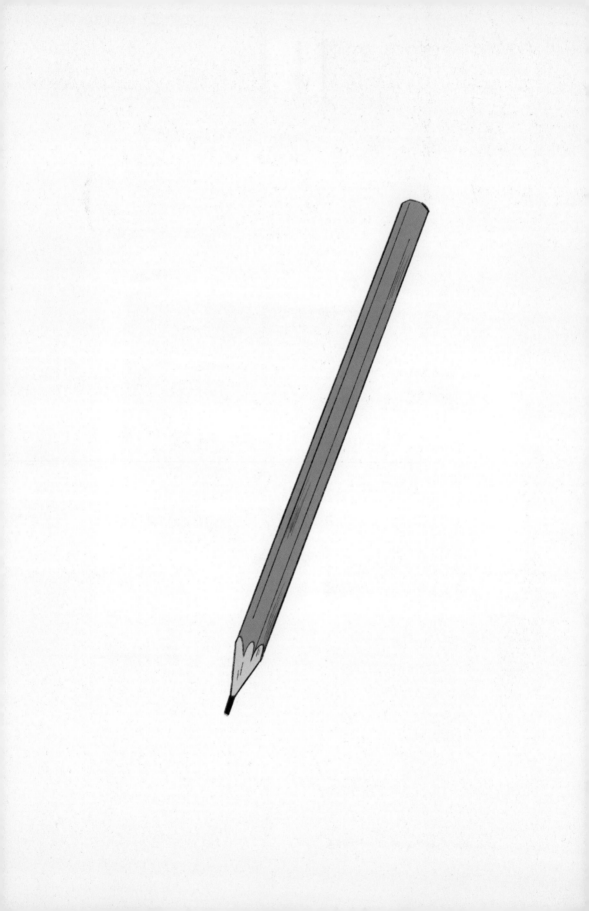

ACKNOWLEDGEMENTS

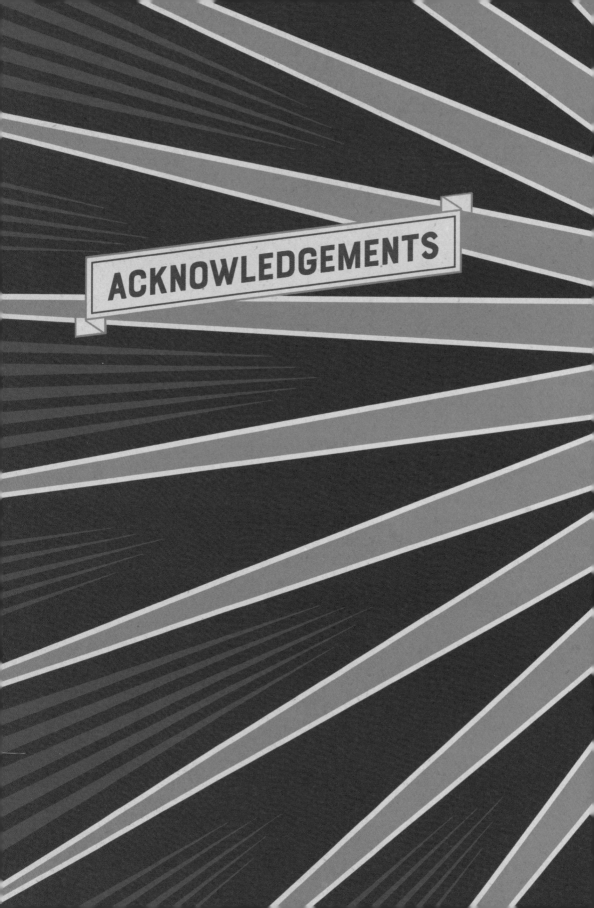

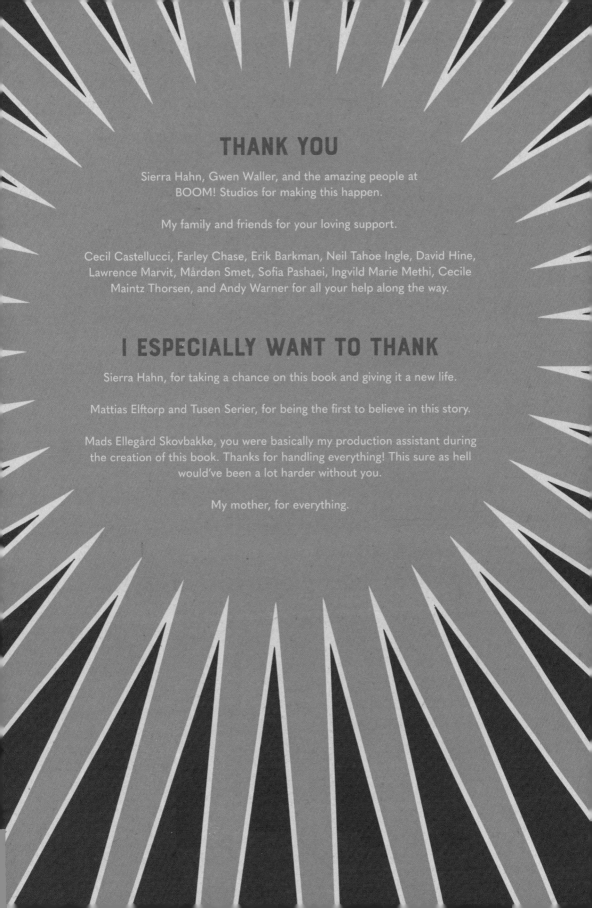

THANK YOU

Sierra Hahn, Gwen Waller, and the amazing people at
BOOM! Studios for making this happen.

My family and friends for your loving support.

Cecil Castellucci, Farley Chase, Erik Barkman, Neil Tahoe Ingle, David Hine,
Lawrence Marvit, Mårdøn Smet, Sofia Pashaei, Ingvild Marie Methi, Cecile
Maintz Thorsen, and Andy Warner for all your help along the way.

I ESPECIALLY WANT TO THANK

Sierra Hahn, for taking a chance on this book and giving it a new life.

Mattias Elftorp and Tusen Serier, for being the first to believe in this story.

Mads Ellegård Skovbakke, you were basically my production assistant during
the creation of this book. Thanks for handling everything! This sure as hell
would've been a lot harder without you.

My mother, for everything.

ABOUT THE AUTHOR

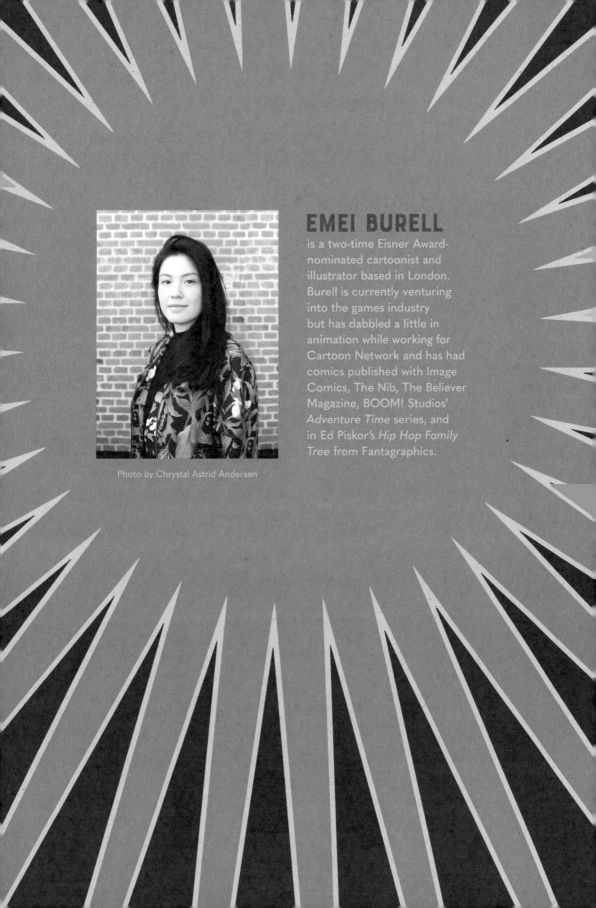

EMEI BURELL

is a two-time Eisner Award-nominated cartoonist and illustrator based in London. Burell is currently venturing into the games industry but has dabbled a little in animation while working for Cartoon Network and has had comics published with Image Comics, The Nib, The Believer Magazine, BOOM! Studios' *Adventure Time* series, and in Ed Piskor's *Hip Hop Family Tree* from Fantagraphics.

Photo by Chrystal Astrid Andersen

DISCOVER
GROUNDBREAKING TITLES

ASAF HANUKA
THE
REALIST

LONG WALK
TO VALHALLA
ADAM SMITH · MATTHEW FOX

THE
MARCH
OF THE CRABS
THE CRABBY CONDITION
ARTHUR DE PINS

Jane
ALINE BROSH McKENNA
RAMÓN K. PÉREZ

ROYDEN LEPP
RUST
VOLUME ONE
VISITOR IN THE FIELD

MOUSE GUARD
THE BLACK AXE
DAVID PETERSEN

The Realist
Asaf Hanuka
ISBN: 978-1-60886-688-5 | $24.99 US

The Realist: Plug and Play
Asaf Hanuka
ISBN: 978-1-60886-953-4 | $24.99 US

Long Walk to Valhalla
Adam Smith, Matt Fox
ISBN: 978-1-60886-692-2 | $24.99 US

The March of The Crabs
Arthur De Pins
Volume 1: The Crabby Condition
ISBN: 978-1-60886-689-2 | $19.99 US
Volume 2: The Empire of the Crabs
ISBN: 978-1-68415-014-4 | $19.99 US

Jane
Aline Brosh McKenna, Ramón K. Pérez
ISBN: 978-1-60886-981-7 | $24.99 US

Rust
Royden Lepp
Volume 0: The Boy Soldier
ISBN: 978-1-60886-806-3 | $10.99 US
Volume 1: Visitor in the Field
ISBN: 978-1-60886-894-0 | $14.99 US
Volume 2: Secrets of the Cell
ISBN: 978-1-60886-895-7 | $14.99 US

Mouse Guard
David Petersen
Mouse Guard: Fall 1152
ISBN: 978-1-93238-657-8 | $24.95 US
Mouse Guard: Winter 1152
ISBN: 978-1-93238-674-5 | $24.95 US
Mouse Guard: The Black Axe
ISBN: 978-1-93639-306-0 | $24.95 US

The Cloud
K.I. Zachopoulos, Vincenzo Balzano
ISBN: 978-1-60886-725-7 | $24.99 US

Cursed Pirate Girl Coloring Book
Jeremy A. Bastian
ISBN: 978-1-60886-947-3 | $16.99 US

ARCHAIA™

AVAILABLE AT YOUR LOCAL COMICS SHOP AND BOOKSTORE
To find a comics shop in your area, visit www.comicshoplocator.com
WWW.**BOOM-STUDIOS**.COM

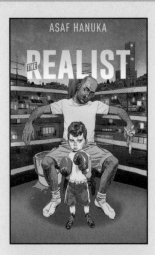

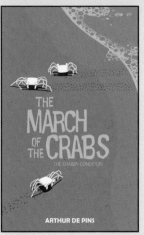

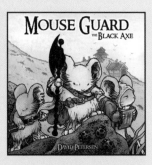

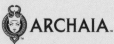